AAT

INTERACTIVE TEXT

Technician Unit 18

Preparing Business Taxation Computations (FA 2000)

In this August 2000 edition

- Layout designed to be easy on the eye and easy to use

- Icons to guide you through a fast track approach if you wish

- Numerous activities throughout the text reinforce learning

- The text fully reflects the Finance Act 2000

- The Text is focused as it takes account of information received from the AAT and the Chief Assessor

FOR DEVOLVED ASSESSMENTS UNDER FINANCE ACT 2000

BPP Publishing
August 2000

Fourth edition August 2000

ISBN 0 7517 6224 5 (Previous edition 0 7517 6179 6)

British Library Cataloguing-in-Publication Data
A catalogue record for this book
is available from the British Library

Published by

BPP Publishing Limited
Aldine House, Aldine Place
London W12 8AW

www.bpp.com

Printed in England by DA COSTA PRINT
35 – 37 Queensland Road
LONDON
(Tel 0207 700 1000)

We are grateful to the Lead Body for Accounting for permission to reproduce extracts from the Standards of Competence for Accounting, and to the AAT for permission to reproduce extracts from the mapping and Guidance Notes.

TAX RATES AND ALLOWANCES

A   INCOME TAX

1   *Rates*

	1999/00	%	2000/01	%
	£		£	
Starting rate	1 - 1,500	10	0 – 1,520	10
Basic rate	1,501 - 28,000	23	1,521 – 28,400	22
Higher rate	28,001 and above	40	28,401 and above	40

In 2000/01 savings (excl. Dividend) income is taxed at 20% if it falls in the basic rate band. Dividend income in the basic rate band is taxed at 10%. Dividend income within the higher rate band is taxed at 32.5%.

2   *Allowances*

	1999/00	2000/01
	£	£
Personal allowance	4,335	4,385

3   *Capital allowances*

	%
Plant and machinery	
Writing down allowance★	25
First year allowance (acquisitions 2.7.97 - 1.7.98)★★	50
First year allowance (acquisitions after 2.7.98)	40
First year allowance (information and communication technology equipment - period 1.4.00 - 31.3.03)	100
Industrial buildings allowance	
Writing down allowance: post 5.11.62	4
pre 6.11.62	2
Agricultural buildings allowance	
Writing down allowance	4

★ 6% reducing balance for certain long life assets.

★★ 12% for certain long life assets.

B   CORPORATION TAX

1   *Rates*

Financial year	Full rate %	Small companies rate %	Starting rate	Marginal relief Fraction	Lower limit for starting rate £	Upper limit for starting rate £	Upper limit for SCR £	Lower Limit for SCR £
1997	31	21	-	1/40	-	-	1,500,000	300,000
1998	31	21	-	1/40	-	-	1,500,000	300,000
1999	30	20	-	1/40	-	-	1,500,000	300,000
2000	30	20	10	1/40	10,000	50,000	1,500,000	300,000

2   *Marginal relief*

$(M - P) \times I/P \times$ Marginal relief fraction

BPP PUBLISHING

C RATES OF INTEREST

Official rate of interest: 10% (assumed)

Rate of interest on unpaid/overpaid tax: 10% (assumed)

D CAPITAL GAINS TAX

1 *Lease percentage table*

Years	Percentage	Years	Percentage	Years	Percentage
50 or more	100.000	33	90.280	16	64.116
49	99.657	32	89.354	15	61.617
48	99.289	31	88.371	14	58.971
47	98.902	30	87.330	13	56.167
46	98.490	29	86.226	12	53.191
45	98.059	28	85.053	11	50.038
44	97.595	27	83.816	10	46.695
43	97.107	26	82.496	9	43.154
42	96.593	25	81.100	8	39.399
41	96.041	24	79.622	7	35.414
40	95.457	23	78.055	6	31.195
39	94.842	22	76.399	5	26.722
38	94.189	21	74.635	4	21.983
37	93.497	20	72.770	3	16.959
36	92.761	19	70.791	2	11.629
35	91.981	18	68.697	1	5.983
34	91.156	17	66.470	0	0.000

2 *Retail prices index (January 1987 = 100.0)*

	1982	1983	1984	1985	1986	1987	1988	1989	1990
Jan		82.6	86.8	91.2	96.2	100.0	103.3	111.0	119.5
Feb		83.0	87.2	91.9	96.6	100.4	103.7	111.8	120.2
Mar	79.4	83.1	87.5	92.8	96.7	100.6	104.1	112.3	121.4
Apr	81.0	84.3	88.6	94.8	97.7	101.8	105.8	114.3	125.1
May	81.6	84.6	89.0	95.2	97.8	101.9	106.2	115.0	126.2
Jun	81.9	84.8	89.2	95.4	97.8	101.9	106.6	115.4	126.7
Jul	81.9	85.3	89.1	95.2	97.5	101.8	106.7	115.5	126.8
Aug	81.9	85.7	89.9	95.5	97.8	102.1	107.9	115.8	128.1
Sept	81.9	86.1	90.1	95.4	98.3	102.4	108.4	116.6	129.3
Oct	82.3	86.4	90.7	95.6	98.5	102.9	109.5	117.5	130.3
Nov	82.7	86.7	91.0	95.9	99.3	103.4	110.0	118.5	130.0
Dec	82.5	86.9	90.9	96.0	99.6	103.3	110.3	118.8	129.9

	1991	*1992*	*1993*	*1994*	*1995*	*1996*	*1997*	*1998*	*1999*	*2000★*	*2001★*
Jan	130.2	135.6	137.9	141.3	146.0	150.2	154.4	159.5	163.4	167.5	173.5
Feb	130.9	136.3	138.8	142.1	146.9	150.9	155.0	160.3	163.7	168.0	174.0
Mar	131.4	136.7	139.3	142.5	147.5	151.5	154.4	160.8	164.1	168.5	174.5
Apr	133.1	138.8	140.6	144.2	149.0	152.6	156.3	162.6	165.2	169.0	175.0
May	133.5	139.3	141.1	144.7	149.6	152.9	156.9	163.5	165.6	169.5	175.5
Jun	134.1	139.3	141.0	144.7	149.8	153.0	157.5	163.4	165.6	170.0	176.0
Jul	133.8	138.8	140.7	144.0	149.1	152.4	157.5	163.0	165.1	170.5	176.5
Aug	134.1	138.9	141.3	144.7	149.9	153.1	158.5	163.7	165.5	171.0	177.0
Sept	134.6	139.4	141.9	145.0	150.6	153.8	159.3	164.4	166.2	171.5	177.5
Oct	135.1	139.9	141.8	145.2	149.8	153.8	159.6	164.5	166.5	172.0	178.0
Nov	135.6	139.7	141.6	145.3	149.8	153.9	159.6	164.4	166.7	172.5	178.5
Dec	135.7	139.2	141.9	146.0	150.7	154.4	160.0	164.4	167.3	173.0	179.0

★   Estimated figures.

3   *Annual exemption (individuals)*

	£
1997/98	6,500
1998/99	6,800
1999/00	7,100
2000/01	7,200

4   Taper relief: Disposals after 6 April 2000

Number of complete years after 5.4.98 for which asset held	*Business assets % of gain chargeable*	*Non business assets % of gain chargeable*
0	100	100
1	87.5	100
2	75	100
3	50	95
4	25	90
5	25	85
6	25	80
7	25	75
8	25	70
9	25	65
10 or more	25	60

BPP PUBLISHING

Page

BPP PUBLISHING

HOW TO USE THIS INTERACTIVE TEXT

Aims of this Interactive Text

> To provide the knowledge and practice to help you succeed in the devolved assessment for Technician Unit 18 *Preparing Business Taxation Computations.*

To pass the devolved assessment you need a thorough understanding in all areas covered by the standards of competence.

> To tie in with the other components of the BPP Effective Study Package to ensure you have the best possible chance of success.

Interactive Text
This covers all you need to know for devolved assessment for Unit 18 *Preparing Business Taxation Computations.* Icons clearly mark key areas of the text. Numerous activities and quizzes throughout the text help you practise what you have just learnt.

Devolved Assessment Kit
When you have understood and practised the material in this Interactive Text, you will have the knowledge and experience to tackle the Devolved Assessment Kit for Unit 18 *Preparing Business Taxation Computations.* This aims to get you through the devolved assessment, whether in the form of a simulation or workplace assessment. It contains the AAT's sample simulation for Unit 18 plus other simulations.

Recommended approach to this Interactive Text

- To achieve competence in Unit 18 (and all the other units), you need to be able to do **everything** specified by the standards. Study the Text very carefully and do not skip any of it.

- Learning is an **active** process. Do **all** the activities and quizzes as you work through this Interactive Text so you can be sure you really understand what you have read.

- After you have covered the material in this Interactive Text, work through the **Devolved Assessment Kit.**

Before you take the devolved assessment, check that you still remember the material using the following quick revision plan for each chapter.

(i) Read through the chapter learning objectives. Are there any gaps in your knowledge? If so study the section again.

(ii) Read and learn the key terms.

(iii) Read and learn the key learning points which are a summary of the chapter.

(iv) Do the activities for the chapter again.

(v) Do the quick quiz again. If you know what you are doing it shouldn't take long.

This approach is only a suggestion. Your college may well adapt it to suit your needs.
Remember this is a **practical** course.

(a) Try to relate the material to your experience in the workplace or any other work experience you may have had.

(b) Try to make as many links as you can to your study of the other Units at Technician level.

(c) Keep this text (hopefully) you will find it invaluable in your everyday work too.

TECHNICIAN QUALIFICATION STRUCTURE

The competence-based Education and Training Scheme of the Association of Accounting Technicians is based on an analysis of the work of accounting staff in a wide range of industries and types of organisation. The Standards of Competence for Accounting which students are expected to meet are based on this analysis.

The Standards identify the **key purpose** of the accounting occupation, which is **to operate, maintain and improve systems to record, plan, monitor and report on the financial activities of an organisation,** and a number of **key roles** of the occupation. Each key role is subdivided into **units of competence**, which are further divided into **elements of competences**. By successfully completing assessments in specified units of competence, students can gain qualifications at NVQ/SVQ levels 2, 3 and 4, which correspond to the AAT Foundation, Intermediate and Technician stages of competence respectively.

Whether you are competent in a Unit is demonstrated by means of:

- *either* a Central Assessment (set and marked by AAT assessors)

- *or* a Devolved Assessment (where competence is judged by an Approved Assessment Centre to whom responsibility for this is devolved)

- or *both* Central *and* Devolved Assessment.

Below we set out the overall structure of the Technician (NVQ/SVQ Level 4) stage, indicating how competence in each Unit is assessed. In the next section there is more detail about the Devolved Assessment for Unit 18.

Note that Units 8, 9 and 10 are compulsory. You can choose one of Units 11 to 14, and then three out of Units 15 to 19.

INLAND REVENUE FORMS USED WITHIN THIS INTERACTIVE TEXT

In your Devolved Assessment you are likely to have to either complete or take information from Inland Revenue Forms. We have included the applicable forms within an appendix to this Text for illustrative purposes. You will practice using these forms when you try the Devolved Assessments in BPP's Unit 18 Devolved Assessment Kit.

Please note that at the time this Text was printed 2000/01 versions of the Inland Revenue forms were not available. Where necessary, we have therefore updated the 1999/00 versions of the forms. It is unlikely that the 2000/01 versions will differ significantly from what we have included here, but we do suggest that you contact the Inland Revenue for updated copies before you take your assessment.

NVQ/SVQ **Level 4 – Technician**

Unit of competence

Elements of competence

Unit 8	Contributing to the management of costs and the enhancement of value

Central Assessment *only*

8.1	Collect, analyse and disseminate information about costs
8.2	Make recommendations to reduce costs and enhance value

Unit 9	Contributing to the planning and allocation of resources

Central Assessment *only*

9.1	Prepare forecasts of income and expenditure
9.2	Produce draft budget proposals
9.3	Monitor the performance of responsiblity centres against budgets

Unit 10	Managing accounting systems

Devolved Assessment *only*

10.1	Co-ordinate work activities within the accounting environment
10.2	Identify opportunities to improve the effectiveness of an accounting system
10.3	Prevent fraud in an accounting system

Unit 22	Monitor and maintain a healthy, safe and secure workplace (ASC)

Devolved Assessment *only*

22.1	Monitor and maintain health and safety within the workplace
22.2	Monitor and maintain the security of the workplace

Unit 11	Drafting financial statements (Accounting Practice, Industry and Commerce)

Central Assessment *only*

11.1	Interpret financial statements
11.2	Draft limited company, sole trader and partnership year end financial statements

Unit 12	Drafting financial statements (Central Government)

Central Assessment *only*

12.1	Interpret financial statements
12.2	Draft central government financial statements

Unit 13	Drafting financial statements (Local Government)

Central Assessment *only*

13.1	Interpret financial statements
13.2	Draft local authority financial statements

Technician qualification structure

Unit of competence

Elements of competence

Unit 14 Drafting financial statements (National Health Service)
Central Assessment *only*

14.1	Interpret financial statements
14.2	Draft NHS accounting statements and returns

Unit 15 Operating a cash management and credit control system
Devolved Assessment *only*

15.1	Monitor and control cash receipts and payments
15.2	Manage cash balances
15.3	Grant credit
15.4	Monitor and control the collection of debts

Unit 16 Evaluating current and proposed activities
Devolved Assessment *only*

16.1	Prepare cost estimates
16.2	Recommend ways to improve cost ratios and revenue generation

Unit 17 Implementing auditing procedures
Devolved Assessment *only*

17.1	Contribute to the planning of an audit assignment
17.2	Contribute to the conduct of an audit assignment
17.3	Prepare related draft reports

Unit 18 Preparing business taxation computations
Devolved Assessment *only*

18.1	Adjust accounting profits and losses for trades and professions
18.2	Prepare capital allowances computations
18.3	Prepare Capital Gains Tax computations
18.4	Account for Income Tax payable or recoverable by a company
18.5	Prepare Corporation Tax computations and returns

Unit 19 Preparing personal taxation computations
Devolved Assessment *only*

19.1	Calculate income from employment
19.2	Prepare computations of property and investment income
19.3	Prepare Capital Gains Tax computations
19.4	Prepare personal tax returns

UNIT 18 STANDARDS OF COMPETENCE

The structure of the Standards for Unit 18

The Unit commences with a statement of the **knowledge and understanding** which underpin competence in the Unit's elements.

The Unit is then divided into **elements of competence** describing activities which the individual should be able to perform.

Each element includes:

- A set of **performance criteria** which define what constitutes competent performance

- A **range statement** which defines the situations, contexts, methods etc in which competence should be displayed

- **Evidence requirements,** which state that competence must be demonstrated consistently, over an appropriate time scale with evidence of performance being provided from the appropriate sources

- **Sources of evidence,** being suggestions of ways in which you can find evidence to demonstrate that competence.

The elements of competence for Unit 18 *Preparing Business Taxation Computations* are set out below. Knowledge and understanding required for the Unit as a whole are listed first, followed by the performance criteria, range statements, evidence requirements and sources of evidence for each element. Performance criteria are cross-referenced to chapters in the Unit 18 *Preparing Business Taxation Computations* Interactive Text.

Unit 18: Preparing Business Taxation Computations

What is the Unit about?

This Unit relates to preparing tax computations for businesses. The candidate is required to carry out tax computations and be responsible in each case for taking account of current tax law and Revenue practice and submitting returns within the timescale. The Unit involves the provision of advice to clients as well as consulting with the Inland Revenue when necessary.

Elements contained within this unit are:

Element 18.1   Adjust accounting profits and losses for trades and professions

Element 18.2   Prepare capital allowances computations

Element 18.3   Prepare capital gains tax computations

Element 18.4   Account for income tax payable or recoverable by a company

Element 18.5   Prepare corporation tax computations and returns

This unit is assessed by devolved assessment only.

Knowledge and understanding

The business environment

- A general understanding of the duties and responsibilities of the taxation practitioner (Elements 18.1, 18.2, 18.3, 18.4, 18.5)

- A general understanding of the issues of taxation liability (Elements 18.1, 18.2, 18.3, 18.4 and 18.5)

  Relevant legislation and guidance from Inland Revenue (Elements 18.1, 18.2, 18.3, 18.4 and 18.5)

Taxation principles and theory

- The basic law and practice relating to all issues covered in the range and referred to in the performance criteria (Elements 18.1, 18.2, 18.3, 18.4 and 18.5)

- The need to adjust accounting profits and losses for tax purposes (Element 18.1)

- Regulations relating to disallowed expenditures private use, capital expenditure, business entertainment (Element 18.1)

- The treatment of bad debts and bad debts provision (Element 18.1)

- The treatment of bank interest (Element 18.1)

- Basis of periods for assessment (Element 18.1)

- Availability and types of allowances: initial allowance; writing down allowance; disposals; balancing charges and gains (relevant to plant and machinery, industrial buildings and hotels, agricultural buildings, motor vehicles and short-life assets); private use reductions (Element 18.2)

- Treatment of capital allowances for companies (Element 18.2)

- Rates of CGT for companies (Element 18.3)

- Exemptions and reliefs from CGT (Element 18.3)

- Methods of calculation: the rollover principle; reinvestment relief; holdover relief (Element 18.3)

- Indexation allowances (Element 18.3)

- The computation of profit for corporation tax purposes: income; capital gain; franked investment income (Element 18.5)

- Rules of self assessment (Element 18.5)

The organisation

- Understanding that the taxation liabilities of an organisation are affected by its legal structure and the nature of its business transactions (Elements 18.1, 18.2, 18.3, 18.4 and 18.5)

- An understanding of the organisation's legal structure and knowledge of its business transactions (Elements 18.1, 18.2, 18.3, 18.4 and 18.5)

Element 18.1 Adjust accounting profits and losses for trades and professions

Performance criteria	Chapters in the Interactive Text
1 The adjusted profit is calculated and made available for inclusion on the tax return	2
2 In the case of partnerships, profits and losses are correctly divided amongst partners in accordance with agreed procedures	6
3 The bases of assessment, including the special rules, are correctly applied	2
4 Computations and submissions are made in accordance with current tax law and take account of current revenue practice	1, 2, 3, 4, 5, 6
5 Consultation with Inland Revenue staff is conducted openly and constructively	13
6 Returns are submitted within the Inland Revenue's timescale	13
7 Timely and constructive advice is given to clients on the maintenance of accounts and the recording of information relevant to tax returns	13
8 Confidentiality of the client is maintained at all times	13

Range statement

1   Clients: Sole Traders; Partnerships

2   Profits and losses from: trades and professions under Schedule D cases I and II

3   Special rules on: admission and retirement of partners; commencement and cessation of a sole trader's business

Element 18.2 Prepare capital allowances computations

Performance criteria	Chapters in the Interactive Text
1 Computations and submissions are made in accordance with current tax law and take account of current revenue practice	3, 4
2 Expenditure on capital assets is classified in accordance with the statutory distinction between capital and revenue expenditure	3
3 Entries and calculations relating to the computation of capital allowances are correct	3, 4
4 Consultation with Inland Revenue staff is conducted openly and constructively	13
5 Computations are included in the appropriate return	13
6 Timely and constructive advice is given to clients on the maintenance of accounts and the recording of information relevant to tax returns	13
7 Confidentiality of the client is maintained at all times	13

Range statement

1   Capital expenditure on: plant and machinery; industrial buildings and hotels; agricultural buildings; motor vehicles; short-life assets

BPP PUBLISHING

Element 18.3 Prepare Capital Gains Tax computations

	Performance criteria	Chapters in the Interactive Text
1	Computations and submissions are made in accordance with current tax law and take account of current revenue practice	7, 8, 9, 10, 11, 12
2	Chargeable assets disposed of are correctly identified and valued	7, 13
3	Chargeable gains, allowable losses and annual exemptions are correctly determined	8, 9, 10
4	Reliefs and transactions relating to shares and securities are taken into account	9, 11, 12
5	Claims for deferrals are correctly identified and submitted to the Inland Revenue within statutory time limits	11, 12
6	Relevant details are accurately and legibly recorded in the corporation tax return	14
7	Consultation with Inland Revenue staff is conducted openly and constructively	14
8	Returns are submitted within the Inland Revenue's timescale	14
9	Timely and constructive advice is given to clients on the maintenance of accounts and the recording of information relevant to tax returns	14
10	Confidentiality of the client is maintained at all times	14

Range statement

1	Computations of: capital gains arising from the sale, gift, loss and destruction of chargeable assets for companies
2	Reliefs: retirement relief; relief for gifts
3	Transactions relating to shares and securities: pooling; short term transactions; bonus and rights issues

Element 18.4 Account for Income Tax payable or recoverable by a company

Performance criteria	Chapters in the Interactive Text
1 Computations and submissions are made in accordance with current tax law and take account of current revenue practice	15
2 Details of charges and credits are correctly identified and entered on appropriate documentation	15
3 Tax due and recoverable is calculated in accordance with established procedures	15
4 Quarterly returns and payments are made within statutory time limits	15
5 Consultation with Inland Revenue staff is conducted openly and constructively	14
6 Timely and constructive advice is given to clients on the maintenance of accounts and the recording of information relevant to tax returns	14
7 Confidentiality of the client is maintained at all times	14

Range statement

1   Income Tax deducted from annual charges

2   Credits: income credits on income received (unfranked investment income)

BPP PUBLISHING

Element 18.5 Prepare Corporation Tax computations and returns

Performance criteria	Chapters in the Interactive Text
1 Adjusted trading profits/losses, capital allowances, charges and loss reliefs, investment income liable to corporation tax and capital gains are correctly calculated	2, 14, 16, 17
2 Income tax deductions and credits are correctly identified	15, 17
3 Corporation tax due is correctly calculated and relevant details are correctly entered onto corporation tax return	14, 15, 16, 17
4 Consultation with Inland Revenue staff is conducted openly and constructively	14
5 Tax returns and relevant claims and elections are submitted within statutory time limits	14
6 Timely and constructive advice is given to clients on the maintenance of accounts and the recording of information relevant to tax returns	14
7 Computations, submissions and payments are made in accordance with current tax law and take account of current revenue practice	14
8 Confidentiality of the client is maintained at all times	14

Range statement

1   Computations and returns for UK resident companies

2   Losses: trade losses; non-trade losses

ASSESSMENT STRATEGY

This Unit is assessed entirely by means of **devolved assessment**.

Devolved Assessment

Devolved assessment is a means of collecting evidence of your ability to carry out practical activities and to operate effectively in the conditions of the workplace to the standards required. Evidence may be collected at your place of work, or at an Approved Assessment Centre by means of simulations of workplace activity, or by a combination of these methods.

If the Approved Assessment Centre is a workplace, you may be observed carrying out accounting activities as part of your normal work routine. You should collect documentary evidence of the work you have done, or contributed to, in an **accounting portfolio**. Evidence collected in a portfolio can be assessed in addition to observed performance or where it is not possible to assess by observation.

Where the Approved Assessment Centre is a **college or training organisation**, devolved assessment will be by means of a combination of the following.

(a) Documentary evidence of activities carried out at the workplace, collected by you in an **accounting portfolio.**

(b) Realistic **simulations** of workplace activities. These simulations may take the form of case studies and in-tray exercises and involve the use of primary documents and reference sources.

(c) **Projects and assignments** designed to assess the Standards of Competence.

If you are unable to provide workplace evidence you will be able to complete the assessment requirements by the alternative methods listed above.

BPP PUBLISHING

Part A

Business taxation

Chapter 1 The taxation of business income on individuals

Chapter topic list

1 Taxes in the UK

2 The administration of taxation

3 The schedular system, income received gross and income taxed at source

4 The aggregation of income

5 Charges on income

6 Allowances deducted from STI

7 Charitable donations

8 The layout of personal tax computations

Learning objectives

On completion of this chapter you will be able to:

	Performance criteria	Range Statement
• calculate the income tax payable by an individual in business during a tax year	18.1.4	-
• recognise the different treatment of savings income	18.1.4	-
• allocate the correct personal allowance to individuals	18.1.4	-
• identify different sources of income	18.1.4	-
• identify different annual payments made by an individual which may reduce his overall tax bill for the year	18.1.4	-

BPP
PUBLISHING

1 TAXES IN THE UK

1.1 Central government raises revenue through a wide range of taxes. Tax law is made by **statute** and as this can be notoriously ambiguous and difficult to understand, the Revenue are currently involved in a project to rewrite it in simpler more user-friendly language.

Statute is interpreted and amplified by **case law**. The Inland Revenue also issue:

(a) **statements of practice**, setting out how they intend to apply the law;

(b) **extra-statutory concessions**, setting out circumstances in which they will not apply the strict letter of the law;

(c) a wide range of **explanatory leaflets**;

(d) **business economic notes**. These are notes on particular types of business, which are used as background information by the Inland Revenue and are also published;

(e) the **Tax Bulletin**. This is a newsletter giving the Inland Revenue's view on specific points. It is published every two months;

(f) the **Internal Guidance**, a series of manuals used by Inland Revenue staff.

However, none of these Inland Revenue publications has the force of law.

A great deal of information and the Inland Revenue publications can now be found on the Revenue's internet site.

1.2 The main taxes suffered by individuals in business are income tax and capital gains tax. You will study these taxes in this unit. Companies suffer corporation tax. You will also study corporation tax in this unit, but we will leave our study of corporation tax until later in this Text.

1.3 **As a general rule, income tax is charged on receipts which might be expected to recur** (such as weekly wages) **whereas capital gains tax is charged on one-off gains** (for example from selling a painting owned for 20 years). Both taxes are charged for tax years.

> **KEY TERM**
>
> The **tax year**, or **fiscal year**, or **year of assessment** runs from 6 April to 5 April. For example, the tax year 2000/01 runs from 6 April 2000 to 5 April 2001.

1.4 **Finance Acts** are passed each year, incorporating proposals set out in the **Budget**. They make changes which apply mainly to the tax year ahead. This text includes the provisions of the Finance Act 2000.

2 THE ADMINISTRATION OF TAXATION

2.1 The **Treasury** formally imposes and collects taxation. The management of the Treasury is the responsibility of the Chancellor of the Exchequer. The Treasury appoint the **Board of Inland Revenue** (sometimes referred to as the **Commissioners of Inland Revenue (CIR)**), a body of civil servants. The Board administers income tax, capital gains tax and corporation tax.

2.2 For income tax purposes, the UK is divided into a number of **regions** (each under a regional controller). Each region is subdivided into **districts** (although some specialist offices, such as the Superannuation Funds Office dealing with pensions, also exist). Each district has a **district inspector** in charge and he is assisted by other inspectors and clerical staff. The official title for an inspector is **HM Inspector of Taxes** (HMIT). The main work of the districts consists of examining tax returns and accounts.

2.3 The collection of tax is not the responsibility of inspectors but of **collectors** of taxes. The collector will pursue the debt through the courts. In extreme circumstances, the collector may seize the assets of the taxpayer.

2.4 Although the functions of 'Collectors' and Inspectors' are currently kept separate the Treasury is considering combining them and has enacted legislation which enables 'Collectors' and 'Inspectors' to be interchangeable terms in the legislation. The term **'Officer of the Board'** is now generally used in legislation.

2.5 The structure of offices set out above is also being changed. **Taxpayer service offices** are being set up to do routine checking, computation *and* collection work, while **Taxpayer district offices** investigate selected accounts and enforce the payment of tax. **Taxpayer assistance offices** handle enquiries and arrange specialist help for taxpayers.

2.6 The **General Commissioners** (not to be confused with the CIR) are appointed by the Lord Chancellor to hear **appeals** against Revenue decisions. They are part-time and unpaid. They are appointed for a local area (a **division**). They appoint a clerk who is often a lawyer or accountant and who is paid for his services by the Board of Inland Revenue.

2.7 The **Special Commissioners** are also appointed by the Lord Chancellor. They are full-time paid professionals. They generally hear the more complex appeals.

2.8 **Many taxpayers arrange for their accountants to prepare and submit their tax returns. The taxpayer is still the person responsible for submitting the return and for paying whatever tax becomes due: the accountant is only acting as the taxpayer's agent.**

3 THE SCHEDULAR SYSTEM, INCOME RECEIVED GROSS AND INCOME TAXED AT SOURCE

3.1 Some income is received in full, with no tax deducted in advance. An example of such income is gilt interest (interest paid on government securities) which is normally received gross. National Savings Bank interest is also received gross.

3.2 **Other income is received after deduction of tax. This is income taxed at source.** The taxable income for a tax year is the **gross** amount (that is, adding back any tax deducted at source). For example, bank interest is normally received after the deduction of 20% tax at source. This means that if £80 interest is received you must gross it up by multiplying by 100/80. The gross amount of £100 (£80 × 100/80) is included in the individual's income tax computation.

3.3 **Dividends on UK shares are received net of a 10% tax credit.** The taxable income for a tax year is the gross dividend (the dividends received multiplied by 100/90). For example if a dividend of £180 is received, include the gross dividend of £200 (£180 × 100/90) in the income tax computation.

Activity 1.1: Gross dividends and interest

Harriet receives dividends of £2,250 and building society interest (net of 20% tax) of £2,400 in 2000/01. What are the gross amounts of dividends and interest to be included in her income tax computation for 2000/01?   2500   3000

5

The schedular system

3.4 **Each type of income is taxed under a set of rules known as a schedule.** Schedules D and E are divided into cases.

Schedule A	Income from land and buildings (rents and so on) in the UK
Schedules B and C	Abolished
Schedule D	

Case I	Profits of trades
Case II	Profits of professions or vocations
Case III	Interest
Case VI	Income not falling under any other schedule or case

Schedule E	Income from an office or employment including salaries, bonuses, benefits in kind and pensions. Most tax is collected under the PAYE system.
Schedule F	UK dividends.

Foreign income may be taxed under Schedule D Cases IV and V but this is not assessable in Unit 18.

3.5 **The schedules and cases are important because each has its own set of rules.** Once we have decided that income is taxed under, say, Schedule A, the rules of Schedule A determine the amount of income taxed in any year. Each type of income assessable at Unit 18 is considered in detail later in this text.

3.6 Although the devolved assessment for Unit 18 is concerned with business taxation, you may need to know broadly how to compute an individual's income tax liability in order to give advice on, for example, utilising business losses. The remainder of this chapter, therefore, gives some details of this computation. If you study Unit 19 *Preparing Personal Tax Computations* you will deal with the personal tax computations in more detail.

4 THE AGGREGATION OF INCOME

4.1 **An individual's income from all sources is brought together in a personal tax computation. We split income into dividend income, savings (excl. dividend) income and non-savings income.**

4.2 Interest and dividends are **'savings income'** All other income is non-savings income.

Interest received net of 20% tax

4.3 The following interest income is received by **individuals** net of 20% tax.

(a) Interest paid by UK companies on debentures and loan stocks
(b) Bank and building society interest (but not National Savings Bank interest)

The amount received must be grossed up by multiplying by 100/80 and it must be included gross in the income tax computation.

Note that companies receive bank and building society interest gross.

DEVOLVED ASSESSMENT ALERT

In the devolved assessment you may be given either the net or the gross amount of such income: read the question carefully. If you are given the net amount (the amount received or credited), you should gross up the figure at the rate of 20%. However, if you are given the gross amount include the figure you are given in the income tax computation.

4.4 Although building society and bank deposit interest are generally paid net of 20% tax a recipient who is not liable to tax can recover the tax suffered For example, net building society interest of £160 is equivalent to gross income of £160 × 100/80 = £200 on which tax of £40 (20% of £200) has been suffered and a non-taxpayer can get the £40 tax suffered repaid to him. Alternatively, he can certify in advance that he is a non-taxpayer and get the interest paid gross.

Dividends on UK shares

4.5 Dividends received on UK shares are received net of a 10% tax credit. This means a dividend received of £90 has a £10 tax credit, giving gross income of £100 to be included in the tax computation. The tax credit attached to dividends **cannot be repaid to non-taxpayers but it is offsettable and can be set against a taxpayer's tax liability.**

4.6 Once income from all sources has been aggregated, charges and the personal allowance are deducted to arrive at taxable income. We will look at these items in more detail later in this chapter but now let us see an example of the layout of the computation of taxable income.

RICHARD: INCOME TAX COMPUTATION 2000/01

	Non-savings income	Savings (excl dividend) income	Dividend income	Total
	£	£	£	£
Schedule D Case I (business profits)	38,000			
Building society interest		1,000		
National savings bank interest		320		
UK dividends			1,000	
	38,000	1,320	1,000	
Less charges on income	(2,000)			
Statutory total income (STI)	36,000	1,320	1,000	38,320
Less personal allowance	(4,385)			
Taxable income	31,615	1,320	1,000	33,935

4.7 Now follow the above layout to try the next activity for yourself.

Activity 1.2: Taxable income

An individual has the following income in 2000/01.

	£
Business profits	16,000
Building society interest received	4,800
Dividends received	7,875
Premium bond prize	5,000

His personal allowance is £4,385. What is his taxable income?

4.8 To calculate an individual's tax liability on taxable income **deal with non-savings income first, then savings (excl. dividend) income and then dividend income.** There is one set of income tax bands that applies to all the income.

4.9 For non-savings income, the first £1,520 is taxed at the starting rate (10%), the next £26,880 is taxed at the basic rate (22%) and the rest at the higher rate (40%).

4.10 Any savings (excl. dividend) income that falls within the starting rate band is taxed at 10% **but income in the basic rate band is taxed at 20% (not 22%).** Such income in excess of the basic rate threshold of £28,400 is taxed at 40%.

4.11 Any dividend income from UK company shares falling within the starting or basic rate bands is taxed at 10%. UK dividend income in excess of the basic rate threshold is taxed at 32.5%.

4.12 Continuing Richard's income tax computation above, the tax liability is:

	£
Non savings income	
£1,520 × 10%	152
£26,880 × 22%	5,914
£3,215 × 40%	1,286
Savings (excl. dividend) income	
£1,320 × 40%	528
Dividend income	
£1,000 × 32.5%	325
Tax liability	8,205

Savings (excl. dividend) and the dividend income are both above the higher rate threshold of £28,400 so they are taxed at 40% and 32.5% respectively.

Activity 1.3: Income tax calculation

An individual has total taxable income of £50,000 for 2000/01. All of his income is non-savings income. What is the total income tax liability?

4.13 Once the tax liability has been calculated, any tax suffered or deducted at source (for example, PAYE tax) and the tax credit on dividend income are deducted to arrive at tax payable. Tax suffered on savings (excl. dividend) income is repayable if it exceeds the individual's tax liability. The tax credit on UK dividends is never repayable.

Activity 1.4: Income tax payable

Kate, who is single and entitled to a personal allowance of £4,385, has a salary of £10,430 (PAYE tax deducted at source £1,000) and building society interest received of £4,000. Calculate Kate's tax payable for 2000/01.

Activity 1.5: Tax credit on dividends

Doris received dividend income of £30,600 in 2000/01. She has no other income. Her personal allowance to deduct from dividend income is £4,385. Calculate the tax payable.

5 CHARGES ON INCOME

5.1 Charges on income are deducted in computing taxable income.

> ### KEY TERM
>
> A **charge on income** is a payment by the taxpayer which income tax law allows as a deduction.

5.2 Examples of charges on income are:

(a) eligible interest;
(b) patent royalties;
(c) copyright royalties.

5.3 **Charges on income fall into two categories: those from which basic rate (22%) income tax is first deducted by the payer (charges paid net) and those which are paid without any deduction (charges paid gross).**

5.4 Patent royalties are an example of a charge on income which is paid net. Eligible interest and copyright royalties are paid gross.

5.5 **We always deduct the gross figure in the payer's tax computation.** If a charge is paid net you must gross it up by multiplying by 100/78. For example if Sue pays a patent royalty of £1,014 you must gross it up to £1,300 (£1,014 × 100/78) and deduct the gross figure in Sue's income tax computation.

Activity 1.6: Charges on income

In 2000/01 Harriet pays a patent royalty of £3,900 and a copyright royalty of £1,000. What is the total amount that Harriet can deduct as charges on income in her income tax computation for 2000/01?

5.6 If you are preparing the personal tax computation of someone who *receives* a charge, for example the owner of a patent who gets royalties from someone who exploits the patent, do the following.

(a) Include the **gross** amount under non-savings income. If the charge is paid gross, the gross amount is the amount received. If it is paid net, the gross amount is the amount received × 100/78.

(b) If the charge was received net, then under the heading 'less tax suffered' (between tax liability and tax payable) include the tax deducted. This is the gross amount × 22%.

Eligible interest

5.7 **Interest on a loan is a charge when the loan is used for one of the following purposes.**

(a) **To invest in a partnership.**

(b) **To purchase ordinary shares in a close company.** A close company is broadly a company that is controlled by 5 or fewer shareholders or its directors.

(c) **To invest in a co-operative.**

(d) **To purchase shares in an employee-controlled company.**

(e) **By a partner to purchase plant or machinery used in the business.**

(f) **By an employee to purchase plant or machinery used by him in the performance of his duties.**

(g) **By personal representatives to pay inheritance tax**

(h) To replace of other qualifying loans.

Interest on an overdraft or on a credit card debt does not qualify as a charge on income.

Business interest

5.8 A taxpayer paying interest wholly and exclusively for business purposes is allowed to deduct such interest in the computation of his profit under Schedule D Case I, instead of as a charge. The interest need not fall into any of the categories outlined above, and it may be on an overdraft or a credit card debt.

5.9 Note that where interest is allowable as a Schedule D Case I deduction, the amount *payable* (on an accruals basis) is deducted. Only interest *paid* in the tax year may be set against total income as a charge.

Charges in personal tax computations

5.10 The gross amount of any charge is deducted from the taxpayer's income to arrive at Statutory Total Income (STI).

5.11 Deduct charges from non-savings income then from savings (excl. dividend income) and lastly from dividend income.

5.12 If a charge has been paid net, the basic rate income tax deducted (22% of the gross amount) is added into the tax liability. The taxpayer gets tax relief by deducting the gross amount of the payment in computing his STI: he cannot keep the basic rate tax withheld from the payment as well, but he must pay it to the Inland Revenue. This means that the final step in computing the tax liability should be to add on any tax withheld on charges paid net. Note that this addition is made **after** the deduction of tax reducers (see below).

5.13 EXAMPLE

Three taxpayers have the following schedule D Case I income and allowances for 2000/01. Taxpayers A and B pay a patent royalty of £176 (net). Taxpayer C pays a patent royalty of £1,248 (net).

	A	B	C
	£	£	£
Schedule D Case I Income	5,000	3,000	34,615
Less: charge on income (× 100/78)	(226)	(226)	(1,600)
	4,774	2,774	33,015
Less: personal allowance	(4,385)	(4,385)	(4,385)
Taxable income	389	–	28,630
Income tax			
10% on £389/-/£1,520	39	–	152
22% on -/-/£26, 880			5,914
40% on -/-/£230			92
	39	–	6,158
Add: 22% tax retained on charge	50	50	352
Tax liability	89	50	6,510

Activity 1.7: Charges in personal tax computations

John, who is single and entitled to a personal allowance of £4,385, has schedule D case I profits of £8,000 in 2000/01. He also received building society interest of £14,000 and dividends of £450. He paid a patent royalty of £9,360. Show John's income tax liability for 2000/01.

6 ALLOWANCES DEDUCTED FROM STI

6.1 All persons (including children) are entitled to the personal allowance of £4,385.

6.2 Once taxable income from all sources has been aggregated and any charges on income deducted, the remainder is the taxpayer's statutory total income (STI). The personal allowance is then deducted from STI. Like charges, it comes off non-savings income first, then savings (exl dividend) income and then dividend income.

7 CHARITABLE DONATIONS

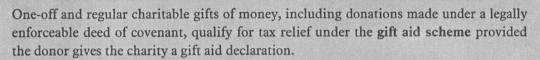

KEY TERM

One-off and regular charitable gifts of money, including donations made under a legally enforceable deed of covenant, qualify for tax relief under the **gift aid scheme** provided the donor gives the charity a gift aid declaration.

7.1 **Gift aid declarations can be made in writing, electronically through the internet or orally over the phone. A declaration can cover a one off gift or any number of gifts for the future or retrospectively.**

7.2 **A gift aid donation is treated as though it was paid net of basic rate tax (22%, 2000/01).**

7.3 **Additional tax relief is given in the personal tax computation by increasing the donor's basic rate band by the gross amount of the gift.**

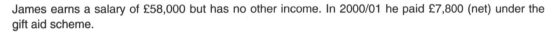

Activity 1.8: Tax relief for gift aid donation

James earns a salary of £58,000 but has no other income. In 2000/01 he paid £7,800 (net) under the gift aid scheme.

Compute James' income tax liability for 2000/01.

7.4 An income tax deduction is available if the whole of any beneficial interest in qualifying shares or securities is given, or sold at an undervalue, to a charity. Broadly, an individual can deduct the market value of the share or securities at the date of disposal in calculating his total income.

8 THE LAYOUT OF PERSONAL TAX COMPUTATIONS

8.1 Now let us work through some complete computations of income tax payable.

BPP
PUBLISHING

8.2   (a)   Kathe has business profits of £10,000 and receives dividends of £4,500.

	Non-savings £	Dividends £	Total £
Schedule D Case I	10,000		
Dividends £4,500 × 100/90		5,000	
STI	10,000	5,000	15,000
Less personal allowance	(4,385)		
Taxable income	5,615	5,000	10,615

	£
Income tax	
Non savings income	
£1,520 × 10%	152
£4,095 × 22%	901
Dividend income	
£5,000 × 10%	500
Tax liability	1,553
Less tax credit on dividend	(500)
Tax payable	1,053

The dividend income falls within the basic rate band so it is taxed at 10% (*not* 22%).

(b)   Jules has business profits of £50,000, net dividends of £6,750 and building society interest of £3,000 net. He pays gross charges of £2,000 and makes a gift aid donation of £780 (net).

	Non-savings £	Savings (excl dividend) £	Dividends	Total £
Schedule D Case I	50,000			
Dividends £6,750 × 100/90			7,500	
Building society interest £3,000 × 100/80		3,750		
	50,000	3,750	7,500	
Less charges	(2,000)			
STI	48,000	3,750	7,500	59,250
Less personal allowance	(4,385)			
Taxable income	43,615	3,750	7,500	54,865

	£
Income tax	
Non savings income	
£1,520 × 10%	152
£26,880 × 22%	5,914
£1,000 (£780 × $\frac{100}{78}$) × 22%	220
£14,215 × 40%	5,686
	11,972
Savings (excl. dividend) income	
£3,750 × 40%	1,500
Dividend income	
£7,500 × 32.5%	2,438
Less tax credit on dividend income	(750)
Less tax suffered on building society interest	(750)
Tax payable	14,410

Savings (excl. dividend) income and dividend income fall above the basic rate threshold so they are taxed at 40% and 32.5% respectively. The basic rate band is extended by the gross amount of the gift aid donation.

The complete proforma

8.3 Here is a complete proforma computation of taxable income. We include it here as you might find it useful to refer back to later.

	Non-savings £	Savings (excl. dividend) £	Dividend £	Total £
Business profits	X			
Less losses set against business profits	(X)			
	X			
Less pension contributions	(X)			
	X			
Wages less pension contributions	X			
Other non-savings (as many lines as necessary)	X			
Building society interest		X		
Other savings (excl. dividends) (as many lines as necessary)		X		
Dividends			X	
	X	X	X	
Less charges	(X)	(X)	(X)	
	X	X	X	
Less losses set against general income	(X)	(X)	(X)	
STI	X	X	X	X
Less personal allowance	(X)	(X)	(X)	
Taxable income	X	X	X	X

Activity 1.9: End of chapter activity

Mary, a single 24 year old, has business profits of £14,000. She also receives building society interest of £6,400 net, dividends of £1,800 (net), and pays a charge of £2,500 (gross) each year. How much cash will she have available to spend in 2000/01?

Key learning points

- In this chapter we have covered both the legal framework of taxation and the basic rules for working out the income tax an individual must pay.

- In a personal income tax computation, we bring together income from all sources, splitting the sources into non-savings income, savings (excl. dividend) income and dividend income. We deduct charges, and then the personal allowance. Finally, we work out income tax on the taxable income.

Quick quiz

1 What are the main UK taxes suffered by businesses?

2 At what rates is income tax charged on non-savings income?

3 Under what schedule and case of income tax are the profits of a trade taxed?

4 What types of income are received by individuals net of 20% tax?

5 What charges on income are paid net?

Answers to quick quiz

1 Income tax, corporation tax and capital gains tax

2 Income tax is charged on the figure of 'taxable income', on the first £1,520 at the starting rate (10%), on the next £26,880 at the basic rate (22%) and on the rest at the higher rate (40%).

3   Schedule D Case I

4   (a)   Interest paid by UK companies on debentures and loan stocks
     (b)   Building society interest
     (c)   Bank deposit interest (but not National Savings Bank interest)

5   Patent royalties

Answers to Activities

Activity 1.1

The gross amounts are:	Dividends (£2,250 × 100/90)	£2,500
	Building society interest (£2,400 × 100/80)	£3,000

Activity 1.2

	Non-savings income £	Savings (excl. dividend) income £	Dividend income £	Total £
Schedule D Case I	16,000	0	0	
Building society interest £4,800 × 100/80	0	6,000	0	
Dividends £7,875 × 100/90	0	0	8,750	
STI	16,000	6,000	8,750	30,750
Less personal allowance	(4,385)			
Taxable income	11,615	6,000	8,750	26,365

Did you remember to gross up dividends by 100/90 and building society interest by 100/80?

Activity 1.3

	£
£1,520 × 10%	152
£26,880 × 22%	5,914
£21,600 × 40%	8,640
	14,706

Activity 1.4

	Non-savings income £	Savings (excl dividend) income) £	Total £
Schedule E	10,430		
Building society interest (× 100/80)		5,000	
	10,430	5,000	15,430
Less personal allowance	(4,385)		
	6,045	5,000	11,045

	£
Tax on non-savings income	
£1,520 × 10%	152
£4,525 × 22%	996
Tax on savings (excl dividend)	
£5,000 × 20%	1,000
Tax Liability	2,148
Less: PAYE	(1,000)
Tax suffered on building society interest	(1,000)
Tax payable	148

The building society interest falls within the basic rate threshold so it is taxed at 20%.

Activity 1.5

	Dividend income £
Dividends (× 100/90)	34,000
Less personal allowance	(4,385)
Taxable income	29,615

Tax on dividend income

	£
£28,400 × 10%	2,840
£1,215 × 32.5%	395
	3,235
Less: Tax credit on dividend (max)	(3,235)
Tax payable	-

The dividend income that falls within the starting and basic rate thresholds is taxed at 10%. Dividend income over the threshold of £28,400 is taxed at 32.5%. The tax credit suffered on the dividend income, £3,400, can be offset against the tax liability to reduce it to £nil. However, the excess tax credit, £165 (£3,400 − £3,235) cannot be repaid. The tax credit is offsettable but not repayable.

Activity 1.6

	£
Patent royalty (£3,900 × 100/78)	5,000
Copyright royalty	1,000
Total to deduct income tax computation	6,000

Copyright royalties are paid gross. The patent royalties are paid net of 22% tax but Harriet will deduct the gross amounts in her income tax computation.

Activity 1.7

	Non-savings Income £	Savings(excl dividend) income £	Dividend income £	
Schedule D Case I	8,000			
Building society interest (× 100/80)		17,500		
Dividends (× 100/90)			500	
Patent royalty (× 100/78)	(8,000)	(4,000)	___	
	-	13,500	500	14,000
Less personal allowance	___	(4,385)	-	
	-	9,115	500	9,165

	£
Income tax savings (excl dividend) income	
£1,520 × 10%	152
£7,595 × 20%	1,519
Dividend income £500 × 10%	50
	1,721
Add: Tax retained on charge	2,640
Income tax liability	4,361

Activity 1.8

	Non-savings £
Salary	58,000
Less: personal allowance	(4,385)
Taxable income	53,615

Income tax	£	£
Starting rate band	1,520 × 10%	152
Basic rate band	26,880 × 22%	5,914
Basic rate band (extended)	10,000 × 22%	2,200
Higher rate band	15,215 × 40%	6,086
	53,615	14,352

The basic rate band is extended by the gross amount of the gift aid donation, £10,000 (£7,800 × $\frac{100}{78}$)

Activity 1.9

	Non-savings £	Savings (excl.dividend) £	Dividend £	Total £
Business profits	14,000			
Building society interest × 100/80		8,000		
Dividends × 100/90			2,000	
	14,000	8,000	2,000	
Less charge	(2,500)	0	0	
Statutory total income	11,500	8,000	2,000	21,500
Less personal allowance	(4,385)	0	0	
Taxable income	7,115	8,000	2,000	17,115

	£
Non-savings income	
Lower rate band £1,520 × 10%	152
Basic rate band £5,595 × 22%	1,231
Savings (excl dividend) income	
£8,000 × 20%	1,600
Dividend income	
£2,000 × 10%	200
	3,183
Less: tax suffered on building society interest	(1,600)
tax credit on dividend income	(200)
Balance of tax still to pay	1,383

	£	£
Profits received		14,000
Building society interest received		6,400
Dividend received		1,800
		22,200
Less: charge paid	2,500	
income tax to pay	1,383	
		3,883
Available to spend		18,317

Chapter 2   Schedule D Cases I and II

Chapter topic list

1   The badges of trade

2   The computation of trading income

3   Basis periods

4   Income Tax forms

Learning objectives

On completion of this chapter you will be able to:

	Performance criteria	Range Statement
• discuss the indicators which point towards a trade being carried on	18.1.1	18.1.2
• calculate taxable profits for a trader starting from the profit and loss account prepared by the business	18.1.1	18.1.2
• indicate for an individual how much business profit will be taxed and in which year	18.1.3	18.1.2 18.1.3

BPP
PUBLISHING

1 THE BADGES OF TRADE

KEY TERM

A trade is defined in the legislation only in an unhelpful manner as including every trade, manufacture, adventure or concern in the nature of a trade. It has therefore been left to the courts to provide guidance. This guidance is often summarised in a collection of principles known as the '**badges of trade**'. These are set out below.

1.1 Trading income is subject to tax under Schedule D Case I.

The subject matter

1.2 **Whether a person is trading or not may sometimes be decided by examining the subject matter of the transaction.** Some assets are commonly held as investments for their intrinsic value: an individual buying some shares or a painting may do so in order to enjoy the income from the shares or to enjoy the work of art. Any subsequent disposal, even at a profit, may produce a gain of a capital nature rather than a trading profit. But **where the subject matter of a transaction is such as would not be held as an investment** (for example 34,000,000 yards of aircraft linen (*Martin v Lowry 1927*) or 1,000,000 rolls of toilet paper (*Rutledge v CIR 1929*)), **it is to be presumed that any profit on resale is a trading profit.**

The frequency of transactions

1.3 Transactions which may be treated in isolation as being of a capital nature will be interpreted as trading transactions where their **frequency indicates the carrying on of a trade.** It was decided that whereas normally the purchase of a mill-owning company and the subsequent stripping of its assets might be a capital transaction, where the taxpayer was embarking on the same exercise for the fourth time he must be carrying on a trade (*Pickford v Quirke 1927*).

The length of ownership

1.4 The courts may infer adventures in the nature of **trade where items purchased are sold soon afterwards.**

Supplementary work and marketing

1.5 **When work is done to make an asset more marketable,** or steps are taken to find purchasers, the courts will be more ready to ascribe a trading motive. When a group of accountants bought, blended and recasked a quantity of brandy they were held to be taxable on a trading profit when the brandy was later sold (*Cape Brandy Syndicate v CIR 1921*).

A profit motive

1.6 The absence of a profit motive will not necessarily preclude a Schedule D Case I assessment, but its presence is a strong indication that a person is trading. The purchase and resale of £20,000 worth of silver bullion by the comedian Norman Wisdom, as a hedge against devaluation, was held to be a trading transaction (*Wisdom v Chamberlain 1969*).

The way in which the asset sold was acquired

1.7 **If goods are acquired deliberately, trading may be indicated.** If goods are acquired unintentionally, for example by gift or inheritance, their later sale is unlikely to constitute trading.

The taxpayer's intentions

1.8 Where a transaction clearly amounts to trading on objective criteria, **the taxpayer's intentions are irrelevant.** If, however, a transaction has (objectively) a dual purpose, the taxpayer's intentions may be taken into account. An example of a transaction with a dual purpose is the acquisition of a site partly as premises from which to conduct another trade, and partly with a view to the possible development and resale of the site.

This intentions test is not one of the traditional badges of trade, but it may be just as important.

Activity 2.1: Trading

Gareth inherited some land. He then bought some adjoining land, drained the combined plot, applied for planning permission and sold the combined plot at a profit. Which badges of trade would indicate that he was trading?

DEVOLVED ASSESSMENT ALERT

If income is received by an individual and on applying the badges of trade the Inland Revenue do not conclude that the income is 'trading income' then they can potentially treat it as Schedule D Case VI income or a capital gain.

2 THE COMPUTATION OF TRADING INCOME

The adjustment of profits

2.1 Although the net profit before taxation shown in the accounts provides the starting point in computing the taxable trading profit, many adjustments may be required to find the profit taxable under the rules of Schedule D Case I. The same rules apply to Case II (profits of a profession or vocation), and we will just refer to Case I from now on.

2.2 Here is an illustrative adjustment.

	£	£
Net profit per accounts		140,000
Add: expenditure charged in the accounts which is not deductible under Schedule D Case I	50,000	
income taxable under Schedule D Case I which has not been included in the accounts	30,000	
		80,000
		220,000
Less: profits included in the accounts but which are not taxable under Schedule D Case I	40,000	
expenditure which is deductible under Schedule D Case I but has not been charged in the accounts	20,000	
		60,000
Profit adjusted for tax purposes		160,000

You may refer to deductible and non-deductible expenditure as allowable and disallowable expenditure respectively. The two sets of terms are interchangeable.

Accounting policies

2.3 **As a rule, accounts drawn up on normal accepted accounting principles are acceptable for tax purposes.** Two special points are worth noting.

- If there is a legal action in progress, the best estimate of the cost should be debited, not the most prudent estimate.

- Under SSAP 9, a loss on a long-term contract is recognised as soon as it is foreseen. Anticipating a loss in this way is not acceptable for tax purposes, so the debit to profit and loss must be added back.

2.4 The profits of a trade, profession or vocation must normally be computed for tax purposes on a basis which gives a true and fair view, subject to any adjustments permitted or required by tax law.

Deductible and non-deductible expenditure

Payments contrary to public policy and illegal payments

2.5 Based on case law fines and penalties are not deductible. However, the Inland Revenue usually allow employees' parking fines incurred in parking their employer's cars while on their employer's business. Fines relating to directors and proprietors, however, are never allowed.

A payment is (by statute) not deductible if making it constitutes an offence by the payer. This covers protection money paid to terrorists, and also bribes. Statute law also prevents any deduction for payments made in response to blackmail or extortion.

Capital expenditure

2.6 **Income tax is a tax solely on income and so capital expenditure is not deductible. The most contentious items of expenditure will often be repairs** (revenue expenditure) **and improvements** (capital expenditure).

- The cost of restoration of an asset by, for instance, replacing a subsidiary part of the asset will be treated as revenue expenditure. It was held that expenditure on a new factory chimney replacement was allowable since the chimney was a subsidiary part of the factory (*Samuel Jones & Co (Devondale) Ltd v CIR 1951*). However, in another case a football club demolished a spectators' stand and replaced it with a modern equivalent. This was held not to be repair, since repair is the restoration by renewal or replacement of subsidiary parts of a larger entity, and the stand formed a distinct and *separate* part of the club (*Brown v Burnley Football and Athletic Co Ltd 1980*).

- The cost of initial repairs to improve an asset recently acquired to make it fit to earn profits is disallowable capital expenditure. In *Law Shipping Co Ltd v CIR 1923* the taxpayer failed to obtain relief for expenditure on making a newly bought ship seaworthy prior to using it.

- The cost of initial repairs to remedy normal wear and tear of recently acquired assets will be treated as allowable. *Odeon Associated Theatres Ltd v Jones 1971* can be contrasted with the *Law Shipping* judgement. Odeon were allowed to charge expenditure incurred on improving the state of recently acquired cinemas.

2.7 Other examples to note include:

- A one-off payment made by a hotel owner to terminate an agreement for the management of a hotel was held to be revenue rather than capital expenditure in *Croydon Hotel & Leisure Co v Bowen 1996*. The payment did not affect the whole structure of the taxpayer's business; it merely enabled it to be run more efficiently.

- A one-off payment to remove a threat to the taxpayer's business was also held to be revenue rather than capital expenditure in *Lawson v Johnson Matthey plc 1992*.

- An initial payment for a franchise (as opposed to regular fees) is capital and not deductible.

2.8 **Two exceptions to the 'capital' rule** are worth noting.

(a) The costs of **registering patents and trade marks** are deductible.

(b) **Incidental costs of obtaining loan finance,** or of attempting to obtain or redeeming it, are deductible other than a discount on issue or a premium on redemption (which are really alternatives to paying interest). This deduction for incidental costs does not apply to companies because they get a deduction for the costs of borrowing in a different way. We will look at companies later in this text.

Appropriations

2.9 **Salary or interest on capital paid to a proprietor, and also depreciation, amortisation and general provisions are not deductible.** A specific provision against a particular trade debt is deductible if it is a reasonable estimate of the likely loss.

The private proportion of payments for motoring expenses, rent, heat and light and telephone expenses of a proprietor is not deductible. Where the payments are to or on behalf of employees, the full amounts are deductible but the employees are taxed on benefits in kind.

Charges and gift payments

2.10 **Charges (such as royalties) and gift aid payments are dealt with in the personal tax computation, so they cannot also be deducted in computing trading profits.**

Entertaining and gifts

2.11 **Entertaining for and gifts to employees are normally deductible** although where gifts are made, or the entertainment is excessive, a charge to tax may arise on the employee under the benefits in kind legislation. **Gifts to customers not costing more than £10 per donee per year are allowed if they carry a conspicuous advertisement for the business and are not food, drink, tobacco or vouchers exchangeable for goods.** Gifts to charities may also be allowed although many will fall foul of the 'wholly and exclusively' rule below.

Tax relief is available for certain donations of trading stock and equipment (see below).

All other expenditure on entertaining and gifts is non-deductible.

Expenditure not wholly and exclusively for the purposes of the trade

2.12 **Expenditure is not deductible if it is not for the purposes of the trade (the remoteness test), or if it reflects more than one purpose (the duality test). If an exact apportionment is possible (as with motor expenses) relief is given on the business element.**

BPP PUBLISHING

2.13 **The remoteness test** is illustrated by the following cases.

- *Strong & Co of Romsey Ltd v Woodifield 1906*
  A customer was injured by a falling chimney when sleeping in an inn owned by a brewery. He obtained compensation from the company.

  Held: the payment was not deductible: 'the loss sustained by the appellant was not really incidental to their trade as innkeepers and fell upon them in their character not of innkeepers but of householders'.

- *Bamford v ATA Advertising Ltd 1972*
  A director misappropriated £15,000.

  Held: the loss was not allowable: 'the loss is not, as in the case of a dishonest shop assistant, an incident of the company's trading activities. It arises altogether outside such activities'.

- Expenditure which is wholly and exclusively to benefit the trades of several companies (for example in a group) but is not wholly and exclusively to benefit the trade of one specific company is not deductible (*Vodafone Cellular Ltd and others v Shaw 1995*).

- *McKnight (HMIT) v Sheppard (1999)* concerned expenses incurred by a stockbroker in defending allegations of infringements of Stock Exchange regulations. It was found that the expenditure was incurred to prevent the destruction of the taxpayer's business and as the expenditure was incurred for business purposes it was deductible. It was also found that although the expenditure also had the effect of preserving the taxpayer's reputation, that was not its purpose, so there was no duality of purpose.

2.14 The **duality test** is illustrated by the following cases.

- *Caillebotte v Quinn 1975*
  A self-employed carpenter spent an average of 40p per day when obliged to buy lunch away from home but just 10p when he lunched at home. He claimed the excess 30p.

  Held: the payment had a dual purpose and was not deductible: 'a Schedule D taxpayer must eat to live not eat to work'.

- *Mallalieu v Drummond 1983*
  The House of Lords held that expenditure by a lady barrister on black clothing to be worn in court (and on its cleaning and repair) was not deductible. The expenditure had been for the dual purpose of enabling the barrister to be warmly and properly clad as well as meeting her professional requirements.

- *McLaren v Mumford 1996*
  The taxpayer, a publican, traded from a public house which had residential accommodation above it. The taxpayer was obliged to live at the public house but he also had another house which he visited regularly. It was held that the private element of the expenditure incurred at the public house on electricity, rent, gas etc, was not incurred for the purpose of earning profits, but for serving the non-business purpose of satisfying the publican's ordinary human needs. The expenditure, therefore had a dual purpose and was disallowed.

2.15 However, the cost of overnight accommodation when on a business trip may be deductible and reasonable expenditure on an evening meal and breakfast in conjunction with such accommodation is then also deductible.

Activity 2.2: Dual purpose

Why might a barrister obtain a deduction for the cost of cleaning his or her gown and wig?

22

Subscriptions and donations

2.16 **There is a general 'wholly and exclusively' rule which determines the deductibility of expenses. Subscriptions and donations are not deductible unless the expenditure is for the benefit of the trade.** The following are the main types of subscriptions and donations you may meet and their correct treatments.

(a) Trade subscriptions (such as to a professional or trade association) are generally deductible.

(b) Charitable donations are deductible only if they are small and to local charities. Tax relief may be available for donations under the gift aid scheme. In this case they are not a deductible Schedule D Case 1 expense.

(c) Political subscriptions and donations are generally not deductible. However, if it can be shown that political expenditure is incurred for the survival of the trade then it may be deducted. This follows a case in which it was held that expenditure incurred in resisting nationalisation was allowable on the grounds that it affected the survival of the business (*Morgan v Tate and Lyle Ltd 1954*).

(d) When a business makes a gift of equipment manufactured, sold or used in the course of its trade to an educational establishment or for a charitable purpose, nothing need be brought into account as a trading receipt or (if capital allowances had been obtained on the asset) as disposal proceeds, so full relief is obtained for the cost. The value of any benefit to the donor from the gift is taxable on him.

(e) Where a donation represents the most effective commercial way of disposing of stock (for example, where it would not be commercially effective to sell surplus perishable food), the donation can be treated as for the benefit of the trade and the disposal proceeds taken as £Nil. In other cases, the amount credited to the accounts in respect of a donation of stock should be its market value.

Legal and professional charges

2.17 **Legal and professional charges relating to capital or non-trading items are not deductible.** These include charges incurred in acquiring new capital assets or legal rights, issuing shares, drawing up partnership agreements and litigating disputes over the terms of a partnership agreement.

Charges incurred are deductible when they relate directly to trading. Deductible items include:

- legal and professional charges incurred defending the taxpayer's title to fixed assets;
- charges connected with an action for breach of contract;
- expenses of the **renewal** (not the original grant) of a lease for less than 50 years;
- charges for trade debt collection;
- normal charges for preparing accounts and assisting with the self assessment of tax liabilities.

2.18 Accountancy expenses arising out of an enquiry into the accounts information in a particular year's return are not allowed where the enquiry reveals discrepancies and additional liabilities for the year of enquiry, or any earlier year, which arise as a result of negligent or fraudulent conduct.

Where, however, the enquiry results in no addition to profits, or an adjustment to the profits for the year of enquiry only and that assessment does not arise as a result of negligent or fraudulent conduct, the additional accountancy expenses are allowable.

Bad and doubtful debts

2.19 **Only bad debts incurred in the course of a business are deductible for taxation purposes.** Thus loans to employees written off are not deductible unless the business is that of making loans, or it can be shown that the writing-off of the loan was an emolument laid out for the benefit of the trade. If a trade debt is released as part of a voluntary arrangement under the Insolvency Act 1986, or a compromise or arrangement under s 425 Companies Act 1985, the amount released is deductible as a bad debt.

2.20 **General doubtful debt provisions are not deductible, but specific provisions and write-offs against individual debts are deductible.** The only adjustment needed to the accounts profit is to add back an increase (or deduct a decrease) in the general provision.

Interest

2.21 **Interest paid by an individual on borrowings for trade purposes is deductible as a trading expense on an accruals basis, so no adjustment to the accounts figure is needed.**

2.22 Companies have different rules for the cost of borrowing. We will look at these later in this text.

2.23 Interest on overdue tax is not deductible.

Activity 2.3: Disallowed expense

A manufacturing business spends the following amounts on legal and professional services.

		£
Debt collection:	trade debts	500
	loan to former employee	230
Defending action for faulty goods		1,900
Preparing accounts		450
Specialist tax consultancy		700
		3,780

How much must be added back in computing the taxable profits?

Miscellaneous deductions

2.24 The **costs of seconding employees to charities or educational establishments are deductible.**

2.25 Expenditure incurred before the commencement of trade **(pre-trading expenditure)** is deductible, provided that:

- it is incurred within seven years of the start of trade; and
- it is of a type that would have been deductible had the trade already started.

It is treated as a trading expense incurred on the first day of trading.

2.26 **Where emoluments for employees are charged in the accounts but have still not been paid to the employees nine months after the end of the period of account, the cost is only deductible for the period of account in which the emoluments are paid.** When a tax computation is made within the nine month period, it is initially assumed that unpaid emoluments will not be paid within that period. The computation is adjusted if they are so paid.

Emoluments are treated as paid at the same time as they are treated as received for Schedule E purposes.

Redundancy payments made when a trade ends are deductible on the earlier of the day of payment and the last day of trading. If the trade does not end, they can be deducted as soon as they are provided for, so long as the redundancy was decided on within the period of account, the provision is accurately calculated and the payments are made within nine months of the end of the period of account.

2.27 Here is a list of various other items that you may meet.

Item	Treatment	Comment
Educational courses for staff	Allow	
Educational courses for proprietor	Allow	If to update existing knowledge or skills, not if to acquire new knowledge or skills
Removal expenses (to new business premises)	Allow	Only if not an expansionary move
Travelling expenses to the trader's place of business	Disallow	*Ricketts v Colquhoun 1925*: unless an itinerant trader (*Horton v Young 1971*)
Redundancy pay in excess of the statutory amount	Allow	If the trade ceases, the limit on allowability is $3 \times$ the statutory amount (in addition to the statutory amount)
Compensation for loss of office and ex gratia payments	Allow	If for benefit of trade: *Mitchell v B W Noble Ltd 1927*
Counselling services for employees leaving employment	Allow	If qualify for exemption from tax charge on employees
Contributions to any of: local enterprise agencies; training and enterprise councils; local enterprise companies; business link organisations individual learning accounts (ILA)	Allow	The ILA must qualify for a discount or grant and contributions must be available to all employees generally.
Pension contributions (to schemes for employees and company directors)	Allow	If paid, not if only provided for; special contributions may be spread over the year of payment and future years
Premiums for insurance: against an employee's death or illness to cover locum costs or fixed overheads whilst the policyholder is ill	Allow	Receipts are taxable
Payments to employees for restrictive undertakings	Allow	Taxable on employee
Damages paid	Allow	If not too remote from trade: *Strong and Co v Woodifield 1906*
Preparation and restoration of waste disposal sites	Allow	Spread preparation expenditure over period of use of site. Pre-trading expenditure is treated as incurred on the first day of trading. Allow restoration expenditure in period of expenditure

BPP PUBLISHING

Item	Treatment	Comment
Improving an individual's personal security	Allow	Trader must be an individual or a partnership (not a company). Provision of a car, ship or dwelling is excluded

DEVOLVED ASSESSMENT ALERT

In the assessment you could be given a copy of a business's profit and loss account and asked to calculate 'taxable profit'. You will have to look at every expense charged in the accounts to decide if it is (or isn't) a 'tax deductible expense'. To help you to achieve this you must become familiar with the many expenses you are likely to see and the correct tax treatment. Look at the above paragraphs again noting what expenses are (and are not) allowable for tax purposes.

Income taxable under Schedule D Case I but excluded from the accounts

2.28 **The usual example is when a proprietor takes goods for his own use. In such circumstances the normal selling price of the goods is added to the accounting profit. In** other words, the proprietor is treated for tax purposes as having made a sale to himself. This rule does not apply to supplies of services, which are treated as sold for the amount (if any) actually paid (but the cost of services to the trader or his household is not deductible).

Accounting profits not taxable under Schedule D Case I

2.29 **There are three types of receipts which may be found in the accounting profits but which must be excluded from the Schedule D Case I computation.** These are:

(a) **capital receipts;**
(b) **income taxed in another way** (at source or under another case or schedule);
(c) **income specifically exempt from tax.**

However, compensation received in one lump sum for the loss of income is likely to be treated as income.

2.30 In some trades, particularly petrol stations and public houses, a wholesale supplier may pay a lump sum to a retailer in return for the retailer's only supplying that wholesaler's products (an **exclusivity agreement**). If the payment must be used for a specific capital purpose, it is a capital receipt. If that is not the case, it is a revenue receipt. If the sum is repayable to the wholesaler but the requirement to repay is waived in tranches over the term of the agreement, each tranche is a separate revenue receipt when the requirement is waived.

Deductible expenditure not charged in the accounts

2.31 **A common instance of such expenditure occurs when a trader deducts an annual sum in respect of the amount taxable under Schedule A on a lease premium which he paid to his landlord.** Normally, the amortisation of the lease will have been deducted in the accounts (and must be added back as an appropriation). Capital allowances (see the following chapters) **are also deductible expenditure not charged in the accounts.**

Activity 2.4: Calculation of Schedule D Case I profit

Here is the profit and loss account of S Pring, a trader.

	£	£
Gross operating profit		30,000
Taxed interest received		860
		30,860
Wages and salaries	7,000	
Rent and rates	2,000	
Depreciation	1,500	
Bad debts written off	150	
Provision against a fall in the price of raw materials	5,000	
Entertainment expenses	750	
Patent royalties	1,200	
Bank interest	300	
Legal expenses on acquisition of new factory	250	
		(18,150)
Net profit		12,710

(a) Salaries include £500 paid to Mrs Pring who works full time in the business.
(b) No staff were entertained.
(c) The provision of £5,000 is charged because of an anticipated trade recession.
(d) Taxed interest and patent royalties were received and paid net but have been shown gross.

Compute the profit taxable under Schedule D Case I.

Rounding

2.32 Where an individual, a partnership or a single company has an annual turnover of at least £5,000,000, and prepares its accounts with figures rounded to at least the nearest £1,000, figures in computations of adjusted profits (including, for companies, non-trading profits but excluding capital gains) may generally be rounded to the nearest £1,000.

The cessation of trades

2.33 **Post-cessation receipts** (including any releases of debts incurred by the trader) **are taxable under Schedule D Case VI**. If they are received in the tax year of cessation or the next six tax years, the trader can elect that they be treated as received on the day of cessation. The time limit for electing is the 31 January which is 22 months after the end of the tax year of receipt.

2.34 **Post-cessation expenses can be deducted so long as they would have been deductible had the trade continued,** and they did not arise as a result of the cessation. Capital allowances which the trader was entitled to immediately before the discontinuance but which remain unrelieved can also be deducted.

2.35 If an individual trader or a partner (not a company) incurs certain expenses within the seven years after ceasing to trade and no deduction from post cessation receipts is possible, he can claim to **deduct them from his total income for the year of payment.**

3 BASIS PERIODS

3.1 **A tax year runs from 6 April to 5 April,** but most businesses do not have periods of account ending on 5 April. **Thus there must be a link between a period of account of a business and a tax year.** The procedure is to **find a period to act as the basis period for a tax year. The profits for a basis period are taxed in the corresponding tax year.** If a basis period is not identical to a period of account, the profits of periods of account are time-apportioned as required. We will assume that profits accrue evenly over a period of account. We will also apportion to the nearest month.

3.2   We will now look at the basis period rules that apply in the opening, continuing and closing years of a business when there is no change of accounting date. Special rules are needed when a trader changes his accounting date but you will not be assessed on these in Unit 18 so they are not considered here.

3.3   The first tax year is the year during which the trade commences. For example, if a trade commences on 1 June 2000 the first tax year is 2000/01.

The first tax year

3.4   The **basis period for the first tax year runs from the date the trade starts to the next 5 April** (or to the date of cessation if the trade does not last until the end of the tax year).

The second tax year

3.5   **If the accounting date falling in the second tax year is at least 12 months after the start of trading, the basis period is the 12 months down to that accounting date.**

3.6   **If the accounting date falling in the second tax year is less than 12 months after the start of trading, the basis period is the first 12 months of trading.**

3.7   **If there is no accounting date falling in the second tax year,** because the first period of account is a very long one which does not end until a date in the third tax year, **the basis period for the second tax year is the year itself (from 6 April to 5 April).**

3.8   The following flowchart may help you determine the basis period for the second tax year.

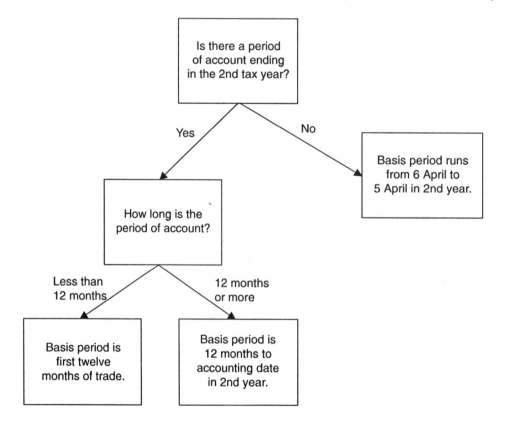

The third tax year

3.9 **If there is an accounting date falling in the second tax year, the basis period for the third tax year is the period of account ending in the third tax year.**

3.10 If there is no accounting date falling in the second tax year, the basis period for the third tax year is the 12 months down to the accounting date falling in the third tax year.

Later tax years

3.11 For later tax years, except the year in which the trade ceases, **the basis period is the period of account ending in the tax year**. This is known as the **current year basis of assessment**.

The final year

3.12 If a trade starts and ceases in the same tax year, the basis period for that year is the whole lifespan of the trade.

3.13 If the final year is the second year, the basis period runs from 6 April at the start of the second year to the date of cessation. This rule overrides the rules that normally apply for the second year.

3.14 If the final year is the third year or a later year, **the basis period runs from the end of the basis period for the previous year to the date of cessation**. This rule overrides the rules that normally apply in the third and later years.

Overlap profits

> **KEY TERM**
>
> Profits which have been taxed more than once are called **overlap profits.**

3.15 When a business starts, some profits may be taxed twice because the basis period for the second year includes some or all of the period of trading in the first year or because the basis period for the third year overlaps with that for the second year.

3.16 **Overlap profits unrelieved when the trade ceases are deducted from the final year's taxable profits.** Any deduction of overlap profits may create or increase a loss. The usual loss reliefs (covered later in this text) are then available.

3.17 EXAMPLE: ACCOUNTING DATE IN 2ND YEAR AT LEAST 12 MONTHS

Jenny trades from 1 July 1995 to 31 December 2000, with the following results.

Period	Profit
	£
1.7.95 - 31.8.96	7,000
1.9.96 - 31.8.97	12,000
1.9.97 - 31.8.98	15,000
1.9.98 - 31.8.99	21,000
1.9.99 - 31.8.00	18,000
1.9.00 - 31.12.00	5,600
	78,600

The profits to be taxed in each tax year from 1995/96 to 2000/01, and the total of these taxable profits are calculated as follows.

Year	Basis period	Working	Taxable profit £
1995/96	1.7.95 - 5.4.96	£7,000 × 9/14	4,500
1996/97	1.9.95 - 31.8.96	£7,000 × 12/14	6,000
1997/98	1.9.96 - 31.8.97		12,000
1998/99	1.9.97 - 31.8.98		15,000
1999/00	1.9.98 - 31.8.99		21,000
2000/01	1.9.99 - 31.12.00	£(18,000 + 5,600 − 3,500)	20,100
			78,600

The overlap profits are those in the period 1 September 1995 to 5 April 1996, a period of seven months. They are £7,000 × 7/14 = £3,500. Overlap profits are either relieved on a change of accounting date (see below) or are deducted from the final year's taxable profit when the business ceases. In this case the overlap profits are deducted when the business ceases. Over the life of the business, the total taxable profits equal the total actual profits.

Activity 2.5: Calculation of taxable profits for six tax years

Peter trades from 1 September 1995 to 30 June 2000, with the following results.

Period	Profit
	£
1.9.95 - 30.4.96	8,000
1.5.96 - 30.4.97	15,000
1.5.97 - 30.4.98	9,000
1.5.98 - 30.4.99	10,500
1.5.99 - 30.4.00	16,000
1.5.00 - 30.6.00	950
	59,450

Show the profits to be taxed in each year from 1995/96 to 2000/01, the total of these taxable profits and the overlap profits.

3.18 EXAMPLE: NO ACCOUNTING DATE IN THE SECOND YEAR

Thelma starts to trade on 1 March 1999. Her first accounts, covering the 16 months to 30 June 2000, show a profit of £36,000. The taxable profits for the first three tax years and the overlap profits are as follows.

Year	Basis period	Working	Taxable profits £
1998/99	1.3.99 - 5.4.99	£36,000 × 1/16	2,250
1999/00	6.4.99 - 5.4.00	£36,000 × 12/16	27,000
2000/01	1.7.99 - 30.6.00	£36,000 × 12/16	27,000

The overlap profits are the profits from 1 July 1999 to 5 April 2000: £36,000 × 9/16 = £20,250.

4 INCOME TAX FORMS

4.1 A copy of the supplementary pages to the income tax return that have to be completed by self employed taxpayers are included in appendix to this text. In Unit 18 you will be expected to be aware of how business income is entered in these supplementary pages. However, completion of the full income tax self assessment return will be assessed in Unit 19 only. Please see page (x) for a note regarding these forms.

Activity 2.6: End of chapter activity

The profit and loss account of Mr Brillo for the year ended 31 December 2000 shows the following.

	£		£
Staff wages	2,416	Gross profit from trading account	10,326
Wife's wages	624	Profit on sale of plant	240
Rent	630	Profit on sale of investment	1,032
Light and heat	171	Bank interest received	54
Motor car expenses	336		
Telephone	79		
Postage, stationery and wrapping	80		
Repairs and renewals	476		
Bad debts written off	100		
Miscellaneous expenses	346		
Advertising	24		
Loan interest	130		

	£		
Depreciation: plant	480		
motor car	120	600	
Net profit		5,640	
		11,652	11,652

Notes

(a) The Revenue have agreed that one third of the expenditure on rent, light and heat relates to living accommodation at the business premises.

(b) One seventh of the motor expenses relate to private motoring.

(c) Repairs and renewals comprise the following.

	£
Painting shop internally	155
Plant repairs	220
Building extension to stockroom	101
	476

(d)

BAD DEBTS ACCOUNT

2000		£	2000		£
31 Dec	Bad debts written off	102	1 Jan	Balances b/f	
	Balances c/f			General	200
	General	400		Specific	360
	Specific	398			560
			31 Dec	Bad debt recovered	240
				Profit & loss account	100
		900			900

(e) Miscellaneous expenses comprise the following.

	£
Donations to the Spastics Society	10
Subscription to the Chamber of Commerce	8
Entertaining customers	90
Christmas gifts to customers:	
bottles of gin costing £8.75 each, one per customer with 'Mr Brillo' labels	70
Payments to employees in lieu of notice	50
Legal expenses re debt collecting	15
Sundries: all allowable	103
	346

(f) The profit on the sale of an investment relates to the sale of a holding of ordinary shares in a company quoted on the Stock Exchange, These shares were purchased by Brillo on 1 January 1997 for £8,460 and sold on 30 June 2000 for £9,492.

(g) Mrs Brillo assists full time in the business.

(h) Gross profit is 15% of selling price and Brillo estimates that he has withdrawn goods costing £340 for his own use.

(i) The staff wages include £260 paid to Brillo.

REQUIREMENT:

Compute Mr Brillo's tax adjusted trading profit before capital allowances for the year ended 31 December 2000.

Key learning points

- The badges of trade can be used to decide whether or not a trade exists. If one does exist, the accounts profits need to be adjusted in order to establish the taxable profits.

- Basis periods are used to link periods of account to tax years.

- In opening and closing years, special rules are applied so that a new trader can start to be taxed quickly, and a retiring trader need not be taxed long after his retirement.

Quick quiz

1 What are the badges of trade?

2 What are the remoteness test and the duality test?

3 What relief is available for pre-trading expenditure?

4 In which period of account are emoluments paid 12 months after the end of the period for which they are charged deductible?

5 When is redundancy pay made on a cessation of trade deductible?

6 How is the basis period for the second tax year of a business found?

7 How is the basis period for the third tax year of a business found?

8 How is the basis period for the final tax year of a business found?

Answers to quick quiz

1   The subject matter, the frequency of transactions, the length of ownership, supplementary work and marketing, a profit motive and the way in which the asset sold was acquired.

2   Expenditure is not deductible if it is not for the purposes of the trade (the remoteness test), or if it reflects more than one purpose (the duality test).

3   Pre-trading expenditure is deductible if:

    •   it is incurred within seven years of the start of trade; and
    •   it is of a type that would have been deductible had the trade already started.

    It is treated as a trading expense incurred on the first day of trading.

4   The cost is deductible in the period of account in which the emoluments are paid.

5   Redundancy payments made when a trade ends are deductible on the earlier of the day of payment and the last day of trading.

6   If the accounting date falling in the second tax year is at least 12 months after the start of trading, the basis period is the 12 months down to that accounting date.

    If the accounting date falling in the second tax year is less than 12 months after the start of trading, the basis period is the first 12 months of trading.

    If there is no accounting date falling in the second tax year, because the first period of account is a very long one which does not end until a date in the third tax year, the basis period for the second tax year is the year itself (from 6 April to 5 April).

7   If there is an accounting date falling in the second tax year, the basis period for the third tax year is the period of account ending in the third tax year.

    If there is no accounting date falling in the second tax year, the basis period for the third tax year is the 12 months down to the accounting date falling in the third tax year.

8   If a trade starts and ceases in the same tax year, the basis period for that year is the whole lifespan of the trade.

    If the final year is the second year, the basis period runs from 6 April at the start of the second year to the date of cessation. This rule overrides the rules that normally apply for the second year.

    If the final year is the third year or a later year, the basis period runs from the end of the basis period for the previous year to the date of cessation. This rule overrides the rules that normally apply in the third and later years.

Answers to Activities

Activity 2.1

Supplementary work and marketing (drainage; obtaining planning permission)

A profit motive

The manner of acquisition (extra land was bought)

Activity 2.2

They are worn in addition to ordinary clothes, and do not significantly add to warmth or decency.

Activity 2.3

£(230 + 700) = £930

Activity 2.4

	£	£
Profit per accounts		12,710
Add: depreciation	1,500	
Provision against a fall in raw material prices	5,000	
Entertainment expenses	750	
Patent royalties paid (to treat as a charge)	1,200	
Legal expenses	250	
		8,700
		21,410
Less interest received (to tax as taxed income)		860
Adjusted trading profit		20,550

Activity 2.5

Year	Basis period	Working	Taxable profits £
1995/96	1.9.95 - 5.4.96	£8,000 × 7/8	7,000
1996/97	1.9.95 - 31.8.96	£8,000 + (£15,000 × 4/12)	13,000
1997/98	1.5.96 - 30.4.97		15,000
1998/99	1.5.97 - 30.4.98		9,000
1999/00	1.5.98 - 30.4.99		10,500
2000/01	1.5.99 - 30.6.00	£(16,000 + 950 - 12,000)	4,950
			59,450

The overlap profits are the profits from 1 September 1995 to 5 April 1996 (taxed in 1995/96 and in 1996/97) and those from 1 May 1996 to 31 August 1996 (taxed in 1996/97 and 1997/98).

	£
1.9.95 - 5.4.96 £8,000 × 7/8	7,000
1.5.96 - 31.8.96 £15,000 × 4/12	5,000
Total overlap profits	12,000

Activity 2.6

	£	£
Profit per accounts		5,640
Add: salary (a)	260	
rent (a)	210	
light and heat (a)	57	
motor expenses (a)	48	
stockroom extension (c)	101	
increase in general provision (a)	200	
donations (b)	10	
entertaining (d)	90	
gifts (e)	70	
depreciation (c)	600	
goods withdrawn at selling price (b)	400	
		2,046
		7,686
Less: profit on sale of plant (c)	240	
profit on sale of investment (c)	1,032	
bank interest received (f)	54	
		1,326
Adjusted trading profit before capital allowances		6,360

Notes

(a) Appropriation of profit

(b) Not expenditure laid out wholly and exclusively for the purpose of trade

(c) Capital items

(d) Entertaining expenses specifically disallowed

(e) Gifts of drink specifically disallowed

(f) Non-trading income

Chapter 3   Capital allowances on plant and machinery

Chapter topic list

1   Capital allowances in general

2   The definition of plant

3   The allowances

4   Short-life assets

5   Hire purchase and leasing

Learning objectives

On completion of this chapter you will be able to:

	Performance criteria	Range Statement
• identify the kind of plant and machinery on which capital allowances can be claimed	18.2.2	18.2.1
• calculate the amount of capital allowances due for an accounting period	18.2.3	18.2.1
• discuss the special treatment accorded to some capital assets	18.2.1	18.2.1

1 CAPITAL ALLOWANCES IN GENERAL

1.1 **Capital expenditure is not in itself an allowable Schedule D Case I deduction, but it *may* attract capital allowances. Capital allowances are treated as a trading expense and are deducted in arriving at Schedule D Case I profits. Balancing charges, effectively negative allowances, are added in arriving at those profits.**

1.2 Capital allowances are available in respect of expenditure on:

- plant and machinery;
- industrial buildings;
- agricultural buildings and works.

For capital expenditure to be allowable it must fall into one of these (or a few other minor) categories.

This chapter deals only with capital allowances on plant and machinery; the next chapter deals with other types of capital allowances.

1.3 For unincorporated businesses, capital allowances are calculated for periods of account. These are simply the periods for which the trader chooses to make up accounts.

1.4 For companies, capital allowances are calculated for accounting periods. We will look at accounting periods for companies later in this text.

1.5 **For capital allowances purposes, expenditure is generally deemed to be incurred when the obligation to pay becomes unconditional.** This will often be the date of a contract, but if for example payment is due a month after delivery of a machine, it would be the date of delivery. However, amounts due more than four months after the obligation becomes unconditional are deemed to be incurred when they fall due.

2 THE DEFINITION OF PLANT

2.1 **There are two sources of the rules on what qualifies as plant and is therefore eligible for capital allowances.** (Machinery is also eligible, but the word 'machinery' may be taken to have its everyday meaning.) **Statute law** lists items which do not qualify, but it does not give a comprehensive list of other items which do qualify. There are then several **cases** in which certain items have been accepted as plant. A few items such as thermal insulation and computer software are also plant by statute.

The statutory exclusions

Buildings

2.2 **Expenditure on a building and on any asset which is incorporated in a building or is of a kind normally incorporated into buildings does not qualify as expenditure on plant unless the asset falls within the list of exceptions given** below. Even if an asset falls within that list, it does not follow that it is plant (although in practice it probably will be, because the list is based on cases in which assets have been held to be plant and on Revenue practice).

2.3 In addition to complete buildings, **the following assets count as 'buildings', and are therefore not plant.**

- Walls, floors, ceilings, doors, gates, shutters, windows and stairs
- Mains services, and systems, of water, electricity and gas

- Waste disposal, sewerage and drainage systems
- Shafts or other structures for lifts etc.

2.4 **The following assets** which would normally count as 'buildings' **can still be plant.**

- Electrical, cold water, gas and sewerage systems:

    (i)   provided mainly to meet the particular requirements of the trade; or
    (ii) provided mainly to serve particular machinery or plant.

- Space or water heating systems and powered systems of ventilation.

- Manufacturing and display equipment.

- Cookers, washing machines, refrigeration equipment, sanitary ware and furniture and furnishings.

- Lifts etc.

- Sound insulation provided mainly to meet the particular requirements of the trade.

- Computer, telecommunication and surveillance systems.

- Sprinkler equipment, fire alarm and burglar alarm systems.

- Any machinery.

- Strong rooms in bank or building society premises; safes.

- Partition walls, where movable and intended to be moved.

- Decorative assets in the hotel, restaurant or similar trades.

- Advertising hoardings.

- Swimming pools.

- Glasshouses which have, as an integral part of their structure, devices which control the plant growing environment automatically.

2.5 In addition, expenditure may qualify as expenditure on plant despite these rules if the assets bought fall within the following categories.

- Caravans provided mainly for holiday lettings
- Movable buildings intended to be moved in the course of the trade

2.6 When a building is sold, the vendor and purchaser can make a joint election to determine how the sale proceeds are apportioned between the building and its fixtures. There are anti-avoidance provisions that ensure capital allowances given overall on a fixture do not exceed the original cost of the fixture.

Activity 3.1: Plant

One side wall of a building consists of a single sheet of wood, 2cm thick, and advertisements are displayed on the outside. Could this wall qualify as plant?

Structures

2.7 **Expenditure on providing structures** and on works involving the alteration of land **does not qualify as expenditure on plant** unless the asset falls within the list of exceptions given below. Even if an asset falls within that list, it does not follow that it is plant (although it probably will be, because the list is based on cases in which assets have been held to be plant and on Revenue practice).

2.8   A 'structure' is a fixed structure of any kind, other than a building.

2.9   **The following assets** and items of expenditure which would normally count as 'structures' **can still be plant.**

- Expenditure on the alteration of land for the purpose only of installing machinery or plant

- Pipelines, and also underground ducts or tunnels with a primary purpose of carrying utility conduits

- Silos provided for temporary storage and storage tanks

- Fish tanks and fish ponds

- A railway or tramway

2.10   In addition, expenditure may qualify as plant despite these rules if the assets bought are items which qualify as plant under the rules in Paragraphs 2.23 and 2.24 below.

Land

2.11   Expenditure on buying an interest in land does not qualify as expenditure on plant and machinery. For this purpose 'land' excludes buildings, structures and assets which are installed or fixed to land in such a way as to become part of the land for general legal purposes.

Case law

2.12   The original case law **definition of plant is 'whatever apparatus is used by a businessman for carrying on his business: not his stock in trade which he buys or makes for sale; but all goods and chattels, fixed or movable, live or dead, which he keeps for permanent employment in the business'.**

2.13   Subsequent cases have refined the original definition and have largely been concerned with the **distinction between plant actively used in the business (qualifying) and the setting in which the business is carried on (non-qualifying). This is the 'functional' test.**

2.14   The whole cost of excavating and installing a swimming pool was allowed to the owners of a caravan park: the pool performed the function of giving 'buoyancy and enjoyment' to the persons using the pool (*Cooke v Beach Station Caravans Ltd 1974*).

2.15   A barrister succeeded in his claim for his law library: 'Plant includes a man's tools of his trade. It extends to what he uses day by day in the course of his profession. It is not confined to physical things like the dentist's chair or the architect's table' (*Munby v Furlong 1977*).

2.16   Office partitioning was allowed. Because it was movable it was not regarded as part of the setting in which the business was carried on (*Jarrold v John Good and Sons Ltd 1963*).

2.17   A ship used as a floating restaurant was regarded as a 'structure in which the business was carried on rather than functional apparatus employed so no capital allowances could be obtained (*Benson v Yard Arm Club 1978*). The same decision was made in relation to a football club's spectator stand. The stand performed no function in the actual carrying out of the club's trade (*Brown v Burnley Football and Athletic Co Ltd 1980*).

2.18 False ceilings containing conduits, ducts and lighting were not plant because they did not perform a function in the business. They were merely part of the setting in which the business was conducted (*Hampton v Fortes Autogrill Ltd 1979*).

2.19 Light fittings, decor and murals can be plant. A company carried on business as hoteliers and operators of licensed premises. The function of the items was the creation of an atmosphere conducive to the comfort and well being of its customers (*CIR v Scottish and Newcastle Breweries Ltd 1982*).

2.20 On the other hand, it has been held that when an attractive floor is provided in a restaurant, the fact that the floor performs the function of making the restaurant attractive to customers is not enough to make it plant. It functions as premises, and the cost therefore does not qualify for capital allowances (*Wimpy International Ltd v Warland 1988*).

2.21 General lighting in a department store is not plant, as it is merely setting. Special display lighting, however, can be plant (*Cole Brothers Ltd v Phillips 1982*).

2.22 Free-standing decorative screens installed in the windows of a branch of a building society have qualified as plant. Their function was not to act a part of the setting in which the society's business was carried on; it was to attract local custom, and accordingly the screens formed part of the apparatus by which the society carried on its business (*Leeds Permanent Building Society v Proctor 1982*).

Expenditure deemed to be on plant and machinery

2.23 Plant and machinery capital allowances are also available on:

- expenditure incurred by a trader in complying with fire regulations for a building which he occupies;
- expenditure by a trader on thermal insulation of an industrial building;
- expenditure by a trader in meeting statutory safety requirements for sports ground;
- expenditure (by an individual or a partnership, not by a company) on *security assets* provided to meet a special threat to an individual's security that arises wholly or mainly due to the particular trade concerned.

On disposal, the sale proceeds for the above are deemed to be zero, so no balancing charge (see below) can arise.

Computer software

2.24 **Capital expenditure on computer software qualifies as** expenditure on **plant and machinery.**

2.25 Where someone has incurred expenditure qualifying for capital allowances on computer software (or the right to use software), and receives a capital sum in exchange for allowing someone else to use the software, that sum is brought into account as disposal proceeds. However, the cumulative total of disposal proceeds is not allowed to exceed the original cost of the software, and any proceeds above this limit are ignored for capital allowances purposes (although they may lead to chargeable gains).

2.26 If software is expected to have a useful economic life of less than two years, its cost may be treated as revenue expenditure.

Activity 3.2: Plant and machinery

Would lights in a factory qualify as plant if they were:

(a) normal background illumination;
(b) powerful spotlights to assist workers engaged in delicate work?

---

3 THE ALLOWANCES

Writing down allowances

> ### KEY TERM
>
> **A writing down allowance (WDA)** is given on expenditure incurred on assets (other than motor cars - see below) **at the rate of 25% a year** (on a reducing balance basis). The WDA is calculated on the written down value (WDV) on all plant on a 'pool' basis, after adding the current period's additions and taking out the current period's disposals.

3.1 It is unnecessary to keep track of individual written down values.

3.2 Allowances are claimed in the tax return. Any business can claim less than the full allowances. This may be to its advantage, if, for example, the trader wants to avoid making such a large loss claim as to lose the benefit of the personal allowance. Higher capital allowances will then be available in later years because the WDV carried forward will be higher.

3.3 When plant is sold the proceeds (but limited to a maximum of the original cost) are taken out of the pool of qualifying expenditure. Provided that the trade is still being carried on, the balance remaining is written down in the future by writing down allowances, even if there are no assets left.

3.4 **Writing down allowances are 25% × months/12:**

(a) for unincorporated businesses where the period of account is longer or shorter than 12 months;

(b) for companies where the accounting period is shorter than 12 months (a company's accounting period for tax purposes is never longer than 12 months), or where the trade concerned started in the accounting period and was therefore carried on for fewer than 12 months.

3.5 Expenditure on plant and machinery by a person about to begin a trade is treated as incurred on the first day of trading. Assets previously owned by a trader and then brought into the trade (at the start of trading or later) are treated as bought for their market values at the times when they are brought in.

First year allowances

Spending by small and medium sized enterprises

3.6 **Expenditure incurred on plant and machinery** (other than leased assets, cars, sea going ships or railway assets) after 2 July 1998 **by small and medium sized enterprises qualifies for a first year allowance** (FYA) of 40%.

3.7 This expenditure qualified for a FYA of 50% if it was incurred in the year to 1 July 1998.

> **KEY TERM**
>
> **A small or medium sized enterprise,** is an individual, partnership or company that either satisfies at least two of the following conditions in the chargeable period/financial year in which the expenditure is incurred.
>
> (a) **Turnover not more than £11.2 million**
> (b) **Assets not more than £5.6 million**
> (c) **Not more than 250 employees**
>
> or which was small or medium sized in the previous year.

Spending by small enterprises on information and communication technology

3.8 Expenditure by **small enterprises on information and communication technology equipment** (computers, software and internet enabled mobile phones) **in the three year period from 1 April 2000 to 31 March 2003 qualifies for a 100% FYA.**

3.9 Equipment acquired for leasing does not qualify for the 100% FYA.

> **KEY TERM**
>
> **A small enterprise** is an individual, partnership or company, which satisfies at least two of the following conditions in the chargeable period/financial year in which the expenditure is incurred:
>
> (a) **Turnover not more than £2.8 million**
> (b) **Assets not more than £1.4 million**
> (c) **Not more than 50 employees**
>
> or which was small in the previous year.

Calculation

3.10 For FYA purposes, the provisions which treat capital expenditure incurred prior to the commencement of trading as incurred on the first day of trading do not apply.

3.11 **First year allowances are given in the place of writing down allowances.** For subsequent years a WDA is given on the balance of expenditure at the normal rate. You should therefore transfer the balance of the expenditure to the pool at the end of the first period.

Activity 3.3: Calculation of taxable profits

Walton starts a trade on 1 March 1997, and has the following results (before capital allowances).

Period of account	Profits
	£
1.3.97 - 31.7.98	42,500
1.8.98 - 31.7.99	36,800
1.8.99 - 31.7.00	32,000

Plant (none of which is information or communication technology equipment) is bought as follows.

Date	Cost
	£
1.3.97	13,000
1.6.97	8,000
1.6.99	5,000
31.7.00	2,000

On 1 May 1999, plant which cost £7,000 is sold for £4,000.

Walton's business is a small or medium sized enterprise for FYA purposes.

Show the Schedule D Case I profits arising in the above periods of account.

3.12 FYAs are given for incurring expenditure. It is irrelevant whether the basis period of expenditure is twelve months or less. FYAs are not scaled up or down by reference to the length of the period.

DEVOLVED ASSESSMENT ALERT

Note the tax planning opportunities available. It may be important to buy plant just before an accounting date, so that allowances become available as soon as possible. On the other hand, it may be worthwhile to claim less than the maximum allowances so as to even out the annual assessments and avoid higher rate tax.

The disposal value of assets

3.13 **The most common disposal value at which assets are entered in a capital allowances computation is the sale proceeds.** But there are a number of less common situations.

3.14 **Where the asset is sold at below market value** (or is given away) **the market value is used instead of the actual sale proceeds.** This general rule has two exceptions. The actual proceeds of sale are used:

  (a) where the buyer will be able to claim capital allowances on the expenditure;

  (b) where an employee acquires an asset from his employer at undervalue (or as a gift) and so faces a charge under the Schedule E benefit-in-kind rules.

If the asset is demolished, destroyed or otherwise lost, the disposal value is taken to be the actual sale proceeds from any resulting scrap, plus any insurance or other compensation moneys.

3.15 With all these rules, there is an overriding rule that the capital allowances **disposal value cannot exceed the original purchase price.**

Activity 3.4: Disposal value of assets

At the start of its accounting period from 1 January to 31 October 2000, a company had a balance on its plant pool of £123,000. Plant which had cost £27,000 was sold for £32,000 on 1 August. What were the capital allowances for this ten month accounting period?

Balancing charges and allowances

3.16 **Balancing charges occur when the disposal value deducted exceeds the balance remaining in the pool. The charge equals the excess and is effectively a negative capital allowance,** increasing profits. Most commonly this happens when the trade ceases and the remaining assets are sold. It may also occur, however, whilst the trade is still in progress.

3.17 **Balancing allowances on the capital allowance pools of expenditure arise only when the trade ceases.** The balancing allowance is equal to the remaining unrelieved expenditure after deducting the disposal value of all the assets. Balance allowances also arise on items which are not pooled (see below) whenever those items are disposed of.

Cars

3.18 **Cars** (but not lorries, vans, short-term hire cars, taxis and vehicles unsuitable for private use) **have a special capital allowance treatment.** There are two categories of cars. **Cars costing more than £12,000 are dealt with on an individual basis (see below). Cars costing £12,000 or less are pooled.**

3.19 **Prior to Finance Act 2000 the car pool was a separate one to that used for general plant and machinery.** However, the separate pool for cars costing £12,000 or less is abolished for companies for accounting periods ending after 31 March 2000. For individuals, it is abolished for periods of account ending after 5 April 2000. The balance that was brought forward on the separate pool at the end of the last period before the abolition is transferred to the main pool.

3.20 Businesses can choose to delay the abolition of the separate car pool until the first accounting period ending after 31 March 2001 or the first period of account ending after 5 April 2001 respectively.

3.21 FYAs are not available on cars.

Assets which are not pooled

3.22 Some items are not pooled. A separate record of allowances and WDV must be kept for each such asset and when it is sold a balancing allowance or charge emerges. The items are:

(a) **assets** not wholly used for business purposes (such as cars **with private use by the proprietor**);

(b) **motor cars costing more than £12,000,** where the maximum WDA is £3,000 a year. The limit is £3,000 × months/12:

    (i)   for short or long periods of account of unincorporated businesses;
    (ii)   for short accounting periods of companies.

(c) **short-life assets** for which an election has been made (see below).

Assets not wholly used for business purposes

3.23 **Where an asset (for example, a car) is used partly for private purposes by a sole trader or a partner, make all calculations on the full cost but claim only the business use proportion of the allowances.** An asset with some private use by an employee (not a proprietor), however, suffers no such restriction. The employee may be taxed on a benefit in kind so the business gets capital allowances on the full cost of the asset.

Activity 3.5: Capital allowances on a car

A trader started to trade on 1 July 1997, making up accounts to 31 December 1997 and each 31 December thereafter. On 1 August 1997 he bought a car for £15,500. The private use proportion is 10%. The car was sold in July 2000 for £4,000. What are the capital allowances?

The cessation of a trade

3.24 **When a business ceases to trade no FYAs or WDAs are given in the final period of account** (unincorporated businesses) or accounting period (companies). Each asset is deemed to be disposed of on the date the trade ceased (usually at the then market value). Additions in the relevant period are brought in and then the disposal proceeds (limited to cost) are deducted from the balance of qualifying expenditure. If the proceeds exceed the balance then a balancing charge arises. If the balance of qualifying expenditure exceeds the proceeds then a balancing allowance is given.

4 SHORT-LIFE ASSETS

4.1 **A trader can elect that specific items of plant be kept separately from the general pool. The election is irrevocable.** For an unincorporated business, the time limit for electing is the 31 January which is 22 months after the end of the tax year in which the period of account of the expenditure ends. For a company, it is two years after the end of the accounting period of the expenditure. **Any asset subject to this election is known as a 'short-life asset'**, and the election is known as a **'de-pooling election'**.

KEY TERM

Provided that the asset is disposed of within four years of the end of the period of account or accounting period in which it was bought, it is a **short life asset** and a balancing charge or allowance is made on its disposal.

4.2 The receipt of a capital sum in return for the right to use computer software does not count as a disposal for this purpose. If the asset is not disposed of in the correct time period, its tax written down value is added to the general pool at the end of that time.

4.3 The election should be made for assets likely to be sold within four years for less than their tax written down values. It should not be made for assets likely to be sold within four years for more than their tax written down values. (These are, of course, only general guidelines based on the assumption that a trader will want to obtain allowances as quickly as possible. There may be other considerations, such as a desire to even out annual taxable profits.)

Activity 3.6: Short life assets

Caithin bought an asset on 1 July 1996 for £12,000 and elected for de-pooling. His accounting year end is 31 March. Calculate the capital allowances due if:

(a) the asset is scrapped for £300 in August 2000;
(b) the asset is scrapped for £200 in August 2001.

4.4 Short-life asset treatment cannot be claimed for:

- motor cars;
- plant used partly for non-trade purposes;
- plant brought into use for the trade following non-business use;
- plant received by way of gift;
- plant in respect of which a subsidy is received.

5 HIRE PURCHASE AND LEASING

Assets on hire purchase

5.1 **Any asset (including a car) bought on hire purchase (HP) is treated as if purchased outright for the cash price.** Therefore:

(a) the buyer normally obtains **capital allowances on the cash price** when the agreement begins;

(b) he may write off the **finance charge as a trade expense** over the term of the HP contract.

Leased assets

5.2 **Under a lease, the lessee merely hires the asset over a period.**

5.3 An expensive car (one costing over £12,000) will attract WDAs limited to £3,000 a year if bought. If it is leased instead, the maximum allowable deduction from trading profits for lease rentals is

$$\frac{£12,000 + P}{2P} \times R$$

where   P = the purchase price (if bought outright)
             R = the annual rental

5.4 This restriction does not apply to the finance charges in hire purchase payments (which could be regarded as payment for the hire of the car), provided the amount payable to acquire the car at the end of the hire period is no more than 1% of the car's retail price when new.

5.5 EXAMPLE: LEASED CARS

A car is used by a business under a lease. The purchase price would have been £20,000. The annual rental is £5,000. The rental allowed for tax purposes is

$$\frac{£12,000 + £20,000}{2 \times £20,000} \times £5,000 = £4,000$$

Since £5,000 is deducted in the profit and loss account, £5,000 - £4,000 = £1,000 is added back in computing taxable profits.

BPP PUBLISHING

5.6 A lessor of plant normally obtains the benefit of capital allowances although there are anti-avoidance provisions which deny or restrict capital allowances on certain finance leases. Leasing is thus an activity which attracts tax allowances and which can be used to defer tax liabilities where the capital allowances given exceed the rental income. For individuals, any losses arising from leasing are available for offset against other income only if the individual devotes substantially all of his time to the conduct of a leasing business.

Activity 3.7: End of chapter activity

Vivace makes up his accounts to 30 June each year.

After claiming allowances based on the period ended 30 June 1997, the balance of his general pool stood at £8,000.

During the years ended 30 June 1998, 1999 and 2000 Vivace recorded the following capital transactions.

14	September 1997	He sold machinery which originally cost £1,800 for £700.
16	September 1997	He bought a new car for a salesman for £4,000. The employee uses it privately for 25% of all its mileage.
1	December 1997	He bought secondhand machinery for £9,232.
5	July 1998	He bought a Mercedes car for his own use costing £22,000. Vivace uses the car 60% for business purposes.
21	March 1999	He sold plant which cost £2,000 in 1996 for £2,500.
22	March 1999	He sold the salesman's car for £3,200.
4	February 2000	He bought a new machine on hire purchase. A deposit of £1,800 was paid immediately. Four further instalments of £1,000 are payable annually in future years. The cash price would have been £4,000.
5	February 2000	He bought a car for the accountant for £3,000. There is no private use.
15	June 2000	He replaced his car. The Mercedes was sold for £4,000; a Volvo was bought for £18,000. 60% business use continued.
30	June 2000	Plant and equipment which originally cost £10,000 was sold for £2,602.

Required

Set out Vivace's capital allowance computations for the periods of account ended 30 June 1998, 1999 and 2000, assuming that maximum claims are made. Assume Vivace's business qualifies for FYA where appropriate.

Key Learning Points

- Statutory rules generally exclude specified items from treatment as plant, rather than include specified items as plant.

- There are several cases on the definition of plant. To help you to absorb them, try to see the function/setting theme running through them.

- With capital allowances computations, the main thing is to get the layout right. Having done that, you will find that the figures tend to drop into place.

- Most expenditure on plant and machinery qualifies for a WDA at 25% every 12 months.

- First year allowances (FYA) may be available for expenditure on plant and machinery in certain time frames.

- Private use assets by sole traders and partners have restricted tax deductible capital allowances.

- Short life asset elections can bring forward the allowances due on an asset.

Quick quiz

1   Are First Year Allowances pro-rated in short accounting periods?

2   What writing down allowances are given in a period of account of less than 12 months?

3   When do balancing allowances arise on the pool of general expenditure?

4   Which assets cannot be treated as short-life assets?

5   What is the formula for restricting allowable lease payments for expensive cars?

Quick quiz answers _____

1   No. FYAs are given for incurring expenditure. It is irrelevant whether the basis period of expenditure is twelve months or less. FYAs are not scaled up or down by reference to the length of the period.

2   Writing down allowances are 25% × months/12.

3   Only when the trade ceases.

4   - motor cars;
    - plant used partly for non-trade purposes;
    - plant brought into use for the trade following non-business use;
    - plant received by way of gift;
    - plant in respect of which a subsidy is received.

5   The formula to calculate the allowable deduction is:

$$\frac{£12,000 + P}{2P} \times R$$

   where   P = the purchase price (if bought outright)
           R = the annual rental

Answers to activities _____

Activity 3.1

No: its principal purpose is to provide a permanent wall.

Activity 3.2

(a) No: they would be part of the setting.
(b) Yes: they would perform a specific function.

Activity 3.3

The capital allowances are as follows.

	FYA £	Pool £	Allowances £
1.3.97 – 31.7.98			
Additions		21,000	
WDA 25% × 17/12		(7,438)	7,438
		13,562	
1.8.98 – 31.7.99			
Disposals		(4,000)	
		9,562	
WDA 25%		(2,391)	2,391
		7,171	
Addition (1.6.99)	5,000		
FYA 40%	(2,000)		2,000
		3,000	4,391
		10,171	
1.8.99 – 31.7.00			
WDA 25%		(2,543)	2,543
		7,628	
Addition (31.7.00)	2,000		
FYA 40%	(800)		800
		1,200	-
TWDV c/f		8,828	
			3,343

The profits of the first three periods of account are as follows.

Period of account	Working	Profits £
1.3.97 – 31.7.98	£(42,500 – 7,438)	35,062
1.8.98 – 31.7.99	£(36,800 – 4,391)	32,409
1.8.99 – 31.7.00	£(32,000 – 3,343)	28,657

Activity 3.4

	Pool £	Allowances £
Balance brought forward	123,000	
Disposals (limited to cost)	(27,000)	
	96,000	
WDA 25% × 10/12	(20,000)	20,000
Balance carried forward	76,000	

Activity 3.5

	Car £	Allowances 90% £
1.7.97 – 31.12.97		
Purchase price	15,500	
WDA 25% × 6/12 of £15,500 = £1,938,		
Limited to £3,000 × 6/12 = £1,500	(1,500)	1,350
	14,000	
1.1.98 – 31.12.98		
WDA 25% of £14,000 = £3,500,		
Limited to £3,000	(3,000)	2,700
	11,000	
1.1.99 – 31.12.99		
WDA 25% of £11,000	(2,750)	2,475
	8,250	
1.1.00 – 31.12.00		
Proceeds	(4,000)	
Balancing allowance	4,250	3,825

Activity 3.6

		£
(a) *Year to 31.3.97*		
Cost		12,000
WDA 25%		(3,000)
		9,000
Year to 31.3.98		
WDA 25%		(2,250)
		6,750
Year to 31.3.99		
WDA 25%		(1,688)
		5,062
Year to 31.3.00		
WDA 25%		(1,266)
		3,796
Year to 31.3.01		
Disposal proceeds		(300)
Balancing allowance		3,496

(b) If the asset is still in use at 31 March 2001, a WDA of 25% × £3,796 = £949 would be claimable in the year to 31 March 2001. The tax written down value of £3,796 - £949 = £2,847 would be added to the general pool at the beginning of the next period of account. The disposal proceeds of £200 would be deducted from the general pool in that period's capital allowances computation.

Activity 3.7

		FYA £	Pool £	Car pool £	Expensive car (60%) £	Allowances £
	WDV b/f		8,000			
Y/e 30.6.98						
14.9.97	Machinery sold		(700)			
			7,300			
16.9.97	Car			4,000		
	WDA 25%		(1,825)	(1,000)		2,825
1.12.97	Machinery	9,232				
	FYA @ 50%	(4,616)				4,616
			4,616			
	WDV c/f		10,091	3,000		
	Total allowances					7,441
Y/e 30.6.99						
5.7.98	Mercedes				22,000	
21.3.99	Plant sold					
	(restricted to cost)		(2,000)			
			8,091			
22.3.99	Car sold			(3,200)		
	Balancing charge			(200)		(200)
	WDA 25%/restricted		(2,023)		(3,000)	3,823
	WDV c/f		6,068		19,000	
	Total allowances					3,623
Y/e 30.6.00						
5.2.00	Car (no FYA)		3,000			
30.6.00	Plant sold		(2,602)			
			6,466			
	WDA 25%		(1,617)			1,617
			4,849			
15.6.00	Mercedes sold				(4,000)	
	Balancing allowance				15,000	9,000
15.6.00	Volvo				18,000	
	WDA restricted				(3,000)	1,800
4.2.00	Machine on HP	4,000				
	FYA @ 40%	(1,600)				1,600
			2,400			
	WDV c/f		7,249		15,000	
	Total allowances					14,017

Note. The separate car pool was abolished with effect from the start of the period of account that includes 6 April 2000 (ie ends after 5 April 2000).

Chapter 4 Capital allowances on industrial and agricultural buildings

---

Chapter topic list

1 Industrial buildings

2 Agricultural buildings

Learning objectives

On completion of this chapter you will be able to:

	Performance criteria	Range Statement
• identify an industrial building	18.2.2	18.2.1
• calculate industrial buildings allowance	18.2.3	18.2.1
• deal with allowances when the building is disposed of	18.2.3	18.2.1
• show an awareness that agricultural buildings are eligible for allowances which are similar to industrial buildings allowances.	18.2.3	18.2.1

1   INDUSTRIAL BUILDINGS

Types of building

1.1   A special type of capital allowance (an **industrial buildings allowance** or IBA) is available in respect of **expenditure on certain types of building**. The types of building are:

- general industrial buildings;
- hotels;
- buildings in enterprise zones.

1.2   The allowance is available to:

- traders;
- landlords who let qualifying buildings to traders.

General industrial buildings

> **KEY TERM**
>
> **Industrial buildings** include:
>
> (a)   all factories and ancillary premises used in:
>
>   (i)   a manufacturing business;
>   (ii)   a trade in which goods and materials are subject to any process;
>   (iii)   a trade in which goods or raw materials are stored;
>
> (b)   staff welfare buildings (such as workplace nurseries and canteens, but not directors' restaurants) where the trade is qualifying;
>
> (c)   sports pavilions in any trade;
>
> (d)   buildings in use for a transport undertaking, agricultural contracting, mining or fishing;
>
> (e)   roads operated under highway concessions. The operation of such roads is treated as a trade for capital allowances purposes, and the operator is treated as occupying the roads.

1.3   The key term in a(ii) above is 'the subjection of goods to any process'.

- The unpacking, repacking and relabelling of goods in a wholesale cash and carry supermarket did not amount to a 'process' but was a mere preliminary to sale (*Bestway Holdings Ltd v Luff* 1998).

- The mechanical processing of cheques and other banking documents was a process but pieces of paper carrying information were not 'goods' and thus the building housing the machinery did not qualify (*Girobank plc v Clarke* 1998).

1.4   Estate roads on industrial estates qualify, provided that the estate buildings are used wholly or mainly for a qualifying purpose.

1.5   Dwelling houses, retail shops, showrooms or offices are not industrial buildings.

1.6 Warehouses used for storage often cause problems in practice. A warehouse used for storage which is merely a transitory and necessary incident of the conduct of the business is not an industrial building. Storage is only a qualifying purpose if it is an end in itself.

1.7 Any building is an industrial building if it is constructed for the welfare of employees of a trader whose trade is a qualifying one (that is, the premises in which the trade is carried on are industrial buildings).

1.8 Sports pavilions provided for the welfare of employees qualify as industrial buildings. In this case, it does not matter whether the taxpayer is carrying on a trade in a qualifying building or not. Thus a retailer's sports pavilion would qualify for IBAs.

1.9 Drawing offices which serve an industrial building are regarded as industrial buildings themselves (*CIR v Lambhill Ironworks Ltd 1950*).

Hotels

1.10 Allowances on hotels are given as though they were industrial buildings.

KEY TERM

For a building to qualify as a 'hotel' for industrial buildings allowance purposes:

(a) it must have at least ten letting bedrooms;

(b) it must have letting bedrooms as the whole or main part of the sleeping accommodation;

(c) it must offer ancillary services including at least:

    (i) breakfast;
    (ii) evening meals;
    (iii) the cleaning of rooms; and
    (iv) the making of beds; and

(d) it must be open for at least four months during the April to October season.

Buildings in enterprise zones

1.11 **Any commercial building** or hotel **built in an enterprise zone qualifies for industrial buildings allowances,** provided that the construction expenditure is contracted for within ten years of the zone's designation, and actually incurred within 20 years of the zone's designation.

A commercial building is any building that is used for trading purposes or as offices. Dwelling houses are not commercial buildings.

Activity 4.1: Industrial building

A retailer buys a shop, a staff canteen, a staff sports pavilion and a warehouse, none of these buildings being in an enterprise zone. Will any of them qualify as industrial buildings?

Eligible expenditure

1.12 Capital **allowances are computed on the amount of eligible expenditure incurred on qualifying buildings**. The eligible expenditure is:

- the original cost of a building if built by the trader; or
- the purchase price if the building was acquired from a person trading as a builder.

If the building was acquired other than from a person trading as a builder, the eligible expenditure is the lower of the purchase price and the original cost incurred by the person incurring the construction expenditure.

1.13 **Where part of a building qualifies as an industrial building and part does not, the whole cost qualifies for IBAs, provided that the cost of the non-qualifying part is not more than 25% of the total expenditure.** If the non-qualifying part of the building does cost more than 25% of the total, its cost must be excluded from the capital allowances computation.

Activity 4.2: Eligible expenditure

Sue purchased an industrial building for £2,500,000. This cost was made up of:

	£
Factory	2,100,000
Land	400,000
	2,500,000

The costs attributable to showrooms and offices within the factory were £400,000 and £200,000 respectively.

What is the expenditure qualifying for industrial buildings allowances?

1.14 Difficulties arise in practice where non-qualifying buildings (particularly offices and administration blocks) are joined to manufacturing areas. In *Abbott Laboratories Ltd v Carmody* a covered walkway linking manufacturing and administrative areas was not regarded as creating a single building. The administrative area was treated as a separate, non-qualifying building.

1.15 The cost of land is disallowed but expenditure incurred in preparing land for building does qualify.

1.16 Professional fees, for example architects' fees, incurred in connection with the construction of an industrial building qualify. The cost of repairs to industrial buildings also qualifies, provided that the expenditure is not deductible as a trading expense.

Writing down allowances

1.17 **A writing down allowance (WDA) is given to the person holding the 'relevant interest'.** Broadly, the relevant interest is the interest of the first acquirer of the industrial building and may be a freehold or leasehold interest.

1.18 Where a long lease (more than 50 years) has been granted on an industrial building, the grant may be treated as a sale so that allowances may be claimed by the lessee rather than the lessor. A claim for this must be made by the lessor and lessee jointly.

1.19 **The WDA is given for a period (accounting period (companies) or period of account (sole traders and partners)) provided that the industrial building was in use as such on the last day of the period concerned.**

1.20 **If the building was not in use as an industrial building at the end of the relevant period it may have been:**

- **unused** for any purpose; or
- **used for a non-industrial purpose.**

The distinction is important in ascertaining whether WDAs are due to the taxpayer. **Providing that any disuse is temporary and previously the building had been in industrial use, WDAs may be claimed in exactly the same way as if the building were in industrial use.** Unfortunately, the legislation does not define 'temporary' but in practice, any subsequent qualifying use of the building will usually enable the period of disuse to be regarded as temporary.

Non-industrial use has different consequences but you will not be expected to deal with these in your assessment.

1.21 **The WDA is 4%** of the eligible expenditure incurred by the taxpayer. For expenditure before 6 November 1962, the rate is 2%.

The allowance is calculated on a straight line basis (in contrast to WDAs on plant and machinery which are calculated on the reducing balance), starting when the building is brought into use.

1.22 **The WDA is 4% (or 2%) × months/12 if the period concerned is not 12 months long.**

1.23 **Buildings in enterprise zones qualify for a 100% allowance** when built, without waiting for them to be brought into use (unlike other buildings). However, not all the allowance need be taken, and any expenditure not so allowed is written off straight line, at 25% of the full cost each year, over a period of up to four years starting when the building is brought into use.

1.24 Buildings always have a **separate computation for each building**. They are never pooled.

Activity 4.3: Writing down allowance

Fraser Ltd acquired a factory for £600,000 and started to use it for industrial purposes on 1 July 2000. What industrial buildings allowances are available to Fraser Ltd in its nine month accounting period to 30 September 2000?

Balancing adjustments on sale

1.25 **The 'tax life' of an industrial building is 25 years** (hence the 4% straight line WDA) after it is first used, or 50 years if constructed before 6 November 1962. Balancing adjustments apply *only* if a building is sold within its tax life of 25 or 50 years.

1.26 On a sale between connected persons, the parties may jointly elect that the transfer price for IBAs purposes should be the lower of the market value and the residue of unallowed expenditure before the sale. This avoids a balancing charge.

1.27 **The seller's calculation is quite straightforward.** It takes the following form.

	£
Cost	X
Less allowances previously given	(X)
Residue before sale	X
Less proceeds (limited to cost)	(X)
Balancing (charge)/allowance	(X)

1.28 **The buyer obtains annual straight line WDAs for the remainder of the building's tax life** (25 years if constructed after 5 November 1962). This life is calculated to the nearest month. The allowances are granted on the residue after sale which is computed thus.

	£
Residue before sale	X
Plus balancing charge or less balancing allowance	X
Residue after sale	X

This means that **the second owner will write off the lower of his cost or the original cost.**

Activity 4.4: - Calculation of IBAs

Frankie, who prepares accounts to 31 December, bought an industrial building for £100,000 (excluding land) on 1 October 1996. He brought it into use as a factory immediately. On 1 September 2000 he sells it for £120,000 to Holly, whose accounting date is 30 September and who brought the building into industrial use immediately. Show the IBAs available to Frankie and to Holly.

DEVOLVED ASSESSMENT ALERT

The Inland Revenue allow IBA's equal to the fall in value of a building over the trader's use of that building.

If an industrial building is sold for more than its original cost a balancing charge equal to the allowances given to date will arise. This is because there was no fall in value so no allowances are actually due.

If sold for less than original cost we could calculate the fall in value of the building and that would equal the allowances available for this building. If we compare this to the allowances already given, the difference would be the balancing adjustment due on the sale.

In the above question if Frankie sold the building Holly for £90,000:

	£
Fall in value (£100,000 – £90,000) = allowances due	10,000
Less: allowances already given to Frankie	16,000
Balancing adjustment = Balancing charge	6,000

Over the use of the building by Frankie £16,000 of IBA's were claimed. On the sale of the building the fall in value is calculated as £10,000. Thus Frankie should only have received £10,000 of allowances not £16,000. So £6,000 is paid back as a balancing charge.

2 AGRICULTURAL BUILDINGS

2.1 The system of allowances for agricultural buildings is similar to the industrial buildings allowances system.

2.2 Expenditure which qualifies for agricultural buildings allowances is **capital expenditure on the construction of farmhouses, farm buildings, cottages, fences, drainage and similar**

works. The cost of land does not qualify and qualifying expenditure on farmhouses is restricted to one third of the total expenditure on the house.

The allowances

2.3 An annual **writing down allowance of 4% a year straight line** is given to the person incurring the qualifying expenditure. The WDA is first given for the period of account or accounting period in which the expenditure was incurred. The 25 year tax life runs from the start of that period and the allowance is 4% × months in the period/12. The allowance for the period at the end of the tax life is whatever is needed to make the total allowances equal the original expenditure.

Disposals

2.4 **There are two available methods for dealing with the allowances when an agricultural building is sold during its tax life. The first, which applies automatically unless an election is made to override it, time-apportions the writing down allowances.** The seller is entitled to a proportion of the WDA for the time he owned the building during *his* period of sale. The buyer is entitled to a proportion for the time he owned the building during *his* period of purchase.

2.5 **Under the alternative method a balancing allowance is given to, or a balancing charge imposed on, the seller.** The buyer obtains allowances on the tax written down value plus any balancing charge or minus any balancing allowance. This equals the lower of the original cost and the sale proceeds. This is very similar to the system on disposal of an industrial building.

Activity 4.5: End of chapter activity

Cuckold Ltd makes up accounts to 31 March each year. It is considering the purchase of an additional, secondhand factory on 1 April 2001. It has decided to spend £150,000 and the following details refer to four possible factories which could each be acquired for that sum. All are equally suitable for Cuckold Ltd's purposes and all have been used for qualifying industrial purposes throughout their lives.

	Original cost to first owner £	Date of first use
(i)	100,000	31 March 1977
(ii)	80,000	31 March 1976
(iii)	160,000	31 March 1999
(iv)	120,000	31 March 1993

Required

Advise Cuckold Ltd of the amount of industrial buildings allowances which would be available as a result of purchasing each of the above factories, indicating the periods for which the allowances would be available. Which building would you advise it to purchase?

BPP PUBLISHING

Key learning points

- The computations for industrial buildings are a little more complicated than those for plant and machinery, but there is less case law to learn.

- The agricultural building allowance system is very similar to the industrial buildings allowance system.

Quick quiz

1   Which buildings cannot be industrial buildings?

2   Are drawing offices industrial buildings?

3   What are the conditions for a hotel to qualify for allowances?

4   What are the conditions for the non qualifying part of an industrial building to qualify for allowances?

5   What allowances are available for buildings in enterprise zones?

Quick quiz answers

1   Dwelling houses, retail shops, showrooms and offices are not industrial buildings.

2   Drawing offices which serve an industrial building are regarded as industrial buildings themselves (*CIR v Lambhill Ironworks Ltd 1950*).

3   For a 'hotel' to qualify for industrial buildings allowances:

    (a)   it must have at least ten letting bedrooms;

    (b)   it must have letting bedrooms as the whole or main part of the sleeping accommodation;

    (c)   it must offer ancillary services including at least:

        (i)   breakfast;

        (ii)   evening meals;

        (iii)   the cleaning of rooms; and

        (iv)   the making of beds; and

    (d)   it must be open for at least four months during the April to October season.

4   The cost of the non qualifying part of the building must not exceed 25% of the total expenditure on the qualifying and non qualifying parts.

5   There is a 100% initial allowance. If all of the initial allowance is not claimed then there are 25% straight line writing down allowances on the unrelieved expenditure commencing in the period in which the initial allowance is claimed.

Answers to activities

Activity 4.1

Only the sports pavilion will qualify.

Activity 4.2

The showrooms and offices are non-qualifying parts of the building. As the cost of the non qualifying parts, £600,000, is more than 25% of the total expenditure on the building, industrial buildings allowances are not available on it. The cost of the land is not qualifying expenditure.

Therefore, the qualifying expenditure for industrial buildings allowance purposes is £1,500,000 (£2,100,000 – £600,000)

Activity 4.3

The building was in industrial use at the end of the accounting period so an industrial buildings allowance of 4% of cost per annum is available. The allowance in the nine months to 30.9.00 is, therefore, 9/12 × £600,000 × 4% = £18,000

Activity 4.4

Frankie	£
Cost 1.10.96	100,000
Y/e 31.12.96 to y/e 31.12.99 WDA 4 × 4%	(16,000)
Residue before sale	84,000
Y/e 31.12.00 Proceeds (limited to cost)	(100,000)
Balancing charge	(16,000)

Holly	£
Residue before sale	84,000
Balancing charge	16,000
Residue after sale	100,000

The tax life of the building ends on 1.10.96 + 25 years = 30.9.2021
The date of Holly's purchase is 1.9.00
The unexpired life is therefore 21 years 1 month

	£
Y/e 30.9.00 WDA £100,000/21.083333	4,743
Next 20 accounting periods at £4,743 a year	94,860
Y/e 30.9.21 (balance)	397
	100,000

Activity 4.5

Cuckold Ltd should acquire factory (i), as shown in the working below.

Factory (ii) is clearly unattractive since, with its tax life expired, industrial buildings allowances cannot be claimed. Factories (iii) and (iv) have greater total allowances available than factory (i) but the annual allowance is much smaller.

Working: industrial buildings allowances on alternative factories

	Factory (i)	Factory (ii)	Factory (iii)	Factory (iv)
Residue after sale*	£100,000	£80,000	£150,000	£120,000
Remaining tax life**	1 yr	0	23 yrs	17 yrs
Allowances available	£100,000	0	£150,000	£120,000
in y/e 31.3.2002	1 yr		23 yrs	17 yrs
	= £100,000		= £6,522	= £7,059

* The residue after sale is the lower of the price paid by the new purchaser and the original cost.

** The tax life of an industrial building begins when it is first brought into use and ends 25 years later (except for expenditure incurred before 6 November 1962, when the relevant period is 50 years rather than 25 years).

Chapter 5   *Trading losses*

Chapter topic list

1   Losses

2   Carry forward of trading losses: s 385 ICTA 1988

3   Setting losses against income: s 380 ICTA 1988

4   Trade charges: s 387 ICTA 1988

5   Losses in the early years of a trade: s 381 ICTA 1988

6   Businesses transferred to companies: s 386 ICTA 1988

Learning objectives

On completion of this chapter you will be able to:

	Performance criteria	Range Statement
• offset a trading loss against the income of an individual to reduce the income tax bill	18.1.4	18.1.2
• offset a trading loss agaisnt the capital gains of an individual to reduce the CGT bill.	18.1.4	18.1.2
• recognise which trading losses can be utilised in which tax years and choose the best use of the loss if more than one option for utilisation is available.	18.1.4	18.1.2

BPP PUBLISHING

1 LOSSES

1.1 This chapter considers how losses are calculated and how a loss-suffering taxpayer can use a Schedule D Case I trading loss to reduce his tax liability. Losses arising in professions and vocations (Schedule D Case II) are treated in exactly the same way.

1.2 **The rules covered in this chapter apply only to individuals,** trading alone or in partnership. Loss reliefs for companies are completely different and are covered later in this text.

1.3 **Losses of one spouse cannot be relieved against income of the other spouse.**

1.4 When computing tax adjusted trading profits, profits may turn out to be negative, that is a loss has been made in the basis period. **A loss is computed in exactly the same way as a profit,** making the same adjustments to the accounts profit or loss.

1.5 **If there is a loss in a basis period, the taxable income for the tax year based on that basis period is nil.**

2 CARRY FORWARD OF TRADING LOSSES: S 385 ICTA 1988

2.1 A trading loss not relieved in any other way may be **carried forward to set against the first available profits of the same trade.** Losses may be carried forward for any number of years.

2.2 EXAMPLE: CARRYING FORWARD LOSSES

B has the following results.

Year ending	£
31 December 1998	(6,000)
31 December 1999	5,000
31 December 2000	11,000

B's taxable profits, assuming that he claims loss relief only under s 385 are:

	1998/99		*1999/00*		*2000/01*
	£		£		£
Schedule D Case I	0		5,000		11,000
Less s 385 relief	0	(i)	5,000	(ii)	1,000
Profits	0		0		10,000

Loss memorandum		£
Trading loss, y/e 31.12.98		6,000
Less: claim in y/e 31.12.99	(i)	(5,000)
claim in y/e 31.12.00 (balance of loss)	(ii)	(1,000)
		0

3 SETTING LOSSES AGAINST INCOME: S 380 ICTA 1988

3.1 **Instead of carrying a loss forward against future trading income, it may be relieved against current income of all types.**

The computation of the loss

3.2 EXAMPLE

The loss for a tax year is the loss in the basis period for that tax year. However, if basis periods overlap then a loss in the overlap period is a loss for the earlier tax year only. Here is an example of a trader who starts to trade on 1 July 2000 and makes losses in opening years.

Period of account	Loss
	£
1.7.00 - 31.12.00	9,000
1.1.01 - 31.12.01	24,000

Tax year	Basis period	Working	Loss for the tax year
			£
2000/01	1.7.00 - 5.4.01	£9,000 + (£24,000 × 3/12)	15,000
2001/02	1.1.01 - 31.12.01	£24,000 - (£24,000 × 3/12)	18,000

3.3 EXAMPLE

The same rule against using losses twice applies when losses are netted off against profits in the same basis period. Here is an example, again with a commencement on 1 July 2000 but with a different accounting date.

Period of account	(Loss)/profit
	£
1.7.00 - 30.4.01	(10,000)
1.5.01 - 30.4.02	24,000

Tax year	Basis period	Working	(Loss)/Profit
			£
2000/01	1.7.00 - 5.4.01	£(10,000) × 9/10	(9,000)
2001/02	1.7.00 - 30.6.01	£24,000 × 2/12 + £(10,000) × 1/10	3,000

Relieving the loss

3.4 **Relief** under s 380 **is against the income of the tax year in which the loss arose. In addition or instead,** relief may be claimed **against the income of the preceding year.**

If there are losses in two successive years, and relief is claimed against the first year's income both for the first year's loss and for the second year's loss, relief is given for the first year's loss before the second year's loss.

3.5 A claim for a loss must be made by the 31 January which is 22 months after the end of the tax year of the loss: thus by 31 January 2003 for a loss in 2000/01.

3.6 The taxpayer cannot choose the amount of loss to relieve: thus the loss may have to be set against income, part of which would have been covered by the personal allowance. However, the taxpayer can choose whether to claim full relief in the current year and then relief in the preceding year for any remaining loss, or the other way round.

Set the loss against non-savings income then against savings (excluding dividend) income and finally against dividend income.

3.7 Relief is available by carry forward under s 385 for any loss not relieved under s 380.

Activity 5.1: loss relief

In 2000/01 Nicola has a loss of £18,000. Her statutory total income in 2000/01 is non-savings investment income totalling £14,000, and her personal allowance for that year is £4,385. She has no other source of income for any year. If she obtains loss relief as soon as possible, what loss is carried forward under s 385 ICTA 1988?

Activity 5.2: s 380 relief

Janet has a loss in her period of account ending 31 December 2000 of £25,000. Her other income is £18,000 rental income a year, and she wishes to claim loss relief for the year of loss and then for the preceding year. Show her taxable income for each year, and comment on the effectiveness of the loss relief. Assume that tax rates and allowances for 2000/01 have always applied.

Capital allowances

3.8 The trader may adjust the size of the total s 380 claim by not claiming all the capital allowances he is entitled to: a reduced claim will increase the balance carried forward to the next year's capital allowances computation.

Trading losses relieved against capital gains

3.9 Where relief is claimed against total income of a given year, the taxpayer may include **a further claim to set the loss against his chargeable gains for the year** less any allowable capital losses for the same year or for previous years. This amount of net gains is computed ignoring taper relief and the annual exempt amount. Chargeable gains are covered later in this text.

3.10 **The trading loss is first set against total income of the year of the claim, and only any excess of loss is set against capital gains. The taxpayer cannot specify the amount to be set against capital gains, so the annual exempt amount may be wasted.**

3.11 An activity is included below for completeness. You are advised to come back and study it after you have studied chargeable gains which are covered later in this text.

Activity 5.3: Loss relief against income and gains

Sibyl had the following results for 2000/01.

	£
Loss available for relief under s 380	27,000
Income	19,500
Capital gains less current year capital losses	10,000
Annual exemption for capital gains tax purposes	7,200
Capital losses brought forward	4,000

Assume no taper relief is due.

Show how the loss would be relieved against income and gains.

Restrictions on s 380 relief

3.12 **Relief cannot be claimed under s 380 unless a business is conducted on a commercial basis with a view to the realisation of profits;** this condition applies to all types of business.

The choice between loss reliefs

3.13 **When a trader has a choice between loss reliefs, he should aim to obtain relief both quickly and at the highest possible tax rate.** However, do consider that losses relieved against income which would otherwise be covered by the personal allowance are wasted.

3.14 Another consideration is that a trading loss cannot be set against the capital gains of a year unless relief is first claimed under s 380 against income of the same year. It may be worth making the claim against income and wasting the personal allowance in order to avoid a CGT liability.

> ### DEVOLVED ASSESSMENT ALERT
>
> Before recommending S 380 loss relief consider whether it will result in the waste of the personal allowance. Such waste is to be avoided if at all possible.

4 TRADE CHARGES: S 387 ICTA 1988

4.1 Annual charges such as patent royalties, although they may be paid out wholly and exclusively for business purposes, are nevertheless not deducted in arriving at the adjusted Schedule D Case I profit or loss. They are deducted in arriving at STI. If these amounts exceed STI there are 'excess charges'.

Excess trade charges can be carried forward against future profits from the same trade in the same way as losses under s 385. Non-trade charges, however cannot be relieved in this way.

4.2 EXAMPLE: EXCESS TRADE CHARGES

A taxpayer has the following results for 2000/01.

	£
Schedule D Case I	4,000
Other income	1,000
	5,000
Less patent royalty	7,000
STI	0

The excess trade charge available to carry forward and set against future Schedule D Case I profits is £2,000.

5 LOSSES IN THE EARLY YEARS OF A TRADE: S 381 ICTA 1988

5.1 S 381 relief is available for **trading losses incurred in the first four tax years of a trade.**

5.2 Relief is obtained by **setting the allowable loss against total income in the three years preceding the year of loss,** applying the loss to the earliest year first. Thus a loss arising in 2000/01 may be set off against income in 1997/98, 1998/99 and 1999/00 in that order.

5.3 A claim under s 381 applies to all three years automatically, provided that the loss is large enough. The taxpayer cannot choose to relieve the loss against just one or two of the years, or to relieve only part of the loss.

5.4 Do not double-count a loss. If basis periods overlap, a loss in the overlap period is treated as a loss for the earlier tax year only. This is the same rule as applies for s 380 purposes.

5.5 Claims for the relief must be made by the 31 January which is 22 months after the end of the tax year in which the loss is incurred.

5.6 The 'commercial basis' test is stricter for loss relief under s 381 than under s 380. The trade must be carried on in such a way that profits could reasonably have been expected to be realised in the period of the loss or within a reasonable time thereafter.

Activity 5.4: S381 loss relief

Mr A is employed as an auditor until 1 January 1999. On that date he starts up his own business as a scrap metal merchant, making up his accounts to 30 June each year.

His taxable income as an auditor is as follows.

	£
1995/96	5,000
1996/97	6,000
1997/98	7,000
1998/99 (nine months)	6,000

His trading results as a scrap metal merchant are as follows.

	Profit/(Loss) £
Six months to 30 June 1999	(3,000)
Year to 30 June 2000	(1,500)
Year to 30 June 2001	(1,200)
Year to 30 June 2002	0

Assuming that loss relief is claimed as early as possible, show the final Schedule E and Schedule D Case I income for each of the years 1995/96 to 2001/02 inclusive.

---

6 BUSINESSES TRANSFERRED TO COMPANIES: S 386 ICTA 1988

6.1 **Although the set-off under s 385 is restricted to future profits of the same business, this is extended to cover income received from a company to which the business is sold.**

6.2 **The amount carried forward is the total unrelieved trading losses of the business. The set-off must be made against the first available income from the company. The order of set-off is:**

(a) against **salary** derived from the company by the former proprietor of the business; **then**
(b) against **interest and dividends** from the company.

6.3 The consideration for the sale must be wholly or mainly shares, which must be retained by the vendor throughout any tax year in which the loss is relieved; the Revenue treat this condition as being satisfied if 80% or more of the consideration consists of shares.

Activity 5.5: End of chapter activity

Morgan started to trade on 6 April 1997. His business has the following results.

Year ending 5 April		£
1998	Profit	12,000
1999	Profit	16,000
2000	Profit	18,000
2001 (projected)	Profit	15,000
2002 (projected)	Loss	(32,000)

It is expected that the business will show healthy profits thereafter. In addition to his business Morgan has rental income of £8,000 a year.

Required

(a) Outline the ways in which Morgan could obtain relief for his loss.

(b) Prepare a statement showing how the loss would be relieved assuming that relief were to be claimed as soon as possible. Comment on whether this is likely to be the best relief

---

Key learning points

- Trading losses may be relieved against future profits of the same trade, against total income and against capital gains.

- In opening years, a special relief involving the carry back of losses against total income is available.

- It is important for a trader to choose the right loss relief, so as to save tax at the highest possible rate and so as to obtain relief reasonably quickly.

- On the transfer of a business to a company it may be possible to carry forward unutilised trading losses for offset against future income received by the previous owner of the business from the company to which the business was transferred.

Quick quiz

1   Against what income may trading losses carried forward be set off?

2   When a loss is to be relieved against total income, how are losses linked to particular tax years?

3   Against which years' total income may a loss be relieved under s 380 ICTA 1988?

4   What is the relief available under s 381 ICTA 1988?

Quick quiz answers

1   The first available profits of the same trade.

2   The loss for a tax year is the loss in the basis period for that tax year. However, if basis periods overlap then a loss in the overlap period is a loss for the earlier tax year only.

3   The tax year in which the loss was suffered and/or the income of the preceding tax year.

4   This relief is available in respect of trading losses incurred in the first four tax years of a trade.

Relief is obtained by setting the allowable loss against total income in the three years preceding the year of loss, applying the loss to the earliest year first. Thus a loss arising in 2000/01 may be set off against income in 1997/98, 1998/99 and 1999/00 in that order.

A claim under s 381 applies to all three years automatically, provided that the loss is large enough. The taxpayer cannot choose to relieve the loss against just one or two of the years, or to relieve only part of the loss.

Answers to activities

Activity 5.1

£18,000 – £14,000 (s 380 claim) = £4,000

Activity 5.2

The loss-making period ends in 2000/01, so the year of the loss is 2000/01.

	1999/00	2000/01
	£	£
Income	18,000	18,000
Less s 380 relief	(7,000)	(18,000)
STI	11,000	0
Less personal allowance	(4,385)	(4,385)
Taxable income	6,615	0

In 2000/01, £4,385 of the loss has been wasted because that amount of income would have been covered by the personal allowance. If Janet claims s 380 relief, there is nothing she can do about this waste of loss relief. However, Janet might have been best advised to claim relief in 1999/00 before making a claim in 2000/01. This would have had the effect of moving the taxable income to 2000/01 and delaying the payment of the associated income tax.

Activity 5.3

	£
Income	19,500
Less loss relief	(19,500)
STI	0

	£
Capital gains	10,000
Less loss relief: lower of £(27,000 – 19,500) = £7,500 (note 1) and	
£(10,000 - 4,000) = £6,000 (note 2)	(6,000)
	4,000
Less annual exemption	(4,000)
	0

Note 1 This equals the loss left after the S380 claim
Note 2 This equals the gains left after losses b/fwd but ignoring taper relief and the annual exemption.

A trading loss of £(7,500 – 6,000) = £1,500 is carried forward. Sibyl's personal allowance and £(7,200 – 4,000) = £3,200 of her capital gains tax annual exemption are wasted. Her capital losses brought forward of £4,000 are carried forward to 2001/02. Although we deducted this £4,000 in working out how much trading loss we were allowed to use in the claim, we do not actually use any of the £4,000 unless there are gains remaining after the annual exemption.

Activity 5.4

Since reliefs are to be claimed as early as possible, s 381 ICTA 1988 is applied. The losses available for relief are as follows.

	£	£	Years against which relief is available
1998/99 (basis period 1.1.99 - 5.4.99)			
3 months to 5.4.99			
£(3,000) × 3/6		(1,500)	1995/96 to 1997/98
1999/00 (basis period 1.1.99 - 31.12.99)			
3 months to 30.6.99			
(omit 1.1.99 - 5.4.99: overlap)			
£(3,000) × 3/6	(1,500)		
6 months to 31.12.99			
£(1,500) × 6/12	(750)		
		(2,250)	1996/97 to 1998/99
2000/2001 (basis period 1.7.99 - 30.6.00)			
6 months to 30.6.00			
(omit 1.7.99 - 31.12.99: overlap)			
£(1,500) × 6/12		(750)	1997/98 to 1999/00
2001/2002 (basis period 1.7.00 - 30.6.01)			
12 months to 30.6.01		(1,200)	1998/99 to 2000/01

The revised Schedule E income is as follows.

	£	£
1995/96		
Original	5,000	
Less 1998/99 loss	(1,500)	
		3,500
1996/97		
Original	6,000	
Less 1999/00 loss	(2,250)	
		3,750
1997/98		
Original	7,000	
Less 2000/01 loss	(750)	
		6,250
1998/99		
Original	6,000	
Less 2001/02 loss	(1,200)	
		4,800

The Schedule D Case I income for 1998/99 to 2001/02 will all be zero, because there were losses in the basis periods.

Activity 5.5

(a)   Loss relief could be claimed:

(i)   under s 380 ICTA 1988, against other income of the year of loss (2001/02), the Schedule A income of £8,000;

under s 380 ICTA 1988, against other income of the preceding year (2000/01). This would be Schedule D Case I income of £15,000 plus Schedule A income of £8,000;

under s 385 ICTA 1988, against the first available future profits of the same trade.

(b)   *The quickest claim*

The quickest way to obtain relief would be for Morgan to use s 380 ICTA 1988 in both years. The tax computations would then be as follows.

	2000/01	*2001/02*
	£	£
Schedule D Case I	15,000	0
Schedule A	8,000	8,000
	23,000	8,000
Less s 380 loss relief	23,000	8,000
Taxable income	0	0

The balance of the loss, £1,000, would be carried forward and relieved under s 385.

Although s 380 produces loss relief quickly, it has the disadvantage of wasting Morgan's personal allowance in both years. Morgan could, if he chose, delay his relief by carrying the loss forward under s 385 ICTA 1988. The loss would then be set off only against trading income, with the rental income using his personal allowance.

Chapter 6   Partnerships

Chapter topic list

1   Partnerships

2   Inland Revenue forms

Learning objectives

On completion of this chapter you will be able to:

	Performance criteria	Range Statement
• discuss the effect on a partnership of a change in partners	18.1.2	18.1.3
• allocate business profits or losses to individual partners	18.1.2	18.1.2

1   PARTNERSHIPS

1.1   **A partnership is treated like a sole trader for the purposes of computing its profits.** (As usual, 'trade' in this chapter includes professions and vocations.) Partners' salaries and interest on capital are not deductible expenses and must be added back in computing profits, because they are a form of drawings.

1.2   **Once the partnership's profits or losses for a period of account have been computed, they are shared between the partners according to the profit sharing arrangements for that period of account.**

The tax positions of individual partners

1.3   **Each partner is taxed like a sole trader** who runs a business which:

- starts when he joins the partnership;

- finishes when he leaves the partnership;

- has the same periods of account as the partnership (except that a partner who joins or leaves during a period will have a period which starts or ends part way through the partnership's period);

- makes profits or losses equal to the partner's share of the partnership's profits or losses.

Changes in membership

1.4   **When a trade continues but partners join or leave** (including cases when a sole trader takes in partners or a partnership breaks up leaving only one partner as a sole trader), **the special rules for basis periods in opening and closing years do not apply to the people who were carrying on the trade both before and after the change. They carry on using the period of account ending in each tax year as the basis period for the tax year. The commencement rules only affect joiners, and the cessation rules only affect leavers.**

1.5   However, when no-one carries on the trade both before and after the change, as when a partnership transfers its trade to a completely new owner or set of owners, the cessation rules apply to the old owners and the commencement rules apply to the new owners.

Loss reliefs

1.6   **Partners are entitled to the same loss reliefs as sole traders.** Different partners may claim loss reliefs in different ways.

Assets owned individually

1.7   **Where the partners own assets (such as their cars) individually, a capital allowances computation must be prepared for each partner in respect of the assets he owns** (not forgetting any adjustment for private use). **The capital allowances must go into the partnership's tax computation.**

1.8   EXAMPLE: A PARTNERSHIP

Alice and Bertrand start a partnership on 1 July 1997, making up accounts to 31 December each year. On 1 May 1999, Charles joins the partnership. On 1 November 2000, Charles leaves. The profit sharing arrangements are as follows.

	Alice	Bertrand	Charles
1.7.97 - 31.12.97			
Salaries (per annum)	£3,000	£4,500	
Balance	3/5	2/5	
1.1.98 - 30.4.99			
Salaries (per annum)	£3,000	£6,000	
Balance	4/5	1/5	
1.5.99 - 31.10.00			
Salaries (per annum)	£2,400	£3,600	£1,800
Balance	2/5	2/5	1/5
1.11.00 - 31.12.00			
Salaries (per annum)	£1,500	£2,700	
Balance	3/5	2/5	

Profits as adjusted for tax purposes are as follows.

Period	Profit(loss)
	£
1.7.97 - 31.12.97	22,000
1.1.98 - 31.12.98	51,000
1.1.99 - 31.12.99	39,000
1.1.00 - 31.12.00	15,000

Show the Schedule D Case I profits for each partner for 1997/98 to 2000/01.

1.9 SOLUTION

We must first share the profits for the periods of account between the partners, remembering to adjust the salaries for periods of less than a year.

	Total £	Alice £	Bertrand £	Charles £
1.7.97 - 31.12.97				
Salaries	3,750	1,500	2,250	
Balance	18,250	10,950	7,300	
Total (P/e 31.12.97)	22,000	12,450	9,550	
1.1.98 - 31.12.98				
Salaries	9,000	3,000	6,000	
Balance	42,000	33,600	8,400	
Total (y/e 31.12.98)	51,000	36,600	14,400	
1.1.99 - 31.12.99				
January to April				
Salaries	3,000	1,000	2,000	
Balance	10,000	8,000	2,000	
Total	13,000	9,000	4,000	
May to December				
Salaries	5,200	1,600	2,400	1,200
Balance	20,800	8,320	8,320	4,160
Total	26,000	9,920	10,720	5,360
Total for y/e 31.12.99	39,000	18,920	14,720	5,360

	Total £	Alice £	Bertrand £	Charles £
1.1.00 - 31.12.00				
January to October				
Salaries	6,500	2,000	3,000	1,500
Balance	6,000	2,400	2,400	1,200
Total	12,500	4,400	5,400	2,700
November and December				
Salaries	700	250	450	
Balance	1,800	1,080	720	
Total	2,500	1,330	1,170	
Total for y/e 31.12.00	15,000	5,730	6,570	2,700

1.10 The next stage is to work out the basis periods and hence the taxable profits for the partners. All of them are treated as making up accounts to 31 December, but Alice and Bertrand are treated as starting to trade on 1 July 1997 and Charles as trading only from 1 May 1999 to 31 October 2000. Applying the usual rules gives the following basis periods and taxable profits.

Alice

Year	Basis period	Working	Taxable profits £
1997/98	1.7.97 - 5.4.98	£12,450 + (£36,600 × 3/12)	21,600
1998/99	1.1.98 - 31.12.98		36,600
1999/00	1.1.99 - 31.12.99		18,920
2000/01	1.1.00 - 31.12.00		5,730

Note that for 1997/98 we take Alice's total for the year ended 1998 and apportion that, because the partnership's period of account runs from 1 January to 31 December 1998.

Alice will have overlap profits for the period 1 January to 5 April 1998 (£36,600 × 3/12 = £9,150) to deduct when she ceases to trade.

Bertrand

Year	Basis period	Working	Taxable profits £
1997/98	1.7.97 - 5.4.98	£9,550 + (£14,400 × 3/12)	13,150
1998/99	1.1.98 - 31.12.98		14,400
1999/00	1.1.99 - 31.12.99		14,720
2000/01	1.1.00 - 31.12.00		6,570

Bertrand's overlap profits are £14,400 × 3/12 = £3,600.

Charles

Year	Basis period	Working	Taxable profits £
1999/00	1.5.99 - 5.4.00	£5,360 + (£2,700 × 3/10)	6,170
2000/01	6.4.00 - 31.10.00	£2,700 × 7/10	1,890

Because Charles ceased to trade in his second tax year of trading, his basis period for the second year starts on 6 April and he has no overlap profits.

Activity 6.1: New partner

A partnership makes profits as follows.

Year ended 31 December

	£
1999	34,200
2000	45,600

A partner joins on 1 September 1999, and is entitled to 20% of the profits. What are his taxable profits for 1999/00 and 2000/01?

DEVOLVED ASSESSMENT ALERT

Partners are effectively taxed in the same way as sole traders with just one difference. Before you tax the partner you need to take each set of accounts (as adjusted for tax purposes) and divide the profit (or loss) between each partner.

Then carry on as normal for a sole trader - each partner is that sole trader in respect of his profits or losses for each accounting period.

2 INLAND REVENUE FORMS

2.1 A sample of the supplementary pages to the income tax return form that may have to be completed by a member of a partnership is included in the appendix to this text. Each partner must enter their share of the partnership's profits or losses on these pages. For Unit 18 you are expected to be aware of how partnership profits or losses are entered on this form. Completion of the full self assessment income tax return is expected only in Unit 19 *Preparing personal tax computations*. Please see page (x) for a note regarding the version of the form used.

2.2 In addition, a partnership tax return must be completed and submitted to the Revenue on behalf of the partnership as a whole. We have included a sample partnership tax return form in the appendix to this text. Please see page (x) for a note regarding the version of the form that we have used.

Activity 6.2: End of chapter activity

Adam, Bert and Charlie started in partnership as secondhand car dealers on 6 April 1997, sharing profits in the ratio 2:2:1, after charging annual salaries of £1,500, £1,200 and £1,000 respectively.

On 5 July 1998 Adam retired and Bert and Charlie continued, taking the same salaries as before, but dividing the balance of the profits in the ratio 3:2.

On 6 May 2000 Dick was admitted as a partner on the terms that he received a salary of £1,800 a year, that the salaries of Bert and Charlie should be increased to £1,800 a year each and that of the balance of the profits, Dick should take one tenth and Bert and Charlie should divide the remainder in the ratio 3:2.

The profits of the partnership as adjusted for tax purposes were as follows.

Year ending 5 April	Profits
	£
1998	10,200
1999	20,800
2000	12,600
2001	18,000

Required

Show the taxable profits for each partner for 1997/98 to 2000/2001 inclusive.

Key learning points

- A partnership is simply treated as a source of profits and losses for trades being carried on by the individual partners.

- Commencement and cessation rules apply to partners individually when they join or leave.

- A partnership tax return must be completed by the partnership. In addition each individual partner must enter his share of partnership profit or losses on the supplementary pages of his self assessment return.

Quick quiz

1   How are individual partners taxed on the partnership's profits?

2   How is a partner taxed on partnership profits when other partners join or leave the partnership?

Quick quiz answers

1   The partnership's profits for a period of account are shared between the partners according to the profit sharing arrangements for that period of account.

Each partner is taxed like a sole trader who runs a business which:

- starts when he joins the partnership;

- finishes when he leaves the partnership;

- has the same periods of account as the partnership (except that a partner who joins or leaves during a period will have a period which starts or ends part way through the partnership's period);

- makes profits or losses equal to the partner's share of the partnership's profits or losses.

2   When a trade continues but partners join or leave, the special rules for basis periods in opening and closing years do not apply to the people who were carrying on the trade both before and after the change. They carry on using the period of account ending in each tax year as the basis period for the tax year. The commencement rules only affect joiners, and the cessation rules only affect leavers.

Answers to activities

Activity 6.1

Year	Basis period	Working	Taxable profits
			£
1999/00	1.9.99 - 5.4.00	(£34,200 × 20%) × 4/12 +	
		(£45,600 × 20%) × 3/12	4,560
2000/01	1.1.00 - 31.12.00	£45,600 × 20%	9,120

Activity 6.2

	Total £	A £	B £	C £	D £
Year ending 5 April 1998					
Salaries	3,700	1,500	1,200	1,000	
Balance	6,500	2,600	2,600	1,300	
Total	10,200	4,100	3,800	2,300	
Year ending 5 April 1999					
6 April to 5 July					
Salaries	925	375	300	250	
Balance	4,275	1,710	1,710	855	
Total (3/12)	5,200	2,085	2,010	1,105	
6 July to 5 April					
Salaries	1,650		900	750	
Balance	13,950		8,370	5,580	
Total (9/12)	15,600		9,270	6,330	
Totals for the year	20,800	2,085	11,280	7,435	
Year ending 5 April 2000					
Salaries	2,200		1,200	1,000	
Balance	10,400		6,240	4,160	
Total	12,600		7,440	5,160	
Year ending 5 April 2001					
6 April - 5 May					
Salaries	183		100	83	
Balance	1,317		790	527	
Total (1/12)	1,500		890	610	
6 May to 5 April					
Salaries	4,950		1,650	1,650	1,650
Balance	11,550		6,237	4,158	1,155
Total (11/12)	16,500		7,887	5,808	2,805
Totals for the year	18,000		8,777	6,418	2,805

Taxable profits are as follows.

	A £	B £	C £	D £
Year				
1997/98	4,100	3,800	2,300	
1998/99	2,085	11,280	7,435	
1999/00		7,440	5,160	
2000/01		8,777	6,418	2,805

Part B

Chargeable gains

Chapter 7   Chargeable gains: An outline

Chapter topic list

1   The charge to tax

2   Chargeable persons, disposals and assets

3   Losses

4   Taper relief

5   Married couples

6   Administration and Inland Revenue form

Learning objectives

On completion of this chapter you will be able to:

	Performance criteria	Range Statement
• identify when a charge to tax will arise	18.3.2	18.3.1
• identify the types of disposal of assets subject to tax	18.3.2	18.3.1
• discuss what to do with losses made on asset disposals	18.3.1	18.3.1
• recognise when taper relief will apply to reduce a chargeable gain	18.3.3	18.3.1
• discuss the treatment of asset disposals beween spouses	18.3.1	18.3.1
• record a capital gain on the appropriate Inland Revenue form	18.3.5	18.3.1

BPP PUBLISHING

1 THE CHARGE TO TAX

Individuals

1.1 An individual pays CGT on any taxable gains arising in the tax year. **Taxable gains are the net chargeable gains (gains minus losses) of the tax year reduced by unrelieved losses brought forward from previous years, a taper relief and the annual exemption.**

1.2 **There is an annual exemption for each tax year.** For 2000/01 it is £7,200. It is the last deduction to be made in the calculation of taxable gains.

Calculating CGT

1.3 Taxable gains are chargeable to capital gains tax as if the gains were an extra slice of savings (excl dividend) income for the year of assessment concerned. This means that CGT may be due at 10%, 20% or 40%.

1.4 The rate bands are used first to cover income and then gains. If a gift aid payment is made, the basic rate can be extended, as for income tax calculations (see Chapter 1).

Activity 7.1: Rates of CGT (1)

In 2000/01, Carol, a single woman, has the following income, gains and losses. Find the CGT payable.

	£
Business profits	32,080
Chargeable gains (not eligible for taper relief - see later)	25,400
Allowable capital losses	8,000

Activity 7.2: Rates of CGT (2)

In 2000/01, Amy had business profits of £28,000 and gains (before the annual exemption) of £22,000. She made a net gift aid payment of £3,900. What is her CGT payable for 2000/01?

Companies

1.5 Companies are not liable to CGT as such but any net chargeable gains which arise in an accounting period, minus unrelieved losses brought forward from previous accounting periods, form part of their profits chargeable to corporation tax. Gains and losses are calculated, broadly, in the same way as for individuals (but see below).

1.6 The gains of companies are charged at normal corporation tax rates. **Companies do not get the annual exemption or taper relief** (see below).

2 CHARGEABLE PERSONS, DISPOSALS AND ASSETS

Chargeable persons

2.1 The following are chargeable persons.

- Individuals
- Partnerships
- Companies

2.2 The following are exempt persons.

- Charities using gains for charitable purposes
- Approved superannuation funds
- Local authorities
- Registered friendly societies
- Approved scientific research associations
- Authorised unit trusts and investment trusts
- Diplomatic representatives

Chargeable disposals

2.3 The following are chargeable disposals.

- Sales of assets or parts of assets
- Gifts of assets or parts of assets
- Receipts of capital sums following the surrender of rights to assets
- The appropriation of assets as trading stock
- The loss or destruction of assets

2.4 A chargeable disposal occurs on the date of the contract (where there is one, whether written or oral), or the date of a conditional contract becoming unconditional. This may differ from the date of transfer of the asset. However, when a capital sum is received on a surrender of rights, the disposal takes place on the day the sum is received.

Where a disposal involves an acquisition by someone else, the date of acquisition is the same as the date of disposal.

2.5 The following are exempt disposals.

- Transfers of assets on death (the heirs inherit assets as if they bought them at death for their then market values, but there is no capital gain or allowable loss on death)

- Transfers of assets as security for a loan or mortgage

- Gifts to charities and national heritage bodies

2.6 Cashbacks, for example on new mortgages or cars, are also not subject to CGT.

2.7 When someone acquires an asset other than as trading stock and then uses it as trading stock, the appropriation to trading stock leads to an immediate chargeable gain or allowable loss, based on the asset's market value at the date of appropriation. The asset's cost for Schedule D Case I purposes is that market value. However, the trader can elect to have no chargeable gain or allowable loss: if he does so, the cost for Schedule D Case I purposes is reduced by the gain or increased by the loss. The time limit for the election, for individuals, is the 31 January which is nearly two years after the end of the tax year which includes the end of the period of account of appropriation. For companies, it is two years after the end of the accounting period of appropriation.

2.8 When an asset which is trading stock is appropriated to other purposes, the trader is treated for Schedule D Case I purposes as selling it for its market value, and for those other purposes as having bought it at the time of the appropriation for the same value.

BPP PUBLISHING

Chargeable assets

2.9 **All forms of property, wherever in the world they are situated, are chargeable assets unless they are specifically designated as exempt.**

2.10 The following are exempt assets (thus gains are not taxable and losses on their disposal are not in general allowable losses.

- Motor vehicles suitable for private use
- Works of art, scientific collections and so on given for national purposes
- Gilt-edged securities (when disposed of by individuals)
- Qualifying corporate bonds (QCBs) (when disposed of by individuals)
- Certain chattels
- Debts (except debts on a security)

DEVOLVED ASSESSMENT ALERT

For a capital gain to arise there needs to be three things:

- chargeable person;
- chargeable disposal; and
- chargeable asset

otherwise no charge to tax occurs.

Activity 7.3: Chargeable disposal

In 1980, J Ltd bought a vintage motor car as an investment. Nobody in the company ever drove it. The car was sold in 2000, making a gain of £75,000. Is the gain chargeable to CGT?

3 LOSSES

3.1 **Allowable capital losses are deductible from chargeable gains in the tax year in which they arise and any loss which cannot be set off in this manner is carried forward for relief in future periods. Losses must be used as soon as possible** (subject to the following paragraph). Losses may not normally be set against income.

3.2 **Allowable losses brought forward are only set off to reduce current year chargeable gains less current year allowable losses to the annual exempt amount. No set-off is made if net chargeable gains for the current year do not exceed the annual exempt amount.** (Companies do not have an annual exempt amount so no such restriction on the set-off of losses applies to them.)

3.3 EXAMPLE: THE USE OF LOSSES

(a) George has chargeable gains for 2000/01 of £10,000 and allowable losses of £6,000. As the losses are *current year losses* they must be fully relieved against the £10,000 of gains to produce net gains of £4,000, despite the fact that net gains are below the annual exemption.

(b) Bob has gains of £11,400 for 2000/01 and allowable losses brought forward of £6,000. Bob restricts his loss relief to £4,200 so as to leave net gains of £(11,400 − 4,200) =

£7,200, which will be exactly covered by his annual exemption for 2000/01. The remaining £1,800 of losses will be carried forward to 2001/02.

(c) Tom has chargeable gains of £5,000 for 2000/01 and losses brought forward from 1999/00 of £4,000. He will leapfrog 2000/01 and carry forward all of his losses to 2001/02. His gains of £5,000 are covered by his annual exemption for 2000/01.

Losses in the year of death

3.4 The only facility to carry back capital losses arises on the death of an individual. **Losses arising in the tax year in which an individual dies can be carried back to the previous three tax years, later years first, and used so as to reduce gains for each of the years to an amount covered by the appropriate annual exemption.** Only losses in excess of gains in the year of death can be carried back.

Activity 7.4: Loss in year of death

Joe dies on 1 January 2001. His chargeable gains (no taper relief available – see later) and allowable loss have been as follows.

	Gain/(loss) £	Annual exemption £
2000/01	2,000	7,200
	(12,000)	
1999/00	7,300	7,100
1998/99	4,000	6,800
1997/98	28,000	6,500

How will the loss be set off?

4 TAPER RELIEF

4.1 **Taper relief may be available to reduce gains realised after 5 April 1998 by individuals. It is not available to reduce gains realised by companies.**

4.2 **Taper relief reduces the percentage of the gain chargeable according to how many complete years the asset had been held since acquisition or 6 April 1998 if earlier. Taper relief is more generous for business assets than for non-business assets.** In unit 18 you will only be expected to compute gains on the disposal of business assets.

4.3 The percentages of gains which remain chargeable after taper relief for disposals after 5 April 2000 are set out below.

Business assets Number of complete years after 5.4.98 for which asset held	*% of gain chargeable*
0	100
1	87.5
2	75
3	50
4 or more	25

4.4 EXAMPLE: COMPLETE YEARS HELD FOR TAPER RELIEF

Peter buys a business asset on 1 January 1998 and sells it on 1 July 2002. For the purposes of the taper Peter is treated as if he had held the asset for 4 complete years after 5 April 1998.

This means that only 25% of the gain remains chargeable after taper relief.

4.5 **Taper relief is applied to net chargeable gains after the deduction of current year and brought forward losses. The annual exemption is then deducted from the tapered gains.**

Activity 7.5: Taper relief

William sold a business asset in December 2000 realising a chargeable gain of £12,000 before taper relief. He had purchased the asset in May 1995. In January 2001 William sold another business asset realising a loss of £1,300 but had made no other disposals in 2000/01. What are William's taxable gains (after the annual exemption) for 2000/01?

4.6 Losses are dealt with **before** taper relief. However losses brought forward are only deducted from net current gains to the extent that the gains exceed the CGT annual exemption.

Activity 7.6: Use of losses and taper relief

Ruby sold a business asset in July 2000 which she had purchased in January 1999. She realised a chargeable gain (before taper relief) of £17,300. She also sold a business asset in 2000/01 realising a capital loss of £6,000. She has a capital loss brought forward from 1998 of £10,000.

4.7 Allocate losses to gains in the way that produces the lowest tax charge. Losses should therefore be deducted from the gains attracting the lowest rate of taper (ie where the highest percentage of the gain remains chargeable).

4.8 EXAMPLE: ALLOCATION OF LOSSES TO GAINS

Alastair made the following capital losses and gains in 2001/2002:

	£
Loss	10,000
Gains (before taper relief)	
Asset A (business asset)	25,000
Asset B (business asset)	18,000

Asset A was purchased in December 1997 and sold in January 2002. Taper relief reduces the gain to 50% of the original gain (3 years business asset). Asset B was purchased on 5 November 1999 and sold on 17 December 2001. Taper relief reduces the gain to 75% of the original gain (2 years; business asset).

The best use of the loss is to offset it against the gain on asset B:

	£	£
Gain – Asset A	25,000	
Gain after taper relief (£25,000 × 50%)		12,500
Gain – Asset B	18,000	
Less loss	(10,000)	
	8,000	
Gain after taper relief £8,000 × 75%		6,000
Gains after taper relief		18,500
Less annual exemption (say)		(9,000)
Taxable gains		9,500

4.9 There are certain special situations which will affect the operation of taper relief:

(a) where there has been a transfer of assets between spouses (a no loss/no gain transfer; see below) the taper on a subsequent disposal will be based on the combined period of holding by the spouses;

(b) where gains have been relieved under a provision which reduces the cost of the asset in the hands of a new owner (such as gift relief, see later in this text) the taper will operate by reference to the holding period of the new owner.

Shares and securities

4.10 Special rules apply to shares and securities. We cover these later in this text.

Business assets

4.11 **A business asset is:**

- an asset **used for the purposes of a trade** carried on by an individual (either alone or in partnership) or by a qualifying company of that individual;

- an asset **held for the purposes of any office or employment** held by that individual with a person carrying on a trade;

- **shares in a qualifying company** held by an individual.

4.12 From 6 April 2000, **a qualifying company** is a trading company (or holding company of a trading group) where:

(a) the company is **not listed** on a recognised stock exchange nor is a 51% subsidiary of a listed company (companies listed on the Alternative Investment Market (AIM) are unlisted for this purpose); or

(b) the shareholder is an **officer or employee** of the company (full-time or part-time), or of a 51% group company, or a company which is under common control with the company in which the shares are held and carries on a complementary business which can reasonably be regarded as one composite undertaking; or

(c) the shareholder holds at least **5% of the voting rights** in the company.

4.13 For the period between 6 April 1998 and 5 April 2000 a qualifying company was a trading company (or holding company of a trading group) in which the individual held shares which entitled him to exercise at least:

(a) 5% of the voting rights in that company and the individual was a full time working officer or employee of that company; or

(b) 25% of the voting rights in that company.

87
BPP PUBLISHING

4.14 If an asset qualifies as a business asset for part of the time of ownership, and part not, the business part and the non-business part are treated as separate assets calculated by time apportionment over the period of ownership of the asset (not just complete years). However, if the asset was acquired before 6 April 1998, only use on or after that date is taken into account. If the asset is owned for more than ten years after 5 April 1998, only the use in the **last ten years** of ownership is taken into account. Taper relief applies to each gain separately.

5 MARRIED COUPLES

5.1 **A husband and wife are taxed as two separate people. Each has an annual exemption, and losses of one spouse cannot be set against gains of the other.**

5.2 **Disposals between spouses who are living together give rise to no gain and no loss, whatever actual price** (if any) **was charged by the person transferring the asset** to their spouse. A couple are treated as living together unless they are separated under a court order or separation deed, or are in fact separated in circumstances which make permanent separation likely.

5.3 Where an asset is jointly owned, the beneficial interests of the spouses will determine the treatment of any gain on disposal. If, for example, there is evidence that the wife's share in an asset was 60%, then 60% of any gain or loss on disposal would be attributed to her. If there is no evidence of the relative interests, the Revenue will normally accept that the asset is held in equal shares. Where a declaration of how income from the asset is to be shared for income tax purposes has been made, there is a presumption that the same shares will apply for CGT purposes.

5.4 If a spouse whose marginal tax rate is 40% wishes to dispose of an asset at a gain and the other spouse would only be taxed on the gain at a lower rate, the asset should first be transferred to the spouse with the lower tax rate. Similarly, assets or parts of assets should be transferred between spouses to use both CGT annual exemptions.

6 ADMINISTRATION AND INLAND REVENUE FORM

6.1 **CGT is charged on individuals for tax years, like income tax. Any gain arising from 6 April 2000 to 5 April 2001 is taxed in 2000/01.**

6.2 Companies pay corporation tax on their chargeable gains. Corporation tax is covered later in this text.

6.3 **CGT is payable on 31 January following the tax year.**

6.4 If the consideration for a disposal of any asset is receivable in instalments over a period exceeding 18 months, the taxpayer may choose to pay the CGT over the shorter of:

(a) the period of instalments;
(b) eight years.

The Revenue decide on the instalments.

6.5 Tax may also be paid by ten equal annual instalments where it arises on certain gifts, if the donor elects in writing. This is covered later in this text.

6.6 A sample of the supplementary pages to the income tax return form that may need to be completed by individual taxpayers with chargeable gains is included in the appendix to this text. Familiarise yourself with these now. At Unit 18 you will be expected to be aware of how gains are entered on these pages. Full completion of an individual's income tax return will be assessed at Unit 19 only. Please see page (x) for a note regarding the version of the form we have used.

Activity 7.7: End of chapter activity

(a) David had business profits of £6,500, gross bank interest of £18,000 and gains of £35,000 in 2000/01.

Required

Calculate David's tax liabilities for 2000/01.

(b) Edwina disposed of assets as follows.

(i) On 1 January 2000 she sold her car at a loss of £10,700.

(ii) On 28 February 2000 she sold a business asset at a loss of £6,300.

(iii) On 1 May 2000 she sold a business asset (acquired August 1999) and realised a gain of £7,500.

(iv) On 1 October 2000 she sold a business asset at a loss of £2,000.

(v) On 1 December 2000 she sold another business asset (acquired July 2000), making a gain of £3,000.

(vi) On 1 April 2001 she sold some gilt-edged securities (acquired May 2000), making a gain of £10,000.

Required

What loss, if any, is available to be carried forward at the end of 2000/01?

Key learning points

- CGT is charged on capital gains accruing to individuals. Individuals have an annual exemption. They pay CGT at income tax rates.

- Companies chargeable gains/allowable losses are calculated in the same way as for individuals but companies have no annual exemption. Companies pay corporation tax on their net chargeable gains.

- Losses are set against gains of the same year or of future years before taper relief.

- For individuals, taper relief reduces the percentage of a gain which is chargeable. The amount of taper relief depends on the number of complete years that the asset has been owned since 6.4.98.

- Taper relief is not available for companies.

- Spouses are treated as separate people. Transfers of assets between spouses give rise to a nil gain.

- CGT is payable by individuals by 31 January that follows the tax year end.

Quick quiz

1   At what rate or rates do individuals pay CGT?

2   Give some examples of chargeable disposals.

3   To what extent can allowable losses of an individual be set against chargeable gains?

Answers to quick quiz_____

1 An individual has **one** set of tax bands, a starting rate band (£1,520) and a basic rate band (£26,880) to use for both taxable income and taxable gains (the gains after deducting losses, taper relief and the annual exemption). Any gains which cannot be fitted into these bands must be taxed at 40%. Gains that fall within the starting rate band are taxed at 10%. Those within the basic rate band are taxed at 20%. The rate bands cover income and then gains.

2 The following are chargeable disposals.

- Sales and gifts of assets or parts of assets
- Receipts of capital sums following the surrender of rights to assets
- The loss or destruction of assets
- The appropriation of assets as trading stock

3 Allowable losses are deductible from chargeable gains in the tax year in which they arise and any loss which cannot be set off in this manner is carried forward for relief in future periods. Losses must be used as soon as possible. Losses may not normally be set against income.

Allowable losses brought forward are only set off to reduce current year chargeable gains less current year allowable losses to the annual exempt amount. No set-off is made if net chargeable gains for the current year do not exceed the annual exempt amount.

Losses are set off before the deduction of taper relief.

Answers to activities _____

Activity 7.1

(a) Carol's taxable income is as follows.

	£
Schedule D Case I	32,080
Less personal allowance	(4,385)
Taxable income	27,695

(b) The gains to be taxed are as follows.

	£
Gains	25,400
Less losses	(8,000)
	17,400
Less annual exemption	(7,200)
Taxable gains	10,200

(c) The tax bands are allocated as follows.

	Total	Income	Gains
Starting rate	1,520	1,520	0
Basic rate	26,880	26,175	705
Higher rate	9,495	0	9,495
		27,695	10,200

(d) The CGT payable is as follows.

	£
£705 × 20%	141
£9,495 × 40%	3,798
Total CGT payable	3,939

Activity 7.2

	£
Schedule D Income	28,000
Less personal allowance	(4,385)
Taxable income	23,615
Basic rate limit	28,400
Add: gift aid £3,900 × 100/78	5,000
Extended basic rate band	33,400
Less: used up by income	(23,615)
Available for gains	9,785
Capital gains	22,000
Less: annual exemption	(7,200)
Taxable gains	14,800

CGT:	£
£9,785 × 20%	1,957
5,015 × 40%	2,006
14,800	3,963

Activity 7.3

No: motor cars are exempt assets.

Activity 7.4

The £10,000 net loss which arises in 2000/01 will be carried back. We must set off the loss against the 2000/01 gains first even though the gains are more than covered by the 2000/01 annual exemption.

£200 of the loss will be used in 1999/00. None of the loss will be used in 1998/99 (because the gains for that year are covered by the annual exemption), and so the remaining £9,800 will be used in 1997/98. Repayments of CGT will follow.

Activity 7.5

The current year loss must be deducted in full from the gain before taper relief is applied:

	£
Gain	12,000
Loss	(1,300)
Net gain	10,700

The asset was owned for 2 years complete years after 5.4.98 so:

	£
Gain after taper relief (75%)	8,025
Less: Annual exemption	(7,200)
Taxable gain	825

Activity 7.6

	£
Gain	17,300
Loss	(6,000)
Current net gains	11,300
Less: brought forward loss	(4,100)
Gains before taper relief	7,200
Gains after taper relief (1 year ownership) £7,200 × 87.5%	6,300
Less: annual exemption	(7,200)
Taxable gains	Nil

BPP PUBLISHING

Note that the benefit of the taper relief is effectively wasted since the brought forward loss reduces the gain down to the annual exemption amount but the taper is then applied to that amount reducing it further.

The loss carried forward is £5,900 (£10,000 – £4,100).

Activity 7.7 _____

(a) TAXABLE INCOME AND GAINS

	£
Non-savings income £(6,500 – 4,385)	2,115
Savings income	18,000
Taxable income	20,115

	£
Gains	35,000
Less annual exemption	(7,200)
Taxable gains	27,800

£1,520 of non-savings income falls within the lower rate band of 10%. The balance is taxed at 22%.

The total of savings and non-savings income falls below the basic rate threshold, so all of the savings income is taxed at 20%.

£8,285 (£28,400 – £20,115) of the gains fall within the basic rate band and are taxed at 20%. The remaining gains are taxed at 40%.

The income tax liability is as follows.

	£
Non-savings income	
£1,520 × 10%	152
£595 × 22%	131
Savings income	
£18,000 × 20%	3,600
Income tax liability	3,883

The capital gains tax liability is as follows.

	£
£8,285 × 20%	1,657
£19,515 × 40%	7,806
	9,463

(b) Motor cars are exempt assets, so the loss brought forward from 1999/00 is £6,300.

The position for 2000/01 is as follows.

	£
Gains	
Business asset (1) (no taper relief)	7,500
Business asset (2) (no taper relief)	3,000
	10,500
Less loss	(2,000)
	8,500
Less loss brought forward	(1,300)
	7,200
Less annual exemption	(7,200)
Chargeable gains	0

Gilt-edged securities are exempt assets. Losses brought forward are (unlike current year losses) only used to bring net gains down to the annual exempt amount.

The loss carried forward at the end of 2000/01 is £(6,300 – 1,300) = £5,000.

Taper relief is not available to reduce either of the gains in 2000/01 because neither of the assets had been held for a complete year.

Chapter 8   The computation of gains and losses

Chapter topic list

1   The basic computation

2   The indexation allowance

3   Assets held on 31 March 1982

4   Valuing assets

5   Connected persons

6   Disposals on a no gain/no loss basis

7   Part disposals

Learning objectives

On completion of this chapter you will be able to:

	Performance criteria	Range Statement
• calculate a gain or loss on the disposal of an asset	18.3.3	18.3.1
• value assets for CGT purposes and thus the sale proceeds used to calculate the capital gain or loss	18.3.2	18.3.1
• dicuss how gains/losses are computed on part disposals	18.3.3	18.3.1

1 THE BASIC COMPUTATION

1.1 **A chargeable gain (or an allowable loss) is generally calculated as follows.**

	£
Disposal consideration (or market value)	45,000
Less incidental costs of disposal	400
Net proceeds	44,600
Less allowable costs	21,000
Unindexed gain	23,600
Less indexation allowance (if available)	8,500
Indexed gain	15,100

For individuals, taper relief may then apply.

1.2 **Incidental costs of disposal** may include:

- valuation fees (but not the cost of an appeal against the Revenue's valuation);
- estate agency fees;
- advertising costs;
- legal costs.

These costs should be deducted separately from any other allowable costs (because they do not qualify for any indexation allowance if it was available on that disposal).

1.3 **Allowable costs** include:

- the original cost of acquisition;
- incidental costs of acquisition;
- enhancement expenditure.

Incidental costs of acquisition may include the types of cost listed above as incidental costs of disposal, but acquisition costs do qualify for indexation allowance (from the month of acquisition) if it is available on the disposal.

1.4 **Enhancement expenditure** is capital expenditure which enhances the value of the asset and is reflected in the state or nature of the asset at the time of disposal, or expenditure incurred in establishing, preserving or defending title to, or a right over, the asset. Excluded from this category are:

- costs of repairs and maintenance;
- costs of insurance;
- any expenditure deductible for income tax purposes;
- any expenditure met by public funds (for example council grants).

Enhancement expenditure may qualify for indexation allowance from the month in which it becomes due and payable.

The consideration for a disposal

1.5 **Usually the disposal consideration is the proceeds of sale of the asset, but a disposal is deemed to take place at market value:**

(a) where the disposal is **not a bargain at arm's length**;
(b) where the disposal is made for a **consideration which cannot be valued**;
(c) where the disposal is by way of a **gift**.

Activity 8.1: Enhancement expenditure

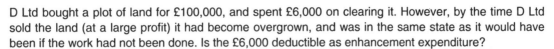

D Ltd bought a plot of land for £100,000, and spent £6,000 on clearing it. However, by the time D Ltd sold the land (at a large profit) it had become overgrown, and was in the same state as it would have been if the work had not been done. Is the £6,000 deductible as enhancement expenditure?

2 THE INDEXATION ALLOWANCE

2.1 Indexation was introduced in 1982. The purpose of having an indexation allowance was to remove the inflationary element of a gain from taxation.

2.2 **Individuals are entitled to an indexation allowance until April 1998, but not thereafter.**

2.3 **The above rule does not apply to companies. Companies are entitled to an indexation allowance until the date of disposal of an asset.**

2.4 EXAMPLE: INDEXATION ALLOWANCE

John bought a painting on 2 January 1987 and sold it on 19 November 2000.

Indexation allowance will be available for the period January 1987 to April 1998 only.

2.5 Indexation is calculated from the month of acquisition of an asset, or March 1982 if later.

DEVOLVED ASSESSMENT ALERT

The indexation factor is:

$$\frac{\text{RPI for month of disposal (or April 1998)} - \text{RPI for month of acquisition (or March 1982)}}{\text{RPI for month of acquisition (or March 1982)}}$$

The calculation is expressed as a decimal and is rounded to three decimal places.

The indexation factor is then multiplied by the cost of the asset to calculate the indexation allowance. If the RPI has fallen, the indexation allowance is zero: it is not negative.

Values of the RPI are given in the Rates and Allowances Tables in this text, including estimated values for January 2000 onwards.

Activity 8.2: The indexation allowance

A business asset is acquired by an individual on 15 February 1983 (RPI = 83.0) at a cost of £5,000. Enhancement expenditure of £2,000 is incurred on 10 April 1984 (RPI = 88.6). The asset is sold for £20,500 on 20 December 2000. Incidental costs of sale are £500. Calculate the indexation allowance.

Indexation and losses

2.6 **The indexation allowance cannot create or increase an allowable loss.** If there is a gain before the indexation allowance, the allowance can reduce that gain to zero, but no further. If there is a loss before the indexation allowance, there is no indexation allowance.

Activity 8.3: Losses

Simon bought a business asset for £97,000 in August 1986, and sold it for £24,000 in April 2000. What is the allowable loss?

3 ASSETS HELD ON 31 MARCH 1982

3.1 **On the disposal of an asset owned on 31 March 1982, we do two calculations. One uses actual cost and the other uses the market value on 31 March 1982. In *both* calculations we base the indexation allowance on the higher of the two.** The final gain or loss is then:

- if both calculations produce gains, the lower gain;

- if both calculations produce losses, the lower loss (so if one produces a loss of £1,000 and the other a loss of £2,000, the allowable loss is £1,000);

- if one calculation produces a gain and the other a loss, or if either produces a result of £nil, no gain and no loss.

3.2 In the computation based on the 31 March 1982 value, that value replaces cost plus all enhancement expenditure up to that date. However, we still use that cost and enhancement expenditure to compute the indexation allowance if they add up to more than the 31 March 1982 value.

Activity 8.4: Assets held on 31 March 1982

Mr A acquired a factory for his business in 1978 at a cost of £28,500. He installed central heating for £1,500 in 1981. The market value of the factory on 31 March 1982 had dropped to £20,000 owing to land subsidence. The property was eventually sold to a property developer in May 2000 for £150,000, the subsidence problem having been rectified at a cost of £15,000 in March 1984.

Compute the chargeable gain before taper relief.

Activity 8.5: Calculation of gain or loss

Mr B acquired a business asset in 1973 for £20,000. The market value of the asset on 31 March 1982 was £150,000. He sold the asset in June 2000 for £180,000. Compute the chargeable gain before taper relief or allowable loss.

3.3 It is possible for taxpayers to make a once-and-for-all election that gains and losses arising on all assets held at 31 March 1982 should be computed by reference to their 31 March 1982 values only. Indexation allowance can then only be based on 31 March 1982 value and later enhancement expenditure.

3.4 Before making the election, the taxpayer should consider the net effect on all his assets owned at 31 March 1982. The effect might be to increase the gain or decrease the loss on some assets.

4 VALUING ASSETS

4.1 **Where market value is used in a CGT computation (see Paragraph 1.5 above), the value to be used is the price which the assets in question might reasonably be expected to fetch on a sale in the open market.**

Shares and securities

4.2 **Quoted shares and securities are valued using prices in The Stock Exchange Daily Official List,** taking the lower of:

- lower quoted price + 0.25 × (higher quoted price - lower quoted price);

- the average of the highest and lowest marked bargains (ignoring bargains marked at special prices).

Activity 8.6: Calculation of CGT value

Shares in A plc are quoted at 100-110p. The highest and lowest marked bargains were 99p and 110p. What would be the market value for CGT purposes?

4.3 Unquoted shares are much harder to value than quoted shares. The Revenue have a special office, the Shares Valuation Division, to deal with the valuation of unquoted shares.

Negligible value claims

4.4 **If a chargeable asset's value becomes negligible a claim may be made to treat the asset as though it were sold, and then immediately reacquired at its current market value.** This will probably give rise to an allowable loss.

The sale and reacquisition are treated as taking place when the claim is made, or at a specified earlier time. The earlier time can be any time up to two years before the start of the tax year in which the claim is made. The asset must have been of negligible value at the specified earlier time.

On a subsequent actual disposal, any gain is computed using the negligible value as the acquisition cost.

5 CONNECTED PERSONS

5.1 **A transaction between 'connected persons' is treated as one between parties to a transaction otherwise than by way of a bargain made at arm's length. The effect of this is that the acquisition and disposal are deemed to take place for a consideration equal to the market value of the asset, rather than the actual price paid.**

5.2 If a loss results, it can be set only against gains arising in the same or future years from disposals to the same connected person and the loss can only be set off if he or she is still connected with the person sustaining the loss.

> **KEY TERM**
>
> **Connected person**
>
> An individual is connected with:
>
> - his spouse;
> - his relatives (brothers, sisters, ancestors and lineal descendants);
> - the relatives of his spouse;
> - the spouses of his and his spouse's relatives.
>
> A company is connected with:
>
> - a person who (alone or with persons connected with him) controls it;
> - another company under common control.

6 DISPOSALS ON A NO GAIN/NO LOSS BASIS

6.1 **Disposals between spouses living together do not give rise to chargeable gains or allowable losses.** For taper relief purposes the transferee is deemed to have acquired the asset when it was acquired by the transferor

6.2 Special rules apply to indexation on no gain/no loss disposals and on later disposals outside the marriage. To illustrate the rules, we assume a husband (H) buys an asset and later transfers it to his wife (W) who then sells it to an outsider. The rules are exactly the same if the roles of H and W are reversed.

- If **H buys the asset before 1 April 1982** treat W as having bought it when H bought it and for the price he paid. Thus W can use the 31 March 1982 value, and can get indexation from March 1982.

- If **H buys the asset after 31 March 1982** W is deemed to have bought the asset when H transferred it to her. Her cost is H's cost plus indexation allowance up to the date of transfer (or 6 April 1998). When W sells the asset, she computes indexation allowance from the time of the transfer. If the transfer was made after 5 April 1998 there is no further indexation allowance.

Activity 8.7: No gain/no loss disposal

Sylvia bought an asset for £15,000 on 1 January 1980. Its value on 31 March 1982 was £18,000. On 1 January 1993 she gave it to her husband Nicholas. On 12 April 2000 he sold it for £50,000. The asset had always been used in Nicholas' business. What is his chargeable gain after taper relief?

7 PART DISPOSALS

7.1 **The disposal of part of a chargeable asset is a chargeable event. The chargeable gain (or allowable loss) is computed by deducting from the disposal value a fraction of the original cost of the whole asset.**

DEVOLVED ASSESSMENT ALERT

The fraction is:

$$\frac{A}{A+B} = \frac{\text{value of the part disposed of}}{\text{value of the part disposed of} + \text{market value of the remainder}}$$

A is the proceeds (for arm's length disposals) *before* deducting incidental costs of disposal.

7.2 The part disposal fraction should not be applied indiscriminately. Any expenditure incurred wholly in respect of a particular part of an asset should be treated as an allowable deduction in full for that part and not apportioned. An example of this is incidental selling expenses, which are wholly attributable to the part disposed of.

Activity 8.8: Part disposals

Mr Heal owns a business asset which originally cost him £27,000 in March 1984. He sold a quarter interest in the asset in July 2000 for £18,000. The market value of the three-quarter share remaining is estimated to be £36,000. What is the chargeable gain after taper relief?

Activity 8.9: Part disposal

Androulla bought a plot of land for use in her business for £150,000 in January 1989. In August 2000, she sold part of the land for £187,000, which was net of legal fees on the sale of £3,000. At that time, the value of the remaining land was £327,000. What expenditure (apart from the indexation allowance) could she deduct in computing her chargeable gain?

Small part disposals of land

7.3 Two special reliefs apply to small part disposals of land. They are only available if the land is freehold or on a lease with at least 50 years to run.

7.4 If the disposal is the result of a compulsory purchase order and the value of the consideration is 'small', the taxpayer may claim to have the consideration received deducted from the base cost of the asset retained, instead of doing a part disposal computation. **'Small' means either 5% or less of the total value of the land immediately before the part disposal or £3,000 or less.**

7.5 If, however, the relief above is not available, an alternative relief may be claimed. If the value of the consideration is 20% or less of the total value of the land immediately before the part disposed and the total consideration in that tax year from all small part disposals of land (excluding disposals under compulsory purchase orders where the consideration is small) does not exceed £20,000, then the taxpayer may claim to deduct the consideration from the base cost of his remaining land instead of doing a part disposal computation.

7.6 The time limit for claims, for individuals, is the 31 January which is nearly twenty two months after the end of the tax year of disposal. For companies, it is two years after the end of the accounting period of disposal.

BPP PUBLISHING

Activity 8.10: End of chapter activity

Hardup made the following disposals in 2000/01. All disposals were to unconnected persons except where otherwise stated.

(a) On 12 May 2000 he sold a business asset for £100,000. He had bought it for £65,000 on 1 July 1988.

(b) On 18 June 2000 he sold a plot of land for £47,000. He had bought it for £2,000 on 14 January 1970, and had spent £5,000 on permanent improvements in July 1972 and £4,000 on defending his title to the land in July 1985. On 31 March 1982, the land was worth £20,000. The land had always been used in Hardup's business.

(c) On 25 June 2000 he exchanged contracts for the sale of a property (which he had always used in his business) for £173,000. Completion took place on 24 July 2000. He had bought the house for £20,000 on 16 October 1978. On 31 March 1982, the property had been worth £65,000.

(d) On 16 October 2000 he sold an antique table to his wife (with whom he was living) for £130,000, its market value. He had bought it a year earlier for £120,000.

(e) On 1 December 2000 he sold a business asset to his brother for £32,000, its market value. He had bought the asset for £35,000 on 15 December 1990.

Hardup's taxable income for 2000/01 is £48,000.

Required

Compute Hardup's capital gains tax liability for 2000/01, and state the date by which it is payable.

Key learning points

- A chargeable gain is computed by taking the proceeds and deducting both the costs and the indexation allowance. For individuals, indexation allowance only runs to April 1998.

- Companies get indexation to the date of disposal of an asset.

- An asset owned on 31 March 1982 needs two computations, one based on its cost and the other based on its value on that date.

- There are special rules for disposals between connected persons and disposals between spouses.

- On a part disposal, the cost must be apportioned between the part disposed of and the part retained.

Quick quiz

1   What enhancement expenditure is allowable?

2   How is the chargeable gain or allowable loss on assets held on 31 March 1982 computed?

3   How are quoted shares valued?

4   What is the importance of a 'connected person' for CGT?

5   How is the allowable expenditure computed on a part disposal?

Answer to quick quiz

1   Allowable enhancement expenditure is capital expenditure which enhances the value of the asset and is reflected in the state or nature of the asset at the time of disposal, or expenditure incurred in establishing, preserving or defending title to, or a right over, the asset. Excluded from this category are:

- costs of repairs and maintenance;
- costs of insurance;
- any expenditure deductible for income tax purposes;

- any expenditure met by public funds (for example council grants).

2   On the disposal of an asset owned on 31 March 1982, we do two calculations. One uses actual cost and the other uses the market value on 31 March 1982. In *both* calculations we base the indexation allowance on the higher of the two. The final gain or loss is then:

- if both calculations produce gains, the lower gain;
- if both calculations produce losses, the lower loss (so if one produces a loss of £1,000 and the other a loss of £2,000, the allowable loss is £1,000);
- if one calculation produces a gain and the other a loss, or if either produces a result of £nil, no gain and no loss.

3   They are valued using prices in The Stock Exchange Daily Official List, taking the lower of:

- lower quoted price + 0.25 × (higher quoted price - lower quoted price);
- the average of the highest and lowest marked bargains (ignoring bargains marked at special prices).

4   A transaction between 'connected persons' is deemed to take place for a consideration equal to the market value of the asset, rather than the actual price paid. In addition, if a loss results, it can be set only against gains arising in the same or future years from disposals to the same connected person and the loss can only be set off if he or she is still connected with the person sustaining the loss.

5   The allowable expenditure is a fraction of the original cost of the whole asset found by multiplying the original cost by A/A + B where A is the disposal proceeds and B is the value of the asset remaining. In addition any expenditure incurred wholly in respect of that particular part of the asset is allowable expenditure.

Answers to activities

Activity 8.1

No: it is not reflected in the state or nature of the asset at the time of disposal.

Activity 8.2

The indexation allowance is available until April 1998 (RPI = 162.6) and is computed as follows.

	£
$\dfrac{162.6 - 83.0}{83.0} = 0.959 \times £5,000$	4,795
$\dfrac{162.6 - 88.6}{88.6} = 0.835 \times £2,000$	1,670
	6,465

Activity 8.3

	£
Proceeds	24,000
Less cost	97,000
Allowable loss	(73,000)

Indexation cannot increase a loss.

BPP PUBLISHING

Activity 8.4

	Cost £	31.3.82 value £
Proceeds	150,000	150,000
Less: cost 1978	(28,500)	
enhancement cost 1981	(1,500)	
31.3.82 value (includes 1981 improvement)		(20,000)
enhancement cost 1984	(15,000)	(15,000)
Unindexed gain	105,000	115,000
Less indexation allowance		
On original cost (March 1982 to April 1998):		
$\dfrac{162.6-79.4}{79.4} = 1.048 \times £28,500$	(29,868)	(29,868)
On enhancement cost 1981 (March 1982 to April 1998):		
$1.048 \times £1,500$	(1,572)	(1,572)
On enhancement cost 1984 (March 1984 to April 1998):		
$\dfrac{162.6-87.5}{87.5} = 0.858 \times £15,000$	(12,870)	(12,870)
	60,690	70,690

The chargeable gain before taper relief is £60,690.

At 31 March 1982 the cost of the factory was £30,000 (£28,500 + £1,500) compared to the equivalent March 1982 market value of £20,000. Thus the indexation allowance available from March 1982 is based on the cost values in this question.

Activity 8.5

	Cost £	31.3.82 value £
Proceeds	180,000	180,000
Less: cost	(20,000)	
31.3.82 value		(150,000)
Unindexed gain	160,000	30,000
Less indexation allowance (March 1982 to April 1998)		
$\dfrac{162.6-79.4}{79.4} = 1.048 \times £150,000$	(157,200)	(30,000)
Indexed gain (indexation cannot create or increase a loss)	2,800	0

There is no chargeable gain and no allowable loss.

Activity 8.6

The value will be the lower of:

(a) $100 + 0.25 \times (110-100) = 102.5$;

(b) $\dfrac{110 + 99}{2} = 104.5$.

The market value for CGT purposes will therefore be 102.5p per share.

Activity 8.7

	Cost	31.3.82 value
	£	£
Proceeds	50,000	50,000
Less cost/31.3.82 value	(15,000)	(18,000)
	35,000	32,000

Less indexation allowance to April 1998

$$\frac{162.6 - 79.4}{79.4} = 1.048 \times £18,000$$

	(18,864)	(18,864)
	16,136	13,136

Nicholas's chargeable gain after taper relief is £9,852 (£13,136 × 75%)

Activity 8.8

The amount of the original cost attributable to the part sold is

$$\frac{18,000}{18,000 + 36,000} \times £27,000 = £9,000$$

	£
Proceeds	18,000
Less cost (see above)	9,000
Unindexed gain	9,000
Less indexation allowance (March 1984 to April 1998)	

$$\frac{162.6 - 87.5}{87.5} = 0.858 \times £9,000$$

	7,722
Indexed gain	1,278

The chargeable gain after taper relief is £959 (£1,278 × 75%)

Activity 8.9

Cost: £150,000 × 190/(190 + 327) = £55,126

Incidental costs of disposal: £3,000

Total: £58,126

Activity 8.10

CAPITAL GAINS TAX COMPUTATION

	£
Business asset £940 (W1) × 75%	705
Plot of land (W2)	0
Property £39,880 (W3) × 75%	29,910
	30,615
Less annual exemption	(7,200)
Taxable gains	23,415

Both business assets were owned for two complete years after 6.4.98 so 75% of the gains are taxable.

Capital gains tax of £23,415 × 40% = £9,366 is due by 31 January 2002.

The table was disposed of between spouses living together, so there is no chargeable gain or allowable loss.

A loss arises on the sale of the business asset to Hardup's brother (W4), but because it was sold to a connected person, the loss can only be set against gains on disposals in the same year or future years to the same connected person while he or she remains connected. A brother cannot, of course, cease to be connected, but a connection by marriage could cease.

Part B: Chargeable gains

Workings

1   *Business asset*

	£
Proceeds	100,000
Less cost	(65,000)
	35,000
Less indexation allowance (July 1988 to April 1998)	

$$\frac{162.6 - 106.7}{106.7} = 0.524 \times £65,000 \qquad (34,060)$$

Chargeable gain before taper relief	940

2   *The plot of land*

	Cost £	31.3.82 value £
Proceeds	47,000	47,000
Less: cost in January 1970	(2,000)	
expenditure in July 1972	(5,000)	
31.3.82 value		(20,000)
expenditure in July 1985	(4,000)	(4,000)
	36,000	23,000
Less indexation allowance to April 1998		

$$\frac{162.6 - 79.4}{79.4} = 1.048 \times £20,000 \qquad (20,960) \qquad (20,960)$$

$$\frac{162.6 - 95.2}{95.2} = 0.708 \times £4,000/(\text{restricted}) \qquad (2,832) \qquad (2,040)$$

	12,208	0

As one calculation produces a gain and the other a result of zero, the result is no gain and no loss.

3   *The property*

	Cost £	31.3.82 value £
Proceeds	173,000	173,000
Less cost/31.3.82 value	(20,000)	(65,000)
	153,000	108,000
Less indexation allowance (March 1982 to April 1998)		

$$\frac{162.6 - 79.4}{79.4} = 1.048 \times £65,000 \qquad (68,120) \qquad (68,120)$$

	84,880	39,880

The gain before taper relief is the lower gain, which is £39,880.

4   *Business asset*

	£
Proceeds	32,000
Less cost	(35,000)
Loss	(3,000)

Chapter 9   Shares and securities

Chapter topic list

1   The matching rules for companies

2   The FA 1985 pool

3   The matching rules for individuals

4   Bonus and rights issues

Learning objectives

On completion of this chapter you will be able to:

	Performance criteria	Range Statement
• match a disposal of shares to a corresponding purchase in order to match sale proceeds to cost and compute the capital gain or loss arising	18.3.4	18.3.3
• discuss the difference between disposals of shares held by individuals and companies	18.3.4	18.3.3
• discuss what happens on the issue of bonus shares or rights shares	18.3.4	18.3.3

BPP PUBLISHING

1 THE MATCHING RULES FOR COMPANIES

1.1 Quoted and unquoted shares and securities and units in a unit trust present special problems when attempting to compute gains or losses on disposal. For instance, suppose that a company buys some quoted shares in X plc as follows.

Date	Number of shares	Cost
		£
5 May 1992	100	150
17 January 1999	100	375

On 15 June 2000, it sells 120 of its shares for £1,450. To determine its chargeable gain, we need to be able to work out which shares out of the two original holdings were actually sold.

1.2 We therefore need **matching rules. These allow us to decide which shares have been sold and so work out what the allowable cost on disposal should be.**

1.3 In what follows, we will use 'shares' to refer to both shares and securities.

1.4 The **matching of shares** sold by a company is in the following order.

 (a) Shares acquired on the **same day**
 (b) Shares acquired in the **previous nine days,** taking earlier acquisitions first
 (c) Shares from the **FA 1985 pool** (see below)

 If a company owns 2% or more of another company, disposals are matched (after same day acquisitions) with shares acquired within one month before or after the disposal (for Stock Exchange transactions) or six months (in other cases) before being matched with shares from the FA 1985 pool.

1.5 Where shares are disposed of within nine days of acquisition, **no indexation allowance is available** even if the acquisition and the disposal fall in different months. Acquisitions matched with disposals under the nine day rule never enter the FA 1985 pool (see below).

DEVOLVED ASSESSMENT ALERT

Learn the 'matching rules' because a crucial first step to getting a shares question right is to correctly match the shares sold to the original shares purchased.

2 THE FA 1985 POOL

2.1 For companies we treat shares as a 'pool' which grows as new shares are acquired and shrinks as they are sold. **The FA 1985 pool** (so called because it was introduced by rules in the Finance Act 1985) **comprises the following shares of the same class in the same company.**

 • **Shares held by a company on 1 April 1985 and acquired by that company on or after 1 April 1982.**

 • **Shares acquired by that company on or after 1 April 1985.**

DEVOLVED ASSESSMENT ALERT

Note that the FA 1985 pool only contains shares acquired on or after 1 April 1982. You will not be required to deal with shares purchased before this date in your Devolved Assessment so they are not considered here.

2.2 In making computations which use the FA 1985 pool, we must keep track of:

    (a) the **number** of shares;

    (b) the **cost** of the shares ignoring indexation;

    (b) the **indexed cost** of the shares.

2.3 Each FA 1985 **pool is started by aggregating the cost and number of shares acquired between 1 April 1982 and 1 April 1985** inclusive. In order to calculate the indexed cost of these shares, an indexation allowance, computed from the relevant date of acquisition of the shares to April 1985, is added to the cost.

2.4 EXAMPLE: THE FA 1985 POOL

Oliver Ltd bought 1,000 shares in Judith plc for £2,750 in August 1984 and another 1,000 for £3,250 in December 1984. The FA 1985 pool at 1 April 1985 is as follows.

2.5 SOLUTION

	No of shares	Cost £	Indexed cost £
August 1984 (a)	1,000	2,750	2,750
December 1984 (b)	1,000	3,250	3,250
	2,000	6,000	6,000

Indexation allowance

See Pg
(iv+v)

$$\frac{94.8 - 89.9}{89.9} = 0.055 \times £2,750 \qquad\qquad 151$$

$$\frac{94.8 - 90.9}{90.9} = 0.043 \times £3,250 \qquad\qquad 140$$

Indexed cost of the pool at 1 April 1985   6,291

2.6 Disposals and acquisitions of shares which affect the indexed value of the FA 1985 pool are termed 'operative events'. **Prior to reflecting each such operative event within the FA 1985 share pool, a further indexation allowance (described as an indexed rise) must be computed up to the date of the operative event concerned from the date of the last such operative event** (or from April 1985 if the operative event in question is the first one).

2.7 **Indexation calculations within the FA 1985 pool** (after its April 1985 value has been calculated) **are not rounded to three decimal places.** This is because rounding errors would accumulate and have a serious effect after several operative events.

If there are several operative events between 1 April 1985 and the date of a disposal, the indexation procedure described above will have to be performed several times over.

Activity 9.1: Value of FA 1985 pool

Following on from the above example, assume that Oliver Ltd acquired 2,000 more shares on 10 July 1986 at a cost of £4,000. Recalculate the value of the FA 1985 pool on 10 July 1986 following the acquisition.

2.8 **In the case of a disposal, following the calculation of the indexed rise to the date of disposal, the cost and the indexed cost attributable to the shares disposed of are deducted from the amounts within the FA 1985 pool. The proportions of the cost and indexed cost to take out of the pool should be computed using the same A/(A + B)**

BPP PUBLISHING

fraction that is used for any other part disposal. However, we are not usually given the value of the remaining shares (B in the fraction). We then just use numbers of shares.

2.9 The indexation allowance is the indexed cost taken out of the pool minus the cost taken out. As usual, the indexation allowance cannot create or increase a loss.

HW
143

Activity 9.2: The FA 1985 pool

Continuing the above exercise, suppose that Oliver Ltd sold 3,000 shares on 10 July 2000 for £17,000. Compute the gain, and the value of the FA 1985 pool following the disposal.

3 THE MATCHING RULES FOR INDIVIDUALS

3.1 **For individuals, the pooling of shares ceased for acquisitions on or after 6 April 1998. This means the time of each post April 1998 acquisition can be recorded enabling the length of ownership for each share to be calculated for tapering purposes.**

3.2 **Share disposals for individuals are matched with acquisitions in the following order.**

(a) Same day acquisitions.

(b) Acquisitions within the following 30 days.

(c) Previous acquisitions after 5 April 1998 identifying the most recent acquisition first (a LIFO basis).

(d) Any shares in the FA 1985 pool at 5 April 1998 (the FA 1985 pool runs from 6 April 1982 (instead of 1 April 1982) to 5 April 1998 for individuals).

3.3 EXAMPLE

Sue acquired the following shares in X plc.

	No of shares
1.4.90	10,000
1.9.98	5,000
10.11.99	7,000
30.12.00	2,000

On 11.12.00 Sue sold 12,000 shares. With which acquisitions is Sue's share disposal matched?

3.4 SOLUTION

Sue will initially match the disposal with the 2,000 shares bought on 30.12.00 (next 30 days). She will then match with the other post April 1998 acquisitions on a LIFO basis, so the 7,000 shares bought on 10.11.99 and 3,000 of the shares bought on 1.9.98 are deemed to be sold. 2,000 of the shares acquired on 1.9.98 and the FA 1985 pool shares remain.

3.5 For all FA 1985 pools held by an individual at 5 April 1998 indexation allowance to April 1998 is calculated and then effectively the pool is closed.

HW
14/3

Activity 9.3: Disposals by individuals

Ron acquired the following shares in First Ltd:

Date of acquisition	No of shares	Cost
9.11.90	10,000	25,000
4.8.99	3,000	11,400
15.7.00	5,000	19,000

He disposed of 18,000 shares on 10 July 2000 for £72,000. The shares are business assets for the purposes of taper relief. Calculate the chargeable gain arising after taper relief but before the deduction of the annual exemption.

4   BONUS AND RIGHTS ISSUES

Bonus issues (scrip issues)

4.1   When a company issues bonus shares all that happens is that the size of the original holding is increased. Since bonus shares are issued at no cost there is no need to adjust the original cost. Instead the numbers purchased at particular times are increased by the bonus. The normal matching rules will then be applied.

4.2   EXAMPLE: BONUS ISSUES

The following transactions by an individual in the ordinary shares of X plc would be matched as shown below

6.4.86	Purchase of 600 shares
6.4.90	Purchase of 600 shares
6.4.99	Purchase of 1,000 shares
6.10.99	Bonus issue of one for four
6.12.00	Sale of 1,500 shares

(a)   Post 6.4.98 acquisition

		No of shares
6.4.99	Purchase	1,000
6.10.99	Bonus	250
		1,250
6.12.00	Sold	(1,250)

(b)   FA 1985 pool

		No of shares
6.4.86	Purchase	600
6.4.90	Purchase	600
		1,200
6.10.99	Bonus	300
		1,500
6.12.00	Sold	(250)
Number of shares remaining in FA 1985 pool		1,250

Rights issues

4.3   The difference between a bonus issue and a rights issue is that in a rights issue the new shares are paid for and this results in an adjustment to the original cost. As with bonus issues, rights shares derived from shares in the 1985 pool go into that holding and for individuals, those derived from post 5.4.98 holdings attach to those holdings. You should add the number and cost of each of right issue to each holding as appropriate.

4.4 The length of the period of ownership for taper relief purposes depends on the date of acquisition of the original holding **not** the date of acquisition of the rights shares.

4.5 Let us try an activity with a rights issue made to an individual.

Activity 9.4: Rights issues for individuals

Simon (aged 36) had the following transactions in the shares of S Ltd.

1.10.95   Bought 10,000 shares (10%) holding) for £15,000
11.9.98   Bought 2,000 shares for £5,000
1.2.99   Took up rights issue 1 for 2 at £2.75 per share
14.10.00   Sold 5,000 shares for £15,000

Compute the gain arising in October 2000, after taper relief (if applicable). The shares are a business asset for taper relief purposes.

4.6 For companies, you will always need to index the value of the FA1985 pool to the date of the rights issue. Add the number and cost of the rights issue shares after you have added the indexation to the pool. Rights issues made to individuals before 6.4.98 should be dealt with in the FA 1985 pool in a similar way.

Activity 9.5: Rights issues for companies

J Ltd had the following transactions in the shares of T plc.

July 1985   Purchased 1,000 shares for £3,000
May 1986   Took up one for four rights issue at £4.20 per share
October 2000   Sold the shares for £10,000

Compute the chargeable gain or allowable loss arising on the sale in October 2000.

Activity 9.6: End of chapter activity

Frances sold her ordinary shares in The Hastings Hardening Company Ltd on 17 May 2000 for £24,000. She had bought ordinary shares in the company on the following dates.

	No of shares	Cost
		£
19 September 1985	2,000	1,700
12 December 1998	2,000	5,500
17 January 2000	2,000	6,000

Required

Calculate, before the annual exemption but after taper relief, the capital gain for 2000/01. The shares are a business asset for the taper relief purposes.

Key learning points

- When dealing with shares held by companies, we usually need to construct a FA 1985 pool which contains all shares acquired since 31 March 1982.

- When dealing with shares held by individuals we need to construct a FA 1985 pool running (with indexation allowance) to 5 April 1998 and then a list of shares acquired from 6 April 1998 onwards.

- The rules for matching shares sold to shares purchased are different for company shareholders and individual shareholders.

- Bonus and right issues attach to the shares to which they relate.

Quick quiz

1   In what order are acquisitions of shares matched with disposals for companies?

2   What shares are included in the FA 1985 pool for companies?

3   What are the matching rules for individuals?

4   What is the difference between a bonus issue and a rights issue?

Quick quiz answer

1   The matching of shares sold is in the following order.

    (a)   Shares acquired on the same day
    (b)   Shares acquired in the previous nine days, taking earlier acquisitions first
    (c)   Shares from the FA 1985 pool

    If a company owns 2% or more of another company, disposals are matched (after same day acquisitions) with shares acquired within one month before or after the disposal (for Stock Exchange transactions) or six months (in other cases) before being matched with shares from the FA 1985 pool.

2   The FA 1985 pool comprises the following shares of the same class in the same company.

    • Shares held by a company on 1 April 1985 and acquired by that company on or after 1 April 1982.

    • Shares acquired by that company on or after 1 April 1985.

3   Disposals are identified with acquisitions in the following order.

    1   Same day acquisitions.
    2   Acquisitions within the following 30 days.
    3   Previous acquisitions after 5.4.98 identifying the most recent acquisition first (a LIFO basis).
    4   Any shares in the FA 1985 pool.

4   The difference between a bonus issue and a rights issue is that in a rights issue the new shares are paid for and this results in an adjustment to the original cost.

Answers to activities

Activity 9.1

	No of shares	Cost £	Indexed cost £
Value at 1.4.85	2,000	6,000	6,291
Indexed rise			
$\dfrac{97.5 - 94.8}{94.8} \times £6{,}291$			179
	2,000	6,000	6,470
Acquisition	2,000	4,000	4,000
Value at 10.7.86	4,000	10,000	10,470

Activity 9.2

	No of shares	Cost £	Indexed cost £
Value at 10.7.86	4,000	10,000	10,470
Indexed rise			

$$\frac{170.5 - 97.5}{97.5} \times £10,470$$

	No of shares	Cost £	Indexed cost £
			7,839
	4,000	10,000	18,309
Disposal	(3,000)		
Cost and indexed cost $\dfrac{3,000}{4,000} \times £10,000$ and £18,309		(7,500)	(13,732)
Value at 10.7.00	1,000	2,500	4,577

The gain is computed as follows:

	£
Proceeds	17,000
Less cost	(7,500)
	9,500
Less indexation allowance £(13,732 – 7,500)	(6,232)
Chargeable gain	3,268

Note that for companies indexation runs to the date of disposal of an asset.

Activity 9.3

Matching of shares

(a)   Acquisition in 30 days after disposal:

	£
Proceeds $\dfrac{5,000}{18,000} \times £72,000$	20,000
Less cost	(19,000)
Gain	1,000

(b)   Post 5.4.98 acquisitions

	£
Proceeds $\dfrac{3,000}{18,000} \times £72,000$	12,000
Less cost	(11,400)
Gain	600

No taper relief is due since the period of ownership was only 11 months.

(c)   FA 1985 pool

	Number of shares	Cost £	Indexed cost £
11.90 Acquisition	10,000	25,000	25,000
Index to 4.98 $\dfrac{162.6 - 130.0}{130.0} \times £25,000$			6,269
Pool closes at 5.4.98	10,000	25,000	31,269
7.00 sales	10,000	25,000	31,269
Gain			

	£
Proceeds $\dfrac{10,000}{18,000} \times £72,000$	40,000
Less cost	25,000
	15,000
Less indexation from FA 1985 pool £(31,269 – 25,000)	6,269
Gain	8,731

The gain after taper relief is £6,548 (75% × £8,731)

Total gains £(1,000 + 600 + 6,548)   **£8,148**

Activity 9.4

(a)   *Post 5.4.98 holding*

	Number	*Cost*
		£
Shares acquired 11.9.98	2,000	5,000
Shares acquired 1.2.99 (rights) 1:2 @ £2.75	1,000	2,750
	3,000	7,750

Gain

	£
Proceeds $\dfrac{3,000}{5,000} \times £15,000$	9,000
Less: cost	(7,750)
Gain	1,250

Taper relief (based on ownership of original holding)

75% (Two years: business asset) × £1,250   **£938**

(b)   *FA 1985 pool*

	Number	*Cost*	*Indexed cost*
		£	*£*
1.10.95	10,000	15,000	15,000
IA to 4.98 $\dfrac{162.6 - 149.8}{149.8} \times £15,000$			1,282
Pool 'closed' at 5.4.98	10,000	15,000	16,282
Rights issues 1.2.99	5,000	13,750	13,750
	15,000	28,750	30,032
14.10.00 Sale	(2,000)	(3,833)	(4,004)
c/F	13,000	24,917	26,028

Gain

	£
Proceeds $\dfrac{2,000}{5,000} \times £15,000$	6,000
Less: cost	(3,833)
Unindexed gain	2,167
Less: indexation £(4,004 – 3,833)	(171)
Indexed gain	1,996

Taper relief (based on original holding)

75% (Two years: business asset) × £1,996   **£1,497**

(c)   *Total gain (after taper relief)*

£(938 + 1,497)   **£2,435**

Part B: Chargeable gains

Activity 9.5

(a)   The FA 1985 pool

	No of shares	Cost £	Indexed cost £
July 1985	1,000	3,000	3,000
Indexed rise to May 1986			
$\dfrac{97.8 - 95.2}{95.2} \times £3,000$			82
May 1986 one for four rights	250	1,050	1,050
	1,250	4,050	4,132
Indexed rise to October 2000			
$\dfrac{172.0 - 97.8}{97.8} \times £4,132$			3,135
	1,250	4,050	7,267
Disposal in October 2000	(1,250)	(4,050)	(7,267)

	£
Proceeds:	10,000
Less cost	(4,050)
	5,950
Less indexation allowance £(7,267 – 4,050)	(3,217)
Chargeable gain	2,733

Note that companies do not get taper relief

Activity 9.6

Post 6.4.98 acquisitions: match on a LIFO basis.

17.1.00

	£
Proceeds $\left(\dfrac{2,000}{6,000} \times £24,000\right)$	8,000
Less: cost	(6,000)
Chargeable gain	2,000

No taper relief

12.12.98

	£
Proceeds $\left(\dfrac{2,000}{6,000} \times £24,000\right)$	8,000
Less: cost	(5,500)
Chargeable gain	2,500

Chargeable gain after taper relief £2,188 (£2,500 × 87$^{1}/_{2}$%)

The FA 1985 pool

	Shares	Cost £	Indexed cost £
Acquisition 19.9.85	2,000	1,700	1,700
Indexation to April 1998 (Pool closes)			
$\dfrac{162.6 - 95.4}{95.4} \times £1,700$			1,197
Value when pool closes (5.4.98)	2,000	1,700	2,897
Disposal 17.5.00	2,000	1,700	2,897
	0	0	0

	£
Proceeds $\dfrac{2,000}{6,000} \times £24,000$	8,000
Less cost	(1,700)
	6,300
Less indexation allowance £(2,897 − 1,700)	(1,197)
Chargeable gain	5,103

The chargeable gain after taper relief is £3,827 (£5,103 × 75%)

The total gains are £(2,000 + 2,188 + 3,827) = £8,015.

Chapter 10 Chattels, wasting assets and leases

Chapter topic list

1   Chattels

2   Wasting assets

3   Leases

Learning objectives

On completion of this chapter you will be able to:

	Performance criteria	Range Statement
• outline the exemptions that apply to	18.3.3	18.3.1
° chattels		
° wasting chattels		
• you will also be able to compute restricted gains and losses on certain chattels, wasting assets and leases	18.3.3	18.3.1

BPP
PUBLISHING

1 CHATTELS

> **KEY TERMS**
>
> A **chattel** is tangible movable property.
>
> A **wasting asset** is an asset with an estimated remaining useful life of 50 years or less.

1.1 Plant and machinery, whose predictable useful life is always deemed to be less than 50 years, is therefore an example of a wasting chattel (unless it is immovable, in which case it will be wasting but not a chattel). Machinery includes, in addition to its ordinary meaning, motor vehicles (unless exempt as cars), railway engines, engine-powered boats and clocks.

1.2 **Wasting chattels are exempt from CGT** (so that there are no chargeable gains and no allowable losses). There is one exception to this: assets used for the purpose of a trade, profession or vocation in respect of which capital allowances have been or could have been claimed. This means that items of plant and machinery used in a trade are not exempt merely on the ground that they are wasting. (However, cars are always exempt.)

1.3 **If a chattel is not exempt under the wasting chattels rule, any gain arising on its disposal will still be exempt from CGT if the asset is sold for gross proceeds of £6,000 or less,** even if capital allowances were claimed on it.

1.4 **If sale proceeds exceed £6,000, any gain is limited** to a maximum of $5/3 \times$ (gross proceeds $-$ £6,000).

Activity 10.1: Gains on chattels

A Ltd purchased a Chippendale chair on 1 June 1984 for £800. On 10 October 2000 it sold the chair at auction for £6,300 (which was net of the auctioneer's 10% commission). What was the chargeable gain?

Losses

1.5 Where a chattel, not exempt under the wasting chattels rule is sold for less than £6,000 and a loss arises, the allowable loss is restricted by assuming that the chattel had been sold for £6,000. This rule cannot turn a loss into a gain, only reduce the loss, perhaps to zero.

Activity 10.2: Computation of gain or loss

E Ltd purchased a rare first edition on 1 July 1992 for £8,000 which it sold in October 2000 at auction for £2,700 (which was net of 10% commission). Compute the gain or loss.

2 WASTING ASSETS

2.1 As we have seen, a wasting asset is one which has an estimated remaining useful life of 50 years or less and whose original value will depreciate over time. **Freehold land is never a wasting asset,** and there are special rules for leases of land, given below.

2.2 **Wasting chattels are exempt except for those on which capital allowances have been** (or could have been) **claimed**. Where capital allowances were available (on any asset, not just a chattel) and a loss would arise, the base cost is reduced by the net capital allowances obtained: the result is no gain and no loss. Gains on such assets may still be exempted or restricted under the chattels rules based on £6,000 as long as the assets are not fixed. Items of fixed plant and machinery are not movable and so are not chattels.

2.3 EXAMPLE: WASTING CHATTEL

X Ltd bought a computer for £17,000 in January 1993. The computer was sold for £8,000 in December 2000. Capital allowances were claimed on the computer which will have equalled £9,000 (£17,000 cost less £8,000 disposal proceeds) in total over the life of the computer.

	£	£
Sale proceeds		8,000
Cost	17,000	
Less net capital allowances claimed	(9,000)	
		(8,000)
Gain on disposal		NIL

Wasting assets other than chattels

2.4 The cost is written down on a straight line basis before calculating the indexation allowance. Thus, if a taxpayer acquires such an asset with a remaining life of 40 years and disposes of it after 15 years (with 25 years remaining) only 25/40 of the cost is deducted from the disposal consideration. Indexation allowance is computed on the written down cost rather than the full original cost.

2.5 Examples of such assets are copyrights (with 50 years or less to run) and registered designs.

2.6 Where the asset has an estimated residual value at the end of its predictable life, it is the cost less residual value which is written off on a straight line basis over the asset's life. Where additional expenditure is incurred on a wasting asset the additional cost is written off over the life remaining when it was incurred.

2.7 Assets eligible for capital allowances and used throughout the period of ownership in a trade, profession or vocation do not have their allowable expenditure written down.

Activity 10.3: Wasting asset

Jeremy bought a copyright on 1 April 1990, when it had 40 years to run. He paid £7,000 for it, and sold it for £23,000 on 1 July 2000. What was the chargeable gain after taper relief? The copyright was a business asset.

---

3 LEASES

Types of disposal

3.1 The gain that arises on the disposal of a lease will be chargeable according to the terms of the lease disposed of. We must consider:

- the assignment of a lease or sub-lease with 50 years or more to run;
- the assignment of a lease or sub-lease with less than 50 years to run.

3.2 **There is an assignment when a lessee sells the whole of his interest. There is a grant when a new lease or sub-lease is created out of a freehold or existing leasehold, the grantor retaining an interest.** The assessor has stated that the rules on the grant of leases will not be assessed.

3.3 The duration of the lease will normally be determined by the contract terms. The expiry date, however, will be taken as the first date on which the landlord has an option to terminate the lease or the date beyond which the lease is unlikely to continue because of, for example, the likelihood that the rent will be substantially increased at that date.

The assignment of a lease with 50 years or more to run

3.4 An **ordinary disposal computation** is made and the whole of any gain on disposal will be chargeable to CGT.

The assignment of a lease with less than 50 years less to run

3.5 **In calculating the gain on the disposal of a lease with less than 50 years to run only a certain proportion of the original expenditure counts as an allowable deduction from the disposal proceeds.** This is because a lease is losing value anyway as its life runs out: only the cost related to the tail end of the lease being sold is deductible. The proportion is determined by a table of percentages, which is reproduced in the Rates and Allowances Tables in this text.

3.6 **The allowable cost is given by original cost $\times$ X/Y, where X is the percentage for the number of years left for the lease to run at the date of the assignment, and Y is the percentage for the number of years the lease had to run when first acquired by the seller.**

3.7 The table only provides percentages for exact numbers of years. Where the duration is not an exact number of years the relevant percentage should be found by adding 1/12 of the difference between the two years on either side of the actual duration for each extra month. Fourteen or more odd days count as a month.

Activity 10.4: The assignment of a short lease

Mr A acquired a 20 year lease on an office block which he used in his business on 1 August 1994 for £15,000. He assigned the lease on 1 August 2000 for £19,000. Compute the chargeable gain arising after taper relief but before the annual exemption.

3.8 **If a lease was acquired before 31 March 1982, then in the calculation based on 31 March 1982 value, 31 March 1982 is treated as the date of acquisition of the lease.**

Activity 10.5: Calculation of gain arising

Mr B acquired a 30 year lease on a factory used in his business on 1 January 1980 for £20,000. He assigned the lease on 1 July 2000 for £28,000. The lease was valued at £15,000 on 31 March 1982. Compute any chargeable gain arising after taper relief.

Activity 10.6: End of chapter activity

(a) Wolf Ltd carried out the following capital transactions:

(i) On 30 June 2000 it assigned the lease of a commercial building for £20,750; the lease expires on 30 June 2016.

The company had acquired the lease for £8,000 on 1 January 1992.

(ii) On 28 July 2000 it sold a racehorse for £25,000. The horse had been bought for £3,000 on 1 July 1995.

Required

Prepare a statement showing Wolf Ltd's capital gains on disposal of the above assets.

(b) Mr Sacramento bought a copyright for use in his business for £37,000 on 4 December 1992, when it had 47 years left to run. He sold it for £62,000 on 4 June 2000. Compute Sacramento's chargeable gain arising after taper relief.

Quick quiz

1 How are gains on non-wasting chattels sold for more than £6,000 restricted?

2 How are losses on non-wasting chattels sold for less than £6,000 restricted?

3 What is the general treatment of intangible wasting assets (eg a copyright)?

4 Distinguish between the grant and the assignment of a lease.

5 When a lease with less than 50 years to run is assigned, what proportion of the cost is allowable?

Answers to quick quiz

1 If sale proceeds exceed £6,000, any gain is limited to a maximum of 5/3 × (gross proceeds – £6,000)

2 Where a chattel, not exempt under the wasting chattels rule is sold for less than £6,000 and a loss arises, the allowable loss is restricted by assuming that the chattel had been sold for £6,000. However, this rule cannot turn a loss into a gain, only reduce the loss, perhaps to zero.

3 The cost is written down on a straight line basis before calculating any indexation allowance. Thus, if a taxpayer acquires such an asset with a remaining life of 40 years and disposes of it after 15 years (with 25 years remaining) only 25/40 of the cost is deducted from the disposal consideration. Indexation allowance is computed on the written down cost rather than the full original cost.

4 There is an assignment when a lessee sells the whole of his interest. There is a grant when a new lease or sub-lease is created out of a freehold or existing leasehold, the grantor retaining an interest.

5 The allowable cost is given by original cost × X/Y, where X is the percentage for the number of years left for the lease to run at the date of the assignment, and Y is the percentage for the number of years the lease had to run when first acquired by the seller.

Answers to activities

Activity 10.1

	£ £
Proceeds	7,000
Less incidental costs of sale	(700)
Net proceeds	6,300
Less cost	(800)
Unindexed gain	5,500
Less indexation allowance (June 1984 to October 2000)	

$$\frac{172.0 - 89.2}{89.2} = 0.928 \times £800 \qquad (742)$$

Indexed gain	4,758

The maximum gain is 5/3 × £(7,000 – 6,000) = £1,667

The chargeable gain is the lower of £4,758 and £1,667, so it is £1,667.

Note: Taper relief is not available to companies. However, indexation is available to the date of disposal of an asset.

Part B: Chargeable gains

Activity 10.2

	£
Proceeds (assumed)	6,000
Less incidental costs of disposal (£2,700 x 10/90)	300
	5,700
Less cost	8,000
Allowable loss (indexation allowance cannot increase a loss)	(2,300)

Activity 10.3

	£
Proceeds	23,000
Less cost £7,000 x 29.75/40	(5,206)
	17,794

Less indexation allowance to April 1998

$$\frac{162.6 - 125.1}{125.1} = 0.300 \times £5,206 \qquad (1,562)$$

	£
Chargeable gain	16,232

Gain chargeable after taper relief £12,174 (£16,232 × 75%)

Activity 10.4

	£
Proceeds	19,000
Less cost £15,000 × $\dfrac{58.971}{72.770}$	(12,156)
Unindexed gain	6,844

Less indexation allowance (August 1994 to April 1998)

$$\frac{162.6 - 144.7}{144.7} = 0.124 \times £12,156 \qquad (1,507)$$

	£
Indexed gain	5,337

The chargeable gain after taper relief is £4,003 (£5,337 × 75%)

58.971 = percentage for 14 years (life from 1.8.00)
72.770 = percentage for 20 years (life from 1.8.94)

Activity 10.5

	Cost £	31.3.82 value £
Proceeds	28,000	28,000
Less: cost		
£20,000 × $\dfrac{44.925}{87.330}$	(10,289)	
31.3.82 value		
£15,000 × $\dfrac{44.925}{84.744}$		(7,952)
Unindexed gain	17,711	20,048
Less indexation allowance (March 1982 to April 1998)		
$\dfrac{162.6 - 79.4}{79.4}$ = 1.048 × £10,289	(10,783)	(10,783)
	6,928	9,265

The chargeable gain is £5,196 (£6,928 × 75%).

Percentages are as follows.

1.7.2000:	9½ years:	$43.154 + (46.695 - 43.154) \times {}^{6}/_{12} = 44.925$
31.3.1982:	27¾ years:	$83.816 + (85.053 - 83.816) \times {}^{9}/_{12} = 84.744$
1.1.1980:	30 years:	87.330

Activity 10.6 _____

(a) (i) *The lease*

	£
Proceeds	20,750
Less $\dfrac{64.116\,(16\text{ years})}{80.361\,(24\frac{1}{2}\text{ years})} \times £8,000$	(6,383)
Unindexed gain	14,367
Less indexation allowance $\dfrac{170.0 - 135.6}{135.6} = 0.254 \times £6,383$	(1,621)
Chargeable gain	12,746

The percentage for 24½ years is $79.622 + (81.100 - 79.622) \times 6/12 = 80.361$.

Note: Taper relief is not available to companies. However, indexation is given to the date of disposal of an asset.

(ii) *The racehorse*

This is a wasting chattel and is therefore exempt.

(b)

	£
Proceeds	62,000
Less cost £37,000 × 39.5/47	(31,096)
	30,904
Less indexation allowance to April 1998	
$\dfrac{162.6 - 139.2}{139.2} = 0.168 \times £31,096$	(5,224)
Chargeable gain before taper relief	25,680
Gain remaining after taper relief (75%).	£10,2C0

Note. Taper relief applies for this business asset with two complete years of ownership post 5 April 1998.

Chapter 11   Holdover reliefs

Chapter topic list

1   Gift relief

2   Compensation and insurance proceeds

Learning objectives

On completion of this chapter you will be able to:

	Performance criteria	Range Statement
• outline which assets qualify for gift relief	18.3.5	18.3.2
• discuss how gift relief operates to defer gains	18.3.5	18.3.2
• outline how chargeable gains arise when an asset is damaged or destroyed	18.3.1	18.3.2

BPP
PUBLISHING

1   GIFT RELIEF

1.1   **If an individual gives away a qualifying asset, an election can be made** by the 31 January which is nearly six years after the end of the tax year of the transfer, **for the transferor's gain be reduced to nil.**

1.2   **If an election is made the transferee is deemed to acquire the asset for market value at the date of transfer less the transferor's deferred gain** (no taper relief given). The transferee will qualify for further indexation allowance (if available) on that reduced base cost from the date of the transfer. The transferee will start a new period for taper relief from the date of his acquisition.

Activity 11.1: Transferee base cost

Tim makes a gain of £50,000 on the gift of an asset to Sue. The market value of the asset on the date of the gift was £120,000 and Sue and Tim elected for Tim's gain to be reduced to £Nil under the gift relief provisions.

At what value is Sue deemed to acquire the gift?

1.3   **If a disposal involves actual consideration rather than being a pure gift but is still not a bargain made at arm's length** (so that the proceeds are deemed to be the market value of the asset), **then any excess of actual consideration over allowable costs** (excluding indexation allowance) **is chargeable immediately and only the balance of the gain is deferred.** Of course, the amount chargeable immediately is limited to the full gain after indexation allowance.

If the gain before gift relief is computed using the 31 March 1982 value, the allowable costs (to be compared with the actual consideration) are the 31 March 1982 value and later enhancement expenditure.

Activity 11.2: Gift relief (1)

On 6 December 2000 Angelo sold to his son Michael a freehold shop valued at £200,000 for £50,000, and claimed gift relief. Angelo had originally purchased the shop from which he had run his business in July 1982 for £30,000. Michael continued to run a business from the shop premises but decided to sell the shop in March 2004 for £195,000. Compute any chargeable gains arising. Assume Finance Act 2000 continues to apply in March 2004.

Qualifying assets

1.4   **Gift relief can be claimed on gifts or sales of business assets at an undervalue.**

1.5   **Transfers of business assets** are transfers of :

*   **Assets used in a trade, profession or vocation** carried on:

   (1)   by the donor;

   (2)   by the donor's personal company or a member of a trading group of which the holding company is his personal company;

KEY TERMS

A 'personal company' is one in which not less than 5% of the voting rights are controlled by the individual disposing of the shares.

A 'trading company' is a company whose business is wholly or mainly the carrying on of a trade or trades. A 'trading group' is a group the business of whose members, taken together, consists wholly or mainly of the carrying on of a trade or trades.

- **Certain agricultural property**

- **Shares and securities in trading companies,** or holding companies of trading groups, where:

    (1) the shares or securities are **not listed on a recognised stock exchange** (but they may be on the AIM);

    (2) the company concerned is the donor's **personal company.**

Activity 11.3: Gift relief (2)

20 years ago, Rupert formed a company with £1,000 in share capital. The company used this money to buy a painting, but has since had no transactions. The painting is now worth £60,000. Rupert wishes to give all of the shares in the company to his daughter, claiming gift relief. Why will gift relief be unavailable?

1.6 If the asset was used for the purposes of the trade, profession or vocation for only part of its period of ownership, the gain to be held over is the gain otherwise eligible × period of such use/total period of ownership (including periods before 31 March 1982).

If the asset was a building or structure only partly used for trade, professional or vocational purposes, only the **part of the gain attributable to the part so used is eligible for gift relief**

Instalments

1.7 Any **CGT payable** on transfers of certain assets **where no gift relief is available** (and any CGT payable because part of a gain cannot be deferred) **can be paid by annual instalments over ten years.** These assets are:

- land;

- a controlling holding of shares or securities in a company;

- minority holdings of shares or securities in a company which is not listed on a stock exchange (but it may be on the AIM).

Note that gift relief must be *unavailable*, not merely not elected for.

1.8 Interest is chargeable on the outstanding balance from the normal due date.

1.9 The first instalment is due on the normal due date. If for example land is given away on 30 June 2000 and the instalment option is claimed, the first instalment will be due for payment on 31 January 2002.

1.10 If the taxpayer wishes, the balance with interest to date may be paid at any time.

2 COMPENSATION AND INSURANCE PROCEEDS

Damaged assets

2.1 **If an asset is damaged and compensation or insurance money is received as a result, then this will normally be treated as a part disposal. By election, however, the taxpayer can avoid a part disposal computation. A capital sum received can be deducted from the cost of the asset rather than being treated as a part disposal if:**

(a) the amount not spent in restoring the asset is small; or
(b) the capital sum is small.

2.2 The Revenue accept a sum as 'small' if it is either less than 5% of the value of the asset or is less than £3,000.

2.3 If the amount not used in restoring the asset is not small, then the taxpayer can elect for the amount used in restoration to be deducted from the cost; the balance will continue to be treated as a part disposal.

Activity 11.4: Damaged assets

Mr J bought an office block for his business which cost £48,000 on 15 April 2000. On 10 September 2000 it was damaged in a fire and, as a result, £27,000 insurance proceeds were received in December 2000. £20,000 was spent to restore the building in October 2000; the market value of the building immediately after restoration was £62,000. What gain arose and what will be the base cost of the building in future computations? Assume that Mr J elects for the amount used in restoration to be deducted from the base cost of the building.

Destroyed assets

2.4 **If an asset is destroyed (as opposed to merely being damaged) any compensation or insurance monies received will normally be brought into an ordinary CGT disposal computation as proceeds. But if all the proceeds are applied for the replacement of the asset within 12 months, any gain can be deducted from the cost of the replacement asset.** If only part of the proceeds are used, the gain immediately chargeable can be limited to the amount not used. The rest of the gain is then deducted from the cost of the replacement.

Activity 11.5: Destroyed assets

Fiona bought a business asset for £25,000 in June 2000. It was destroyed three years and one month later. Insurance proceeds were £34,000, and Fiona spent £32,500 on a replacement asset. Compute the chargeable gain and the base cost of the new asset. Assume FA 2000 provisions continue to apply.

The compulsory purchase of land

2.5 **If land is sold to an authority exercising or having powers of compulsory purchase and the proceeds are applied to buy other land, the gain on the land disposed of may be deducted from the base cost of the land bought** (instead of being chargeable). If only part of the proceeds are reinvested, the balance (up to the amount of the gain) is chargeable.

2.6   The replacement land must be acquired within the period from one year before to three years after the disposal of the land compulsorily purchased.

2.7   If a taxpayer expects to acquire new land, he can make a provisional claim on the tax return which includes the gain on the old land to reduce the gain accordingly.

Activity 11.6: Compulsory purchase

Helen bought a field for use in her business for £7,800 on 12 April 1988. On 10 August 2000, it was compulsorily purchased for £23,000. The next month, Helen bought replacement land for £21,000, and claimed to defer her gain. What was the base cost of the replacement land?

Activity 11.7: End of chapter activity

David bought some unquoted shares in D Ltd (his personal company) for £4,000 on 31 March 1982. In July 2000, when aged 40, he sold the shares to his sister Alison for £25,000, when their market value was £100,000. In September 2000, Alison sold the shares for £270,000. Gift relief was claimed on the transfer in July 2000. In September 2000 Alison's shareholding equals 30% of the company's issued share capital.

Required

Compute the chargeable gains after arising taper relief (if available).

> **Key learning points**
>
> - Gift relief is available on assets both gifts and sales at an undervalue of business assets.
>
> - The gain which would otherwise arise on the receipt of insurance proceeds may, subject to certain conditions, be deferred

Quick quiz

1   Which transfers qualify for gift relief?

2   When may a part disposal computation be avoided on the receipt of insurance proceeds?

3   What relief is available on the compulsory purchase of land?

Quick quiz answers _____

1   Gift relief can be claimed on gifts or sales at an undervalue of business assets.

2   A capital sum received can be deducted from the cost of the asset rather than being treated as a part disposal if:

  (a)   the amount not spent in restoring the asset is small; or
  (b)   the capital sum is small.

3   If land is sold to an authority exercising or having powers of compulsory purchase and the proceeds are applied to buy other land, the gain on the land disposed of may, if the landowner claims, be deducted from the base cost of the land bought (instead of being chargeable). If only part of the proceeds are reinvested, the balance (up to the amount of the gain) is chargeable.

Answer to activities

Activity 11.1

	£
Market value	120,000
Less: gain	(50,000)
Base cost	70,000

Activity 11.2

(a) *Angelo's CGT position (2000/01)*

	£
Proceeds	200,000
Less cost	(30,000)
Unindexed gain	170,000
Less indexation allowance (July 1982 to April 1998)	

$$\frac{162.6 - 81.9}{81.9} = 0.985 \times £30,000 \qquad (29,550)$$

	£
Indexed gain	140,450
Less gain deferred	
£140,450 – £(50,000 – 30,000)	(120,450)
Gain left in charge	20,000
Gain after taper relief (note)	£15,000

(b) *Michael's CGT position (2003/04)*

	£
Proceeds	195,000
Less cost £(200,000 – 120,450)	(79,550)
Gain	115,450
Chargeable gain after taper relief (50%)	£57,725

Note: Taper relief is available for Angelo since the asset disposed of in December 2000 is a 'business asset'. The period of ownership is two complete years. Thus only 75% of the gain will be taxable.

Michael acquired the asset on 6 December 2000 and sold it in March 2004. He therefore owned the asset for three complete years. 50% of the gain is taxable.

Activity 11.3

The company is not a trading company

Activity 11.4

	£	£
The part disposal in December 2000		
Capital sum not used for restoration		
£(27,000 - 20,000)		7,000
Less: part of original cost (incurred April 2000)		

$$£48,000 \times \frac{7,000}{7,000 + 62,000} \qquad 4,870$$

part of restoration cost (incurred October 2000)

$$£20,000 \times \frac{7,000}{7,000 + 62,000} \qquad 2,029$$

	£	£
		(6,899)
Chargeable gain		101

	£	£
The base cost of the restored building		
Original cost		48,000
Restoration expenditure		20,000
		68,000
Less: costs used in part disposal	6,899	
restoration expenditure rolled over	20,000	
		(26,899)
Base cost		41,101

The date of the part disposal is the date of receipt of the insurance monies (December 2000). No taper relief is due as the asset had not been owned for one year.

Activity 11.5

	£
Proceeds	34,000
Less cost	(25,000)
	9,000
Gain immediately chargeable £(34,000 – 32,500)	(1,500)
Deduction from base cost	7,500

The base cost of the new asset is £(32,500 – 7,500) = £25,000.

The gain chargeable of £1,500 qualifies for taper relief (3 complete years of ownership of a business asset). 50% of the gain is charged to tax which equals £750.

Activity 11.6

	£
Proceeds	23,000
Less cost	(7,800)
	15,200
Less indexation allowance to April 1998 $\frac{162.6 - 105.8}{105.8}$ = 0.537 × £7,800	(4,189)
	11,011
Gain immediately chargeable £(23,000 – 21,000) (before taper relief)	(2,000)
Deduction from base cost	9,011

The base cost of the replacement land is (£21,000 – £9,011) = £11,989.

Activity 11.7

We must first compute the gift relief on the July 2000 disposal.

	£
Deemed proceeds	100,000
Less cost	(4,000)
	96,000
Less indexation allowance to April 1998	
$\frac{162.6 - 79.4}{79.4}$ = 1.048 × £4,000	(4,192)
Gain	91,808
Less gain chargeable in 2000 £(25,000 – 4,000)	21,000
Gift relief	70,808

Taper relief for two years of ownership will be available for David on the gain not covered by gift relief (ie £21,000 × 75% = £15,750 chargeable gain).

Alison's chargeable gain is as follows.

	£
Proceeds	270,000
Less deemed cost £(100,000 – 70,808)	(29,192)
Gain	240,808

No taper relief due.

BPP PUBLISHING

Chapter 12 Chargeable gains and businesses

Chapter topic list

1   The replacement of business assets

2   Chargeable gains and capital allowances

3   Retirement relief

4   EIS reinvestment relief

5   Loans to traders

Learning objectives

On completion of this chapter you will be able to:

	Performance criteria	Range Statement
• outline the relief available if the proceeds of the sale of a business asset are fully or partly reinvested in a replacement business asset	18.3.5	18.3.2
• discuss the interaction between CGT and capital allowances	18.3.1	18.3.1
• outline retirement relief; when it applies and how it is calculated	18.3.3	18.3.2
• outline how EIS reinvestment relief operates	18.3.5	18.3.2
• discuss the relief available when losses are made on loans to traders	18.3.5	18.3.2

1 THE REPLACEMENT OF BUSINESS ASSETS

1.1 **A gain may be 'rolled over' (deferred) where it arises on the disposal of a business asset which is replaced.** This is **rollover relief.** A claim cannot specify that only part of a gain is to be rolled over.

1.2 All the following conditions must be met.

- **The old asset sold and the new asset bought are both used only in the trade** or trades carried on **by the person claiming rollover relief.** Where part of a building is in non-trade use for all or a substantial part of the period of ownership, the building (and the land on which it stands) can be treated as two separate assets, the trade part (qualifying) and the non-trade part (non-qualifying). This split cannot be made for other assets.

- **The old asset and the new asset both fall within one** (but not necessarily the same one) **of the following classes.**

  (i) Land and buildings (including parts of buildings) occupied as well as used only for the purpose of the trade

  (ii) Fixed (that is, immovable) plant and machinery

  (iii) Ships, aircraft and hovercraft

  (iv) Goodwill

  (v) Satellites, space stations and spacecraft

  (vi) Milk quotas, potato quotas and ewe and suckler cow premium quotas

  (vii) Fish quota

- **Reinvestment of the proceeds of the old asset takes place in a period beginning one year before and ending three years after the date of the disposal.**

- **The new asset is brought into use in the trade on its acquisition** (not necessarily immediately, but not after any significant and unnecessary delay).

1.3 The new asset can be for use in a different trade from the old asset.

1.4 A rollover claim is not allowed when a taxpayer buys premises, sells part of the premises at a profit and then claims to roll over the gain into the part retained (*Watton v Tippet 1997*). However, a rollover claim is allowed (by concession) when the proceeds of the old asset are spent on improving a qualifying asset which the taxpayer already owns. The improved asset must already be in use for a trade, or be brought into trade use immediately the improvement work is finished.

1.5 **Deferral is obtained by carrying forward the chargeable gain and deducting it from the cost of the new asset. To obtain full relief, the whole of the consideration for the disposal must be reinvested. Where only part is reinvested, a part of the gain equal to the lower of the full gain and the amount not reinvested will be liable to tax immediately.**

1.6 The new asset will have a CGT 'cost' of its purchase price less the gain rolled over into its acquisition.

1.7 If an unincorporated business or a company expects to buy new assets, it can make a provisional rollover claim on the tax return which includes the gain on the old asset. The gain is reduced accordingly. If new assets are not actually acquired, the Revenue collect the tax saved by the provisional claim.

Activity 12.1: Rollover relief

A freehold factory (purchased in October 1999) was sold by a sole trader for £70,000 on 18 May 2000, giving a gain before rollover relief of £17,950. A replacement factory was purchased on 6 June 2000 for £60,000. Compute the base cost of the factory purchased in June 2000, taking account of any rolled over gain from the disposal in May 2000.

1.8 **Rollover relief applies to the untapered gain. Any gain left in charge will then be eligible for taper relief.** When the replacement asset is sold taper relief on that sale will only be given by reference to the holding period for that asset (assuming further rollover relief is not claimed on this disposal). **Effectively, taper relief on the rolled over gain, for the period of ownership of the original asset, is lost.**

Activity 12.2: Rollover relief and taper relief interaction

Karen is a sole trader who bought a business asset for £170,625 on 5 November 1991 and sold it on 31 December 2000 for £491,400. A replacement business asset was acquired on 1 November 2000 at a cost of £546,000. The new asset was sold on 3 September 2005 for £914,550. Karen made a claim for rollover relief on the first asset sale but not on the second asset sale.

Calculate the taxable gains for each asset disposal.

1.9 Where an old asset has not been used in the trade for a fraction of its period of ownership (ignoring periods before 1 April 1982), the amount of the gain that can be rolled over is reduced by the same fraction. If the proceeds are not fully reinvested the restriction on rollover by the amount not reinvested is also calculated by considering only the proportion of proceeds relating to the part of the asset used in the trade or the proportion relating to the period of trade use.

Activity 12.3: Assets with non-business use (1)

John bought a factory for £150,000 on 11 November 1998, for use in his business. From 11 November 1999, he let the factory out to an unconnected company, for a period of two years. He then used the factory for his own business again, until he sold it on 10 May 2003 for £225,000. On 13 December 2003, he purchased another factory for use in his business. This second factory cost £100,000.

Calculate the chargeable gain on the sale of the first factory that is eligible for rollover relief and the base cost of the second factory.

Activity 12.4: Assets with non-business use (2)

Y Ltd bought a factory in July 1990 for £100,000. It sold the factory in November 2000 for £215,000. The company let out a quarter of the factory on commercial terms for the entire period of ownership. Y Ltd bought a replacement factory in August 2000 for £165,000, which was used wholly for its trade.

Calculate the chargeable gain rolled over in the first factory and the base cost of the second factory.

2 CHARGEABLE GAINS AND CAPITAL ALLOWANCES

2.1 The wasting chattels exemption does not apply to chattels on which capital allowances have been claimed or could have been claimed. The chattels rules based on £6,000 do apply.

2.2 Where capital allowances have been obtained on any asset, and a loss would arise before indexation allowance, the allowable cost for chargeable gains purposes must be reduced by the lower of the unindexed loss and the net amount of allowances (taking into account any balancing allowances or charges. The result is no gain and no loss.

Activity 12.5: CGT and capital allowances

David buys a machine for £100,000 in June 1990 and sells it for £70,000 in June 2000. Show the CGT consequences.

3 RETIREMENT RELIEF

3.1 **Retirement relief is available where an individual disposes of 'business assets' and meets certain other conditions.**

3.2 The term **'business assets'** includes:

   (a) the **whole or part of a business**;

   (b) **shares or securities in a 'personal company'** which is either a trading company or the holding company of a trading group;

   (c) **assets which were in use for the taxpayer's business at the time a business ceased,** provided that the owner would have qualified for retirement relief on a disposal of the business.

3.3 **Relief is available to an individual if he is aged 50 or more at the time of disposal. Relief is allowed at an earlier age if the individual has had to retire on the grounds of ill health.**

Except where ill health is claimed, there is no requirement for the individual to cease work: he need not actually retire.

3.4 In 2000/01 the maximum gain which can qualify for retirement relief is:

   (a) £150,000; plus
   (b) 50% of the gain between £150,000 and £600,000.

This gain is calculated as the gain after indexation allowance but before taper relief. **Taper relief reduces gains which remain chargeable after retirement relief.**

3.5 Full retirement relief is available only where the necessary conditions (owning the business, or owning the shares and working in the company) have been satisfied throughout a qualifying period of at least ten years. If the qualifying period is at least one year but less than ten years, the limits of £150,000 and £600,000 are scaled down on a time basis. If the period is less than one year, there is no retirement relief.

Activity 12.6: Retirement relief

Mr A, aged 52, fulfilled the conditions for retirement relief throughout a six year period to the date of sale of his shares in his personal company. These shares are a business asset for taper relief purposes. On 4 March 2001 he realised a gain after indexation but before taper relief of £712,000 on disposal. Compute the chargeable gain after retirement relief and taper relief.

Disposals of businesses or business assets

3.6 Relief is available where a qualifying taxpayer disposes of a whole or part of a business as a going concern. It is also available where a qualifying taxpayer ceases to carry on a business and sells one or more assets previously used in the business.

3.7 The relief is only available for gains made on the disposal of chargeable business assets. These are all the chargeable assets which are used for the purpose of trade, including goodwill but excluding any assets which are held for investment purposes only.

Activity 12.7: Calculation of retirement relief

Mr C, aged 53, had owned his interior design business for seven years. He disposed of his business on 31 January 2001. He made the following disposals on that date.

		Proceeds £	Original cost £	Date of acquisition
(a)	Goodwill	150,000	5,000	January 1994
(b)	Freehold shop	100,000	15,000	January 1994
(c)	Stock	20,000	5,000	July 1998
(d)	Unquoted shares held as an investment	13,000	2,000	August 1994

Compute the gains accruing on the disposal of the above assets before taper relief and calculate the retirement relief available to Mr C.

Disposals of shares or securities in personal companies

KEY TERMS

A 'personal company' is one in which not less than 5% of the voting rights are controlled by the individual disposing of the shares.

A 'trading company' is a company whose business is wholly or mainly the carrying on of a trade or trades. A 'trading group' is a group the business of whose members, taken together, consists wholly or mainly of the carrying on of a trade or trades.

3.8 In order to obtain maximum retirement relief the individual must have **held at least the minimum voting rights in the personal company** for the ten year period up to the date of disposal. He must **also have been a full-time working officer** (such as a director) or employee for that same ten year period. If either of these conditions is not fulfilled for the full ten year period, the retirement relief available is proportionately reduced (as above). To be a full-time working officer or employee an individual must devote substantially the whole of his time to the service of the company in a managerial or technical capacity.

3.9 **Where shares in a personal company are disposed of, the gain on these shares is first calculated in the ordinary way.**

Activity 12.8: Calculation of taxable gain

Mr McGregor is a company director and owns shares giving him half the voting rights in a company.

McGregor bought the shares when he became a director in April 1985 for £200,000 and sold them on 1 January 2001 for £950,000. Calculate the net chargeable gain arising on the disposal after taper relief.

The interaction of gift relief and retirement relief

3.10 **If retirement relief is available to cover any part of the gain arising on a gift eligible for gift relief, retirement relief must be applied first. Gift relief is then computed ignoring retirement relief** (although it cannot of course exceed the gain remaining after retirement relief). Both reliefs are given before taper relief is applied.

Activity 12.9: Gift relief and retirement relief

On 6 December 2000, John, who was aged 64 and had been a full-time working employee in his personal company for the last nine years, transferred shares to his son for a consideration of £210,000. The shares had originally been purchased for £156,631. The gain before any reliefs was £294,100. Father and son jointly claim to have the gain deferred. Compute the chargeable gain after retirement relief and gift relief.

Phasing out of retirement relief

3.11 **Retirement relief is being phased out by a gradual reduction in the relief thresholds and will cease to be available from 6 April 2003.** The relief is being replaced in part by taper relief (from 6 April 1998) which reduces the capital gains tax charge on long-held business assets.

3.12 The maximum retirement relief for the next two years will be as follows:

Year	100% relief on gains to	50% relief on gains between
	£	£
2001/2002	100,000	100,000 – 400,000
2002/2003	50,000	50,000 – 200,000

Activity 12.10: Phasing out of retirement relief

Mr Thompson (age 59) sold his 100% shareholding in Thompson Ltd, his personal company, on 30 March 2001. He was the sole shareholder and a director since incorporation in 1985. The chargeable gain arising on the sale was £1,000,000. Calculate the taxable gain on the disposal and what would be the difference if the sale was delayed by a month?

4   EIS REINVESTMENT RELIEF

EIS reinvestment relief

4.1 A gain arising on the disposal of any type of asset may be deferred by an individual if he invests in a company which is a qualifying company under the Enterprise Investment Scheme (EIS) rules. This is a deferral relief because the deferred gain will become chargeable, for example when the shares are disposed of.

Calculation of relief

4.2 The amount of the gain (before taper relief) that can be deferred is broadly the lower of:

(a)   the amount subscribed by the investor for his shares; and

(b)   the amount specified by the investor in the claim. This can take into account the availability of losses, taper relief and the annual exemption.

Taper relief is then applied to any remaining gain in the usual way.

Activity 12.11: Deferral of gain

Robert made a gain of £196,000 (before taper relief) on the disposal of a property in 2000/01. The property qualifies for two years taper relief as a business asset. He subscribed for some shares in a company which qualified under the EIS rules. What will the gain to defer be if:

(a) the shares cost £200,000 and Robert wants to take the maximum deferral relief possible;

(b) the shares cost £170,000 and Robert wants to take the maximum deferral relief possible;

(c) the shares cost £200,000 and Robert, who has no other chargeable assets, wishes to utilise his annual exemption.

4.3 The EIS shares must be issued to the investor within the period of one year before and three years after the gain to be deferred accrues (or such longer period as the Board of Inland Revenue may allow). If the gain accrues after the issue of the shares, the shares must still be held by the investor at the time that the gain arises.

Gain coming back into charge

4.4 The gain deferred will come back into charge on the following events:

(a) the investor disposing of the shares except by an inter-spouse disposal;

(b) the spouse of an investor disposing of the shares, if the spouse acquired the shares from the investor;

(c) the shares ceasing to be eligible EIS shares.

Note that the gain becomes chargeable in the year of the event, not the year when the original gain was made (if different). It will be charged on the holder of the shares at the date of the event eg. on the investor if he/she still holds the shares or the spouse if the shares have been passed to her/him.

4.5 Taper relief generally applies to the deferred gain with reference to the original asset which gave rise to the deferred gain. No further taper relief can be given to the deferred gain. However, separate taper relief will apply to the holding of the shares.

Activity 12.12: Gain coming back into charge

In 2000/01, Victor made a gain of £160,000 on the disposal of a business asset, qualifying for one year's taper relief. He invested £180,000 in eligible EIS shares on 13 August 2001 and claimed the maximum possible EIS reinvestment relief. The shares were business assets for the purposes of taper relief. Victor sold the shares on 15 October 2003 for £240,000. Show the gains chargeable as a result of the sale.

5 LOANS TO TRADERS

5.1 A debt, except a debt on a security (which is a debt, whether or not secured, represented by a marketable document) is normally an exempt asset, so losses are not allowable.

5.2 **However, certain losses incurred on loans, or guarantees in respect of loans, which are made to traders are allowable losses. The relief for loans applies only to individual lenders, *not* company lenders.** The borrower may be an unincorporated business or a company. The relief for guarantees applies to both individuals and companies.

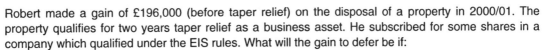

5.3   The taxpayer will be treated as if an allowable loss equal to the irrecoverable loan had arisen on the date of the claim or at a specified earlier time which is up to two years before the start of the tax year in which the claim is made. The amount claimed must have been irrecoverable at the earlier time. Relief is available only for the lost principal of the loan, not for lost interest.

5.4   The taxpayer will be treated as if an allowable loss equal to the payment under the guarantee had arisen on the date that payment was made or at a specified earlier time. An individual can go back in time just as far as for a claim as lender. A company can go back as far as the start of any accounting period which ended within the two years before the claim. In either case, the amount claimed must have been irrecoverable at the earlier time. Interest, as well as principal, paid under a guarantee can qualify.

Recoveries of amounts claimed

5.5   Where the whole or part of the outstanding amount which has given rise to an allowable loss (under a loan or a guarantee) is at any time recovered by the claimant, the claimant is treated as having made a chargeable gain equal to the amount recovered at the date of recovery.

Activity 12.13: Loan losses

Barbara lends £20,000 to Christine for use in her trade on 1 July 1998. The interest rate is 10% per annum compound, and David guarantees the loan. After two years, Christine becomes bankrupt with no assets. She has paid no interest. Barbara obtains full reimbursement from David. What amounts can Barbara and David claim as allowable losses?

Activity 12.14: End of chapter activity

On 5 April 1991, Wire bought 60% of the share capital of Wire Ltd, a trading company, and started to work for the company as its full-time managing director. The shares cost him £49,609.

On 5 October 2000, when Wire was 53, he sold all his shares at arm's length for £286,000. Compute the chargeable gain after retirement relief.

Key learning points

- When assets falling within certain classes are sold and other such assets are bought, it is possible to defer gains on the assets sold.

- The chargeable gains rules are modified for assets eligible for capital allowances.

- Retirement relief is particularly valuable because it exempts a gain completely.

- The EIS reinvestment relief defers gains.

Quick quiz

1   What assets are eligible for rollover relief on the replacement of business assets?

2   Within what time period must reinvestment in a qualifying asset be made if rollover relief is to be claimed in respect of a gain?

3   What are 'business assets' for the purposes of retirement relief?

4   What is the maximum retirement relief available in 2000/01?

5   When is EIS reinvestment relief available?

Quick quiz answers

1   The old asset and the new asset both fall within one (but not necessarily the same one) of the following classes.

  (i)   Land and buildings (including parts of buildings) occupied as well as used only for the purpose of the trade

  (ii) Fixed (that is, immovable) plant and machinery

  (iii) Ships, aircraft and hovercraft

  (iv) Goodwill

  (v)   Satellites, space stations and spacecraft

  (vi) Milk quotas, potato quotas and ewe and suckler cow premium quotas

  (vii) Fish quota

2   Reinvestment must be made in the period starting one year before and ending three years after the disposal of the asset on which the gain was made.

3   The term 'business assets' includes:

  (a)   the whole or part of a business;

  (b)   shares or securities in a 'personal company' which is either a trading company or the holding company of a trading group;

  (c)   assets which were in use for the taxpayer's business at the time a business ceased, provided that the owner would have qualified for retirement relief on a disposal of the business.

4   The maximum amount of gain which can qualify for retirement relief is:

  (a)   £150,000; plus
  (b)   50% of the gain between £150,000 and £600,000.

5   EIS reinvestment relief is available when an individual (but not a company) reinvests a gain on the sale of any asset in EIS shares within the period from one year before to three years after the sale of the asset.

Answers to activities _____

Activity 12.1

	£
Total gain	17,950
Less amount not reinvested £(70,000 - 60,000): gains chargeable immediately	(10,000)
Gain eligible to be rolled over	7,950
Cost of new factory	60,000
Less rolled over gain	(7,950)
Base cost of new factory	52,050

Activity 12.2 _____

31 December 2000 disposal

	£
Sale proceeds	491,400
Cost (5.11.1991)	(170,625)
	320,775
Less: indexation allowance to April 1998	
$\dfrac{162.6 - 135.6}{135.6} = 0.199 \times £170,625$	(33,954)
Chargeable gain before taper relief	286,821

Part B: Chargeable gains

Since the asset was sold for £491,400 and within the required time period a replacement asset was purchased for £546,000 there was a full reinvestment of the sale proceeds. Thus the full gain before taper relief of £286,821 is rolled over against the cost of the new asset.

3 September 2005 disposal

	£	£
Sale proceeds		914,550
Cost (1 November 2000)	546,000	
Less: rollover relief	(286,821)	
		(259,179)
Gain		655,371

Ownership period is 1 November 2000 to 3 September 2005
= 4 complete years of ownership)
Gain after taper relief

Taxable gain (25%) for Karen	£163,843

Activity 12.3

Gain on first factory

	£
Proceeds of sale	225,000
Less: cost	(150,000)
Gain (no indexation allowance)	75,000

Attributable to non business use:

$$\frac{11.11.99 - 10.11.01}{11.11.98 - 10.5.03} = \frac{24\ months}{54\ months} \times £75,000 \qquad £33,333$$

Attributable to business use (remainder ie 30 months):	£41,667

The proceeds of the business element of the factory are:

$$\frac{30}{54} \times £225,000 \qquad\qquad £125,000$$

Proceeds of business element not invested in second factory:

	£
Proceeds of business element	125,000
Less: cost of new factory	(100,000)
Not reinvested	25,000

Therefore of the business gain only £(41,667 - 25,000) = £16,667 is available for rollover relief.

Base cost of second factory.

	£
Cost	100,000
Less rolled over	(16,667)
Base cost	83,333

Activity 12.4

Gain on 1st factory

	Business (75%)	Non business (25%)
	£	£
Proceeds	161,250	53,750
Less: cost	(75,000)	(25,000)
	86,250	28,750
Less: indexation allowance		
$\frac{172.5 - 126.8}{126.8}$ (= 0.360) × £75,000/25,000	(27,000)	(9,000)
Indexed gain	59,250	19,750

£59,250 of the gain can be rolled over.

Base cost of 2nd factory

All of business proceeds are reinvested so full relief is available.

	£
Cost	165,000
Less: rolled over gain	(59,250)
Base cost	105,750

Activity 12.5

The capital allowances after any balancing adjustment, are £(100,000 – 70,000) = £30,000.

	£
Proceeds	70,000
Less reduced cost £(100,000 – 30,000)	70,000
No gain and no loss	0

Activity 12.6

		£	£
Gain			712,000
Less retirement relief			
(a)	60% (6 years/10 years) × £150,000	90,000	
		£	
(b)	60% × £600,000	*360,000	
	60% × £150,000	(90,000)	
	Difference	270,000	
	50% thereof	135,000	
			(225,000)
Chargeable gain (before taper relief)			487,000
Taxable gain after taper relief (75%)			365,250

The complete number of years of ownership post 6 April 1998 is two (6.4.1998 – 5.4.2000). Thus 75% of the business asset gain is taxable.

* Relief is restricted in this case because the gain (£712,000) exceeds the appropriate percentage (60%) of the upper limit (£600,000).

Part B: Chargeable gains

Activity 12.7

Goodwill

	£	Gain/(loss) £
Proceeds	150,000	
Less cost	(5,000)	
Unindexed gain	145,000	
Less indexation allowance (January 1994 to April 1998)		

$$\frac{162.6 - 141.3}{141.3} = 0.151 \times £5,000 \quad (755)$$

		144,245

Freehold shop

	£	Gain/(loss) £
Proceeds	100,000	
Less cost	(15,000)	
Unindexed gain	85,000	
Less indexation allowance (January 1994 to April 1998) 0.151 × £15,000	(2,265)	
		82,735
Gains on chargeable business assets		226,980

Less: retirement relief

	£	
70% × £150,000	105,000	
£(226,980 – 105,000) × 50%	60,990	
		(165,990)
Gains before taper relief		60,990

Stock

These are not chargeable assets and are not subject to CGT on disposal: any profit will be a revenue profit.

Shares

	£
Proceeds	13,000
Less cost	2,000
Unindexed gain	11,000
Less indexed rise (August 1994 to April 1998)	

$$\frac{162.6 - 144.7}{144.7} \times £2,000 \quad (247)$$

	£
Gain before taper relief	10,753

Activity 12.8

	£	£
Proceeds		950,000
Less Cost		(200,000)
Unindexed gain		750,000
Less indexation allowance (April 1985 to April 1998)		

$$\frac{162.6 - 94.8}{94.8} \times £200,000 \text{ (FA 1985 pool shares)} \quad (143,038)$$

	£	£
		606,962
Less retirement relief		
Basic amount	150,000	
£(600,000* – 150,000) × 50%	225,000	
		(375,000)
Chargeable gain		231,962
Taxable gain after taper relief (75%)		173,972

*Upper limit for retirement relief in 2000/01

Activity 12.9

	£	£
Gain		294,100
Less retirement relief		
90% of £150,000	135,000	
50% of £(294,100 - 135,000)	79,550	
		(214,550)
Gain after retirement relief		79,550

Ignoring retirement relief, the gift relief would be as follows.

	£
Gain	294,100
Less excess consideration £(210,000 – 156,631)	(53,369)
	240,731

The maximum gift relief cannot exceed £79,550

The final position is as follows.

	£
Gain	294,100
Less retirement relief	(214,550)
	79,550
Less gift relief	(79,550)
Chargeable gain (before taper relief and annual exemption)	Nil

Activity 12.10

Disposal 30.3.2001

	£
Gain	1,000,000
Less: maximum retirement relief £150,000 + (600,000 – 150,000) x 50%	(375,000)
Chargeable gain	625,000
Taxable gain after taper relief (75%)	£468,750

Disposal 30.4.2001

	£
Gain	1,000,000
Less: maximum retirement relief £100,000 + (400,000 – 100,000) x 50%	(250,000)
	750,000
Taxable gain after taper relief (50%)	£375,000

Activity 12.11

(a) £196,000. The qualifying expenditure on the shares exceeds the gain, so the whole gain can be deferred.

(b) £170,000. The gain deferred is restricted to the qualifying expenditure. The remainder of the gain of £26,000 will remain in charge. If there are no losses to take into account, the gain after taper relief left in charge will be £26,000 × 75% = £19,500.

(c) A claim can be made to defer £186,400. This is calculated as follows:

	£
Gain before relief	196,000
Less; EIS reinvestment relief (balancing figure)	(186,400)
Gain before taper relief	9,600
Gain after taper relief (75%)	7,200
Less annual exemption	(7,200)
Taxable	nil

Activity 12.12

	£
Proceeds	240,000
Less : cost	(180,000)
Gain	60,000
Gain after taper relief (2 years business) (75%)	45,000
Gain deferred recharged after taper relief (1 year business) (87.5%)	140,000
Total gains arising on sale	185,000

Activity 12.13

Barbara: nil, because she has been paid back in full.

David: £20,000 × 1.1 × 1.1 = £24,200.

Activity 12.14

(i)   The gain on the disposal of the shares

	£
Proceeds	286,000
Less cost	(49,609)
	236,391

Less FA 1985 pool indexation to April 1998

$$\frac{162.6 - 133.1}{133.1} \times £49,609 \qquad (10,995)$$

	£
Gain	225,396

(ii)   The retirement relief available
5.4.91 to 5.10.00 is 9 years and 6 months

	£
£150,000 × 95% =	142,500
£(225,396 – 142,500) x 50% =	41,448
	183,948

(iii)   The chargeable gain

	£
Gain	225,396
Less retirement relief (max)	(183,948)
Gain after retirement relief	41,448
Chargeable gain (75%)	31,086

Note: Taper relief is available against the gain chargeable after retirement relief. For a disposal in October 2000 there are two complete years of ownership post 5.4.1998 so the taxable gain is 75% of the original amount.

Part C
Administration

Chapter 13 Administration of income tax and CGT

Chapter topic list

1 Notification of chargeability

2 Tax returns and keeping records

3 Self assessment and claims

4 Payment of tax, interest and penalties

5 Enquiries, determinations and discovery assessments

6 Client confidentiality

Learning objectives

On completion of this chapter you will be able to:

	Performance criteria	Range Statement
• identify the due payment dates for income tax and CGT	18.1.4, 18.3.1	-
• identify the due date of submission of a tax return	18.1.6, 18.3.8	-
• discuss the consequences of not meeting the due submission payment date	18.1.7, 18.3.9	-
• outline the powers of the Inland Revenue	18.1.4, 18.3.1	-
• outline the rights afforded to a taxpayer	18.1.4, 18.3.1	-

1 NOTIFICATION OF CHARGEABILITY

1.1 **Individuals who are chargeable to tax for any tax year and who have not received a notice to file a return are, in general, required to give notice of chargeability to an officer of the Board within six months from the end of the year** ie by 5 October 2001 for 2000/01.

1.2 **The maximum mitigable penalty where notice of chargeability is not given is 100% of the tax assessed which is not paid on or before 31 January following the tax year.**

2 TAX RETURNS AND KEEPING RECORDS

Tax returns

2.1 The tax return comprises a Tax Form, together with supplementary pages for particular sources of income. You will deal with the completion of the tax return if you study Unit 19 *Preparing Personal Tax Computations.*

2.2 Partnerships must file a separate return which includes 'a partnership statement' showing the firm's profits, losses, proceeds from the sale of assets, tax suffered, tax credits, charges on income and the division of all these amounts between partners. The partnership return must normally be made by the senior partner (or whoever else may be nominated by the partnership), but the Revenue have power to require any, all, or some of the partners (or their nominated successors) to submit the return.

2.3 A partnership return must include a declaration of the name, residence and tax reference of each partner, as well as the usual declaration that the return is correct and complete to the best of the signatory's knowledge.

2.4 Each partner must then include his share of partnership profits on his personal tax return.

Time limit for submission of tax returns

> **KEY TERM**
>
> The filing due date for filing a tax return is the later of:
>
> • 31 January following the end of the tax year which the return covers.
> • three months after the notice to file the return was issued.

2.5 **If an individual wishes the Revenue to prepare the self-assessment on their behalf, earlier deadlines apply. The filing date is then the later of:**

• 30 September following the tax year; eg for 2000/01, by 30 September 2001.
• two months after notice to file the return was issued.

Since a partnership return does not include a self-assessment these revised deadlines do not apply to partnership returns. This may, of course, create problems if one of the partners wishes the Revenue to complete his personal self-assessment.

Penalties for late filing

Individual returns

2.6 The maximum penalties for delivering a tax return after the filing due date are:

    (a) **Return up to 6 months late:**   **£100**

    (b) **Return more than 6 months but not more than 12 months late:**   **£200**

    (c) **Return more than 12 months late:**   **£200 + 100% of the tax liability**

2.7 In addition, the General or Special Commissioners can direct that a maximum penalty of £60 per day be imposed where failure to deliver a tax return continues after notice of the direction has been given to the taxpayer. In this case the additional £100 penalty, imposed under (b) if the return is more than six months late, is not charged.

2.8 The fixed penalties of £100/£200 can be set aside by the Commissioners if they are satisfied that the taxpayer had a reasonable excuse for not delivering the return. If the tax liability shown on the return is less than the fixed penalties, the fixed penalty is reduced to the amount of the tax liability. The tax geared penalty is mitigable by the Revenue or the Commissioners.

Partnership returns

2.9 The maximum penalties for late delivery of a partnership tax return are as shown above, save that there is no tax-geared penalty if the return is more than 12 months late. The penalties apply separately to each partner.

Reasonable excuse

2.10 A taxpayer only has a reasonable excuse for a late filing if a default occurred because of a factor outside his control. This might be non-receipt of the return by the taxpayer, serious illness of the taxpayer or a close relative, or destruction of records through fire and flood. Illness is only accepted as a reasonable excuse if the taxpayer was taking timeous steps to complete the return, and if the return is filed as soon as possible after the illness etc.

Returns rejected as incomplete

2.11 If a return, filed before the filing date, is rejected by the Revenue as incomplete later than 14 days before the filing deadline of 31 January, a late filing penalty will not be charged if the return is completed and returned within 14 days of the rejection. This only applies if the omission from the return was a genuine error. It does not apply if a return was deliberately filed as incomplete in the hope of extending the time limit.

Standard accounting information

2.12 'Three line' accounts (ie income less expenses equals profit) only need be included on the tax return of businesses with a turnover (or gross rents from property) of less than £15,000 pa. This is not as helpful as it might appear, as underlying records must still be kept for tax purposes (disallowable items etc) when producing three line accounts.

2.13 Large businesses with a turnover of at least £5 million which have used figures rounded to the nearest £1,000 in producing their published accounts can compute their profits to the nearest £1,000 for tax purposes.

2.14 The tax return requires trading results to be presented in a standard format. Although there is no requirement to submit accounts with the return, accounts may be filed. If accounts accompany the return, the Revenue's power to raise a discovery assessment (see below) is restricted.

Keeping of records

2.15 All taxpayers must keep and retain all records required to enable them to make and deliver a correct tax return.

2.16 **Records must be retained until the later of:**

    (a) (i)   **5 years after the 31 January following the tax year where the taxpayer is in business** (as a sole trader or partner or letting property); or

         (ii)   **1 year after the 31 January following the tax year otherwise;** or

    (b) provided notice to deliver a return is given before the date in (a):

         (i)   **the time after which enquiries by the Inland Revenue into the return can no longer be commenced;** or

         (ii)   **the date any such enquiries have been completed.**

2.17 Where a person receives a notice to deliver a tax return after the normal record keeping period has expired, he must keep all records in his possession at that time until no enquiries can be raised in respect of the return or until such enquiries have been completed.

2.18 **The maximum (mitigable) penalty for each failure to keep and retain records is £3,000 per tax year/accounting period.**

2.19 The duty to preserve records can generally be satisfied by retaining copies of original documents except that original documents which show tax deducted or creditable, (eg. dividend certificates) must be kept.

2.20 Record keeping failures are taken into account in considering the mitigation of other penalties. Where the record keeping failure is taken into account in this way, a penalty will normally only be sought in serious and exceptional cases where, for example, records have been destroyed deliberately to obstruct an enquiry or there has been a history of serious record keeping failures.

3 SELF-ASSESSMENT AND CLAIMS

3.1 **Every personal tax return must be accompanied by a self-assessment.**

KEY TERM

A self assessment is a calculation of the amount of taxable income and gains after deducting reliefs and allowances, and a calculation of the income tax and CGT payable after taking into account tax deducted at source and tax credits.

3.2 **The self-assessment calculation may either be made by the taxpayer or the Revenue.** If a return is filed within certain time limits (normally, 30 September following the tax year to which it relates, see above) an officer of the board must make a self-assessment on the taxpayer's behalf on the basis of the information contained in the return. He must send a copy of the assessment to the taxpayer. These assessments, even though raised by the Revenue, are treated as self-assessments.

3.3 If the taxpayer files a return after the above deadline but without completing the self-assessment, the Revenue will not normally reject the return as incomplete. However the Revenue are not then bound to complete the self-assessment in time to notify the taxpayer of the tax falling due on the normal due date (generally the following 31 January), and it is the taxpayer's responsibility to estimate and pay his tax on time.

3.4 **Within nine months of receiving a tax return, the Revenue can amend a taxpayer's self-assessment to correct any obvious errors or mistakes;** whether errors of principle, arithmetical mistakes or otherwise.

3.5 **Within 12 months of the due filing date (*not* the actual filing date), the taxpayer can give notice to an officer to amend his tax return and self-assessment.** Such amendments by taxpayers are not confined to the correction of obvious errors. They may not be made whilst the Revenue are making enquiries into the return.

3.6 The same rules apply to corrections and amendments of partnership statements and stand alone claims (see below).

Claims

3.7 **All claims and elections which can be made in a tax return must be made in this manner if a return has been issued. A claim for any relief, allowance or repayment of tax must normally be quantified at the time it is made.**

3.8 Certain claims have a time limit that is longer than the time limit for filing or amending a tax return. A claim may therefore be made after the time limit for amending the tax return has expired. Claims not made on the tax return are referred to as **'stand alone' claims.**

3.9 Claims made on a tax return are subject to the administrative rules governing returns, for the making of corrections, enquiries etc.

3.10 Stand alone claims and elections not made in a tax return are governed by provisions which are similar to the rules governing the treatment of tax returns.

Claims involving more than one year

3.11 Self-assessment is intended to avoid the need to reopen earlier years, so relief should be given for the year of the claim. This rule can best be explained by considering a claim to carry back a trading loss to an earlier year of assessment:

(a) the claim for relief is treated as made in relation to the year in which the loss was actually incurred;

(b) the amount of any tax repayment due is calculated in terms of tax of the earlier year to which the loss is being carried back; and

(c) any tax repayment etc is treated as relating to the later year in which the loss was actually incurred.

Error or mistake claims

3.12 **An error or mistake claim may be made for errors in a return or partnership statement where tax would otherwise be overcharged.** The claim may not be made where the tax liability was computed in accordance with practice prevailing at the time the return or statement was made.

3.13 An error or mistake claim may not be made in respect of a claim. If a taxpayer makes an error or mistake in a claim, he may make a supplementary claim within the time limits allowed for the original claim.

3.14 The taxpayer may appeal to the Special Commissioners against any refusal of an error or mistake claim.

4 PAYMENT OF TAX, INTEREST AND PENALTIES

4.1 The self-assessment system may result in the taxpayer making three payments of income tax:

Date	Payment
31 January in the tax year	**1st payment on account**
31 July after the tax year	**2nd payment on account**
31 January after the tax	**Final payment to settle the remaining liability**

KEY TERMS

Payments on account are usually required where the income tax due in the previous year exceeded the amount of income tax deducted at source; this excess is known as 'the **relevant amount**'. Income tax deducted at source includes tax suffered, PAYE deductions and tax credits on dividends.

4.2 **The payments on account are each equal to 50% of the relevant amount for the previous year.**

Activity 13.1: Payments on account

Gordon paid tax for 2000/01 as follows:

		£
Total amount of income tax assessed		9,200
This included:	Tax deducted under PAYE	1,700
	Tax deducted on savings income	1,500
He also paid:	Capital gains tax	4,800

How much are the payments on account for 2001/2002?

4.3 **Payments on account are not required if the relevant amount falls below a de minimis limit of £500. Also, payments on account are not required from taxpayers who paid 80% or more of their tax liability for the previous year through PAYE or other deduction at source arrangements.**

4.4 If the previous year's liability increases following an amendment to a self-assessment, or the raising of a discovery assessment, an adjustment is made to the payments on account due.

4.5 Payments on account are normally fixed by reference to the previous year's tax liability but if a taxpayer expects his liability to be lower than this **he may claim to reduce his payments on account to:**

(a) **a stated amount,** or

(b) **nil.**

The claim must state the reason why he believes his tax liability will be lower, or nil.

4.6 **If the taxpayer's eventual liability is higher than he estimated he will have reduced the payments on account too far. Although the payments on account will not be adjusted, the taxpayer will suffer an interest charge on late payment.**

4.7 A penalty of the difference between the reduced payment on account and the correct payment on account may be levied if the reduction was claimed fraudulently or negligently.

4.8 **The balance of any income tax together with all CGT due for a year, is normally payable on or before the 31 January following the year.**

Activity 13.2: Payments of tax

Giles made payments on account for 2001/02 of £6,500 each on 31 January 2002 and 31 July 2002, based on his 2000/01 liability. He then calculates his total income tax for 2001/02 at £18,000 of which £2,750 was deducted at source. In addition he calculated that his CGT liability for disposals in 2001/02 is £5,120.

What is the final payment due for 2001/02?

4.9 In one case the due date for the final payment is later than 31 January following the end of the year. **If a taxpayer has notified chargeability by 5 October but the notice to file a tax return is not issued before 31 October, then the due date for the payment is three months after the issue of the notice.**

4.10 Tax charged in an amended self-assessment is usually payable on the later of:

(a) the normal due date, generally 31 January following the end of the tax year; and

(b) the day following 30 days after the making of the revised self-assessment.

4.11 Tax charged on a discovery assessment is due thirty days after the issue of the assessment.

Surcharges

> **KEY TERM**
>
> **Surcharges** are normally imposed in respect of amounts paid late:
>
> | *Paid* | *Surcharge* |
> | --- | --- |
> | (a) within 28 days of due date: | none |
> | (b) more than 28 days but not more than six months after the due date: | 5% |
> | (c) more than six months after the due date: | 10% |

4.12 Surcharges apply to:

(a) balancing payments of income tax and any CGT under self-assessment or a determination;

(b) tax due on the amendment of a self-assessment;

(c) tax due on a discovery assessment.

4.13 **The surcharge rules do not apply to late payments on account.**

4.14 No surcharge will be applied where the late paid tax liability has attracted a tax-geared penalty on the failure to notify chargeability to tax, or the failure to submit a return, or on the making of an incorrect return (including a partnership return).

Interest

4.15 **Interest is chargeable on late payment of both payments on account and balancing payments. In both cases interest runs from the due date until the day before the actual date of payment.**

4.16 Interest is charged from 31 January following the tax year (or the normal due date for the balancing payment, in the rare event that this is later), even if this is before the due date for payment on:

(a) tax payable following an amendment to a self-assessment;
(b) tax payable in a discovery assessment; and
(c) tax postponed under an appeal which becomes payable.

4.17 Since a determination (see below) is treated as if it were a self-assessment, interest runs from 31 January following the tax year.

4.18 If a taxpayer claims to reduce his payments on account and there is still a final payment to be made, interest is normally charged on the payments on account as if each of those payments had been the lower of:

(a) the reduced amount, plus 50% of the final income tax liability; and
(b) the amount which would have been payable had no claim for reduction been made.

Activity 13.3: Interest

Herbert's payments on account for 2000/01 based on his income tax liability for 1999/00 were £4,500 each. However when he submitted his 1999/00 income tax return in January 2001 he made a claim to reduce the payments on account for 2000/01 to £3,500 each. The first payment on account was made on 29 January 2001, and the second on 12 August 2001.

Herbert filed his 2000/01 tax return in December 2001. The return showed that his tax liabilities for 2000/01 (before deducting payments on account) were income tax: £10,000, capital gains tax: £2,500. Herbert paid the balance of tax due of £5,500 on 19 February 2002.

For what periods and in respect of what amounts will Herbert be charged interest?

4.19 Where interest has been charged on late payments on account but the final balancing settlement for the year produces a repayment, all or part of the original interest is remitted.

Repayment of tax and repayment supplement

4.20 Tax is repaid when claimed unless a greater payment of tax is due in the following 30 days, in which case it is set-off against that payment.

4.21 Interest is paid on overpayments of:

(a) payments on account;

(b) final payments of income tax and CGT, including tax deducted at source or tax credits **on dividends; and**

(c) **penalties and surcharges.**

4.22 Repayment supplement runs from the original date of payment (even if this was prior to the due date), until the day before the date the repayment is made. Income tax deducted at source and tax credits are treated as if they were paid on the 31 January following the tax year concerned.

Payment of CGT by instalments

4.23 Where the consideration for a disposal of an asset is receivable in instalments over a period exceeding 18 months, the taxpayer has the option to pay the CGT arising in instalments. The Revenue then allow payment of CGT to be spread over the shorter of:

(a) the period of instalments; and

(b) eight years.

5 ENQUIRIES, DETERMINATIONS AND DISCOVERY ASSESSMENTS

Enquiries into returns

5.1 An officer of the Board has a limited period within which to commence enquiries into a return or amendment. The officer must give written notice of his intention by:

(a) **the first anniversary of the due filing date (not the actual filing date); or**

(b) **If the return is filed after the due filing date, the quarter day following the first anniversary of the actual filing date. The quarter days are 31 January, 30 April, 31 July and 31 October.**

5.2 If the taxpayer amended the return after the due filing date, the enquiry 'window' extends to the quarter day following the first anniversary of the date the amendment was filed. Where the enquiry was not raised within the limit which would have applied had no amendment been filed, the enquiry is restricted to matters contained in the amendment.

5.3 Enquiries may be made into partnership returns (or amendments) upon which a partnership statement is based within the same time limits. A notice to enquire into a partnership return is deemed to incorporate a notice, to enquire into each individual partner's return.

5.4 Enquiries may also be made into stand alone claims, provided notice is given by the officer of the Board by the later of:

(a) The quarter day following the first anniversary of the making or amending of the claim;

(b) 31 January next but one following the tax year, if the claim relates to a tax year; or

(c) the first anniversary of the end of the period to which a claim relates if it relates to a period other than a tax year.

5.5 The procedures for enquiries into claims mirror those for enquiries into returns.

5.6 **The officer does not have to have, or give, any reason for raising an enquiry. In particular the taxpayer will not be advised whether he has been selected at random for an audit. Enquiries may be full enquiries, or may be limited to 'aspect' enquiries.**

5.7 In the course of his enquiries **the officer may require the taxpayer to produce documents, accounts or any other information required. The taxpayer can appeal to the Commissioners.**

5.8 During the course of his enquiries an officer may amend a self-assessment if it appears that insufficient tax has been charged and an immediate amendment is necessary to prevent a loss to the Crown. This might apply if, for example, there is a possibility that the taxpayer will emigrate.

5.9 If a return is under enquiry the Revenue may postpone any repayment due as shown in the return until the enquiry is complete. The Revenue have discretion to make a provisional repayment but there is no facility to appeal if the repayment is withheld.

5.10 At any time during the course of an enquiry, the taxpayer may apply to the Commissioners to require the officer to notify the taxpayer within a specified period that the enquiries are complete, unless the officer can demonstrate that he has reasonable grounds for continuing the enquiry.

5.11 An officer must issue a notice that the enquiries are complete, and a statement of the amount of tax that he considers should be included in the tax return, or the amounts which should be contained in the partnership statement, or the amount of the claim. The taxpayer then has thirty days to amend his self-assessment, partnership statement or claim to give effect to the officer's conclusions. He may also make any other amendments that he could have made had the enquiry not been commenced (amendments may not be made whilst enquiries are in progress).

5.12 If the officer is not satisfied with the taxpayer's amendment he has thirty days in which to amend the self-assessment, partnership statement or claim. Also if a claim has been disallowed, but does not affect the self-assessment, he must advise the taxpayer of the extent to which it has been disallowed.

  If the taxpayer is not satisfied with the officer's amendment he may, within 30 days, appeal to the Commissioners.

5.13 Once an enquiry is complete the officer cannot make further enquiries. The Revenue may, in limited circumstances, raise a discovery assessment if they believe that there has been a loss of tax (see below).

5.14 The majority of investigation cases are handled by local inspectors, but serious cases are dealt with by the Special Compliance Office.

5.15 **Where an irregularity is detected, unless it appears to be of a very serious nature, the first overture will often be made by the local inspector writing to the taxpayer or his agent suggesting that he has reason to doubt that full and correct returns have been made and inviting the taxpayer's comments. Correspondence will be followed by**

interviews at which the inspector will try to collect further evidence, and the taxpayer's accountant may be asked to prepare a detailed report showing the estimated tax unpaid.

5.16 The Revenue use various methods to attempt to calculate undisclosed income. Gross profit margins either for previous periods or for similar businesses are standardly used. As a last resort, some indication can be derived from the taxpayer's personal assets. A growth in these, taken together with an assumed level of personal expenditure, can point to an unexplained source, presumably undisclosed income. A sensible taxpayer will co-operate with the Revenue as any resistance on his part at this stage will count heavily against him in the final assessment or penalties.

The Revenue's powers

5.17 **The Revenue's powers include the following.**

(a) **The power to call for documents of taxpayers and others.** The Revenue may require any person to produce any documents which may contain information relevant to any taxpayer's tax liability. The Revenue may also require the taxpayer to provide written answers about questions of fact. The Inspector must give the person holding the documents reasons for applying for the right to demand documents, unless the commissioner is satisfied that giving reasons would prejudice the assessment or collection of tax.

(b) **The power to call for papers of tax accountants.** The Revenue is not normally empowered to demand documents from the taxpayer's accountant. but if he has either:

(i) been convicted of an offence in relation to tax; or
(ii) been penalised for assisting in making an incorrect return,

the Revenue can, in certain circumstances, demand documents relating to the taxpayer's affairs. A tax accountant is anyone (including a barrister or solicitor) who helps a taxpayer to prepare or deliver documents for tax purposes.

(c) **The power of entry with a warrant to obtain documents.** Where there are reasonable grounds for suspecting that an offence involving fraud in connection with tax has been, is being or is about to be committed and that evidence is to be found on certain premises, a warrant can be obtained authorising an officer of the Board to search the premises and remove anything which he has reasonable cause to suppose may be required as evidence.

(d) **The power to obtain information about interest and dividends.** The Revenue can require details from banks and building societies.

Determinations

5.18 The Revenue may only raise enquiries if a return has been submitted.

5.19 If notice has been served on a taxpayer to submit a return but the return is not submitted by the due filing date, an officer of the Board may make a determination of the tax due. Such a determination must be made to the best of the officer's information and belief, and is then treated as if it were a self-assessment. This enables the officer to seek payment of tax, including payments on account for the following year and to charge interest.

BPP PUBLISHING

Discovery assessments

5.20 If an officer of the Board discovers that profits have been omitted from assessment, that any assessment has become insufficient, or that any relief given is, or has become excessive, an assessment may be raised to recover the tax lost.

5.21 If the tax lost results from an error in the taxpayer's return but the return was made in accordance with prevailing practice at the time, no discovery assessment may be made.

5.22 A discovery assessment may only be raised where a return has been made if:

(a) there has been fraudulent or negligent conduct by the taxpayer or his agent; or

(b) at the time that enquiries into the return were completed, or could no longer be made, the officer did not have information to make him aware of the loss of tax.

5.23 These rules do not prevent the Revenue from raising assessments in cases of genuine discoveries, but prevent assessments from being raised due to the Revenue's failure to make timely use of information or to a change of opinion on information made available.

Appeals and postponement of payment of tax

5.24 A taxpayer may appeal against an amendment to a self-assessment or partnership statement, or an amendment to or disallowance of a claim, following an enquiry, or against an assessment which is not a self-assessment, such as a discovery assessment.

5.25 **The appeal must normally be made within 30 days of the amendment or self-assessment.**

5.26 The notice of appeal must state the **grounds** of appeal. These may be stated in general terms. At the hearing the Commissioners may allow the appellant to put forward grounds not stated in his notice if they are satisfied that his omission was not wilful or unreasonable.

5.27 In some cases it may be possible to agree the point at issue by negotiation with the Revenue, in which case the appeal may be settled by agreement. If the appeal cannot be agreed, it will be heard by the General or Special Commissioners.

5.28 An appeal does not relieve the taxpayer of liability to pay tax on the normal due date unless he obtains a 'determination' of the Commissioners or agreement of the Inspector that payment of all or some of the tax may be postponed pending determination of the appeal. The amount not postponed is due 30 days after the determination or agreement is issued, if that is later than the normal due date.

5.29 If any part of the postponed tax becomes due a notice of the amount payable is issued and the amount is payable 30 days after the issue of the notice. Interest, however, is still payable from the normal due date.

6 CLIENT CONFIDENTIALITY

6.1 Whenever you prepare accounts or returns on behalf of a client you should remember that you are bound by the ethical guideline of client confidentiality. This means that you should not discuss a client's affairs with third parties without the client's permission. You should also take care not to leave documents relating to a client's affairs in public places such as on trains or in restaurants.

Activity 13.4: End of chapter activity

Tim is a medical consultant. His total tax liability for 1999/00 was £16,800. Of this £7,200 was paid under the PAYE system, £800 was withheld at source from bank interest and £200 was suffered on dividends received during the year.

Tim's total tax liability for 2000/01 was £22,000. £7,100 of this was paid under PAYE system, £900 was withheld at source from bank interest and there was a £250 tax credit on dividends.

Tim did not make any claim in respect of his payments on account for 2000/01. The Revenue issued a 2000/01 tax return to Tim on 5 May 2001.

Required

State what payments Tim was required to make in respect of his 2000/01 tax liability and the due dates for the payment of these amounts.

Key learning points

- Two payments on account of income tax based on the prior year tax bill are paid on 31 January during the tax year and 31 July after the tax year. On 31 January following the tax year the balance of income tax is due.

- CGT is due to be paid by 31 January following the tax year end. There are no payments on account of CGT.

- A return is due for filing by 31 January following the end of the tax year. However, if the taxpayer wants the Revenue to calculate the amount of tax due in time for him to pay the correct amount by the due date, the return must be submitted by 30 September following the end of the tax year.

- The Revenue have extensive, but not unlimited, powers to enquire into returns.

- There is an extensive regime of interest, surcharges and penalties.

Quick quiz

1   By when must a taxpayer who intends to calculate his own tax submit a tax return?

2   What are the Revenue's powers to obtain documents?

3   What is the time limit for appeals?

4   What is the initial penalty for the late filing of a tax return?

Answers to quick quiz

1   By 31 January that follows the end of the tax year.

2   The Revenue may require any person to produce any documents which may contain information relevant to any taxpayer's tax liability.

3   A written notice of appeal must be given within 30 days of the issue of the assessment, amendment, disallowance or demand.

4   £100.

Answers to activities _____

Activity 13.1

	£
Total income tax	9,200
Less: tax credits (1,700 + 1,500)	(3,200)
	6,000

Payments on account for 2001/02:

31 January 2002: Income tax £6,000 × 1/2	£3,000
31 July 2002 As before, income tax	£3,000

There is no requirement to make payments on account of capital gains tax.

Activity 13.2 _____

Income tax: £18,000 - £2,750 - £6,500 - £6,500 = £2,250. CGT = £5,120.

Final payment due on 31 January 2003 for 20001/02 £2,250 + £5,120 = £7,370

Activity 13.3 _____

Herbert made an excessive claim to reduce his payments on account, and will therefore be charged interest on the reduction. The payments on account should have been £4,500 each based on the 1999/00 liability (not £5,000 each based on the 2000/01 liability). Interest will be charged as follows:

(a)   first payment on account

    (i)   on £3,500 - nil - paid on time
    (ii)   on £1,000 from due date of 31 January 2001 to day before payment, 18 February 2002

(b)   second payment on account

    (i)   on £3,500 from due date of 31 July 2001 to day before payment, 11 August 2001
    (ii)   on £1,000 from due date of 31 July 2001 to day before payment, 18 February 2002

(c)   balancing payment

    (i)   on £3,500 from due date of 31 January 2002 to day before payment, 18 February 2002

Activity 13.4 _____

Tim's Payments on Account for 2000/01 were based on the excess of his 1999/00 tax liability over amounts deducted under the PAYE system, amounts deducted at source and tax credits on dividends:

	£
1999/00 tax liability	16,800
Less: PAYE	(7,200)
Tax deducted at source	(800)
Tax credit on dividends	(200)
Total payments on account for 2000/01	8,600

Two equal payments on account of £4,300 (£8,600 / 2) were required. The due dates for these payments were 31 January 2001 and 31 July 2001 respectively.

The final payment in respect of Tim's 2000/01 tax liability was due on 31 January 2002 and was calculated as follows:

	£
2000/01 tax liability	22,000
Less: PAYE	(7,100)
Tax deducted at source	(900)
Tax credit on dividends	(250)
	13,750
Less: Payments on account	(8,600)
Final payment due 31.1.02	5,150

Part D
Corporation tax

Chapter 14   An outline of corporation tax

Chapter topic list

1   The scope of corporation tax

2   Profits chargeable to corporation tax

3   Charge to corporation tax

4   The corporate venturing scheme

Learning objectives

On completion of this chapter you will be able to:

	Performance criteria	Range Statement
• calculate the profit chargeable to corporation tax (PCTCT) for a company accounting period	18.5.1	18.5.1
• outline how to deal with long and short accounting periods	18.5.1	18.5.1
• outline the period for which financial years run and their importance	18.5.1	18.5.1
• calculate the corporation tax due on the PCTCT for an accounting period	18.5.3	18.5.1

BPP
PUBLISHING

1 THE SCOPE OF CORPORATION TAX

1.1 **Corporation tax is paid by companies. It is charged on the profits (including chargeable gains) arising in each accounting period. Corporation tax is not charged on dividends received from companies resident in the UK.**

> ### KEY TERM
>
> A 'company' is any corporate body (limited or unlimited) or unincorporated association.

Accounting periods

1.2 Corporation tax is chargeable in respect of accounting periods and it is important to understand the difference between an accounting period and a period of account. A period of account is any period for which a company prepares accounts; usually this will be 12 months in length but it may be longer or shorter than this. An accounting period starts when a company commences to trade or otherwise becomes liable to corporation tax, or immediately after the previous accounting period finishes. An accounting period finishes on the earliest of:

- 12 months after its start;
- the end of the company's period of account;
- the commencement of the company's winding up;
- the company's ceasing to be resident in the UK;
- the company's ceasing to be liable to corporation tax.

1.3 **If a company has a long period of account, exceeding 12 months, it is split into two accounting periods: the first 12 months and the remainder.**

1.4 Where the period of account differs from the corporation tax accounting periods (as in the above example), there is the problem of **allocating profits between the relevant periods.** In such cases the following rules apply.

- **Trading income** before capital allowances is apportioned on a **time basis.**

- **Capital allowances** and balancing charges are **calculated for each accounting period.**

- **Other income is allocated to the period to which it relates** (for example rents to the period when accrued). Schedule D Case VI income, however, is apportioned on a time basis.

- **Chargeable gains** are taken into account for the accounting **period in which they are realised.**

- **Charges on income** are deducted from the profits of the accounting **period in which they are paid.**

1.5 **Companies' taxable profits are always computed for accounting periods, not tax years. There are no basis period rules, there is no personal allowance and there is no taper relief or annual exemption for capital gains.**

Activity 14.1: Long accounting period

A company has the following results for the 17 months from 1 January 1999 to 31 May 2000.

	£
Trading profit (there are no capital allowances)	341,700
Rent accrued 6 months to 30.6.99	3,000
accrued 6 months to 31.12.99	3,000
accrued to 31.5.00	4,200
Chargeable gains: 1.10.99	10,800
1.2.00	6,200

Compute the total profits for the two accounting periods covered by this period of account.

2   PROFITS CHARGEABLE TO CORPORATION TAX

2.1   **The profits chargeable to corporation tax (PCTCT) for an accounting period are derived as follows.**

	£
Schedule D Case I	X
Schedule D Case III	X
Schedule D Case VI	X
Schedule A	X
Taxed income (gross)	X
Chargeable gains	X
Total profits	X
Less charges on income (gross)	(X)
Profits chargeable to corporation tax (PCTCT) for an accounting period	X

DEVOLVED ASSESSMENT ALERT

It would be of great help in the assessment if you could learn the above proforma to calculate PCTCT. Then when answering a corporation tax question you could immediately reproduce the proforma and insert the appropriate numbers into the proforma as you are given the information in the question.

2.2   **The Schedule D Case I income of companies is derived from the net profit figure in the accounts, adjusted as follows.**

	£	£
Net profit per accounts		X
Add expenditure not allowed for taxation purposes		X
		X
Less: income not taxable under Schedule D Case I	X	
expenditure not charged in the accounts but allowable for the purposes of taxation	X	
capital allowances	X	
		X
Schedule D Case I income		X

2.3   The adjustment of profits computation shown above broadly follows that for computing business profits subject to income tax.

2.4   Charges are added back in the calculation of adjusted profit. They are treated instead as a deduction from total profits and the amount allowed is the cash paid (grossed up if the charge was paid net). The amounts added back (on an accruals basis) and deducted (on a cash paid basis) may differ.

2.5 Similarly, investment income including rents is deducted in arriving at trading profit but brought in again further down in the computation.

DEVOLVED ASSESSMENT ALERT

When adjusting profits as supplied in a profit and loss account confusion can arise as regards whether figures are net or gross. Properly drawn up company accounts should normally include all income gross. Charges should also be shown gross. However, some questions mention 'net' figures. Read the question carefully.

2.6 **The calculation of capital allowances follows income tax principles. For companies, there is never any reduction of allowances to take account of any private use of an asset. The director or employee suffers a taxable benefit instead.**

Rental income

2.7 The Schedule A rules for companies are set out in detail below but to first summarise them here:

- All UK rental activities are treated as a single source of income calculated in the same way as Schedule D Case I profits.

- Capital allowances are taken into account when computing these Schedule A profits or losses.

2.8 **A company with rental income is treated as running a 'Schedule A business'. All the rents and expenses for all properties are pooled, to give a single profit or loss. Profits and losses are computed in the same way as trading profits are computed for Schedule D Case I purposes,** on an accruals basis. Expenses will often include rent payable, where a landlord is himself renting the land which he in turn lets to others.

2.9 **Capital allowances are given on plant and machinery used in the Schedule A business and on industrial and agricultural buildings, in the same way as they are given for a Schedule D Case I business.** Capital allowances are not available on plant or machinery used in a dwelling, so someone who lets property furnished cannot claim capital allowances on the furniture. Instead, he can choose between the renewals basis and the 10% wear and tear allowance.

- Under the *renewals* basis, there is no deduction for the cost of the first furniture provided, but the cost of replacement furniture is treated as a revenue expense. However, the part of the cost attributable to improvement, as opposed to simple replacement, is not deductible.

- Under the *10% wear and tear* basis, the actual cost of furniture is ignored. Instead, an annual deduction is given of 10% of rents. The rents are first reduced by amounts which are paid by the landlord but are normally a tenant's burden. These amounts include any water rates and council tax paid by the landlord.

2.10 If plant and machinery is used partly in a dwelling house and partly for other purposes a just and reasonable apportionment of the expenditure can be made.

2.11 Rent for furniture supplied with premises is taxed as part of the rent for the premises, unless there is a separate trade of renting furniture.

Premiums on leases

2.12 **When a premium or similar consideration is received on the grant** (that is, by a landlord to a tenant) **of a short lease (50 years or less), part of the premium is treated as rent received in the year of grant.** A lease is considered to end on the date when it is most likely to terminate.

The premium taxed under Schedule A is the whole premium, less 2% of the premium for each complete year of the lease, except the first year.

This rule does not apply on the *assignment* of a lease (one tenant selling his entire interest in the property to another).

Activity 14.2: Taxable premium received

On 1 June 2000 D granted a lease to E for a period of ten years. E paid a premium of £30,000. Calculate the amount treated as rent out of the premium received by D.

Premiums paid by traders

2.13 **Where a trader (taxed under Schedule D Case I or II) pays a premium for a lease he may deduct an amount from his taxable profits in each year of the lease. The amount deductible is the figure treated as rent received by the landlord divided by the number of years of the lease.** For example, suppose that B, a trader, pays A a premium of £30,000 for a ten year lease. A is treated as receiving £30,000 – (£30,000 × (10 – 1) × 2%) = £24,600. B can therefore deduct £24,600/10 = £2,460 in each of the ten years. He starts with the accounts year in which the lease starts and apportions the relief to the nearest month.

Premiums for granting subleases

2.14 **A tenant may decide to sublet property and to charge a premium on the grant of a lease to the subtenant. This premium is treated as rent received in the normal way** (because this is a grant and not an assignment, the original tenant retaining an interest in the property). **Where the tenant originally paid a premium for his own head lease, this deemed rent is reduced by:**

$$\text{Rent part of premium for head lease} \times \frac{\text{duration of sub} - \text{lease}}{\text{duration of head lease}}$$

If the relief exceeds the part of the premium for the sub-lease treated as rent (including cases where there is a sub-lease with no premium), the balance of the relief is treated as rent payable by the head tenant, spread evenly over the period of the sub-lease. This rent payable is an expense, reducing the overall Schedule A profit.

2.15 Schedule A losses are:

- first set off against non-Schedule A income and gains of the company for the current period; and any excess is

- carried forward for set off against future income (of all descriptions)

Interest paid on Schedule A property loans

2.16   Interest paid by a company on a loan to buy or improve property is not a Schedule A expense. The loan relationship rules will apply instead. These are covered later in this chapter.

Income received net of tax

2.17   **Income which suffers a deduction of tax at source is included within the profits chargeable to corporation tax at its gross equivalent.** For example £5,000 of debenture interest received net of tax would need to be grossed up by multiplying by 100/80 to include £6,250 within the profits chargeable to corporation tax. The way in which credit is given for the tax credit so included is covered later in this text. Essentially, if tax suffered on income received net exceeds tax deducted from charges and interest paid net, the difference is subtracted from the corporation tax to find the final amount due (the mainstream corporation tax).

2.18   Examples of income received net of tax are:

(a)   interest received from another UK company (such as debenture or loan stock interest): tax at 20%;

(b)   patent royalties: tax at 22%;

(c)   interest on most gilt edged securities is received gross but in certain limited circumstances it is received net of tax at 20%.

2.19   The pro-forma computation shows a line for taxed income. This will include items received net of 22% tax, such as patent royalties. Interest, however, will go under Schedule D Case III or Case I, as explained below, even if it is received net of 20% income tax.

Interest received gross

2.20   **UK companies receive interest gross from banks and building societies.** Interest on most gilts is received gross.

Chargeable gains

2.21   **Companies do not pay capital gains tax. Instead their chargeable gains are included in the profits chargeable to corporation tax.** A company's capital gains or allowable losses are computed in a similar way to individuals but with a few major differences:

- Indexation allowance calculations may include periods of ownership after 6 April 1998

- The FA 1985 pool for shares does not close at 5 April 1998 and there are different matching rules for shares if the shareholder is a company

- The taper relief does not apply

- No annual exemption is available

Borrowing and lending (loan relationships)

2.22   **If a company borrows or lends money it has a loan relationship. This can be a creditor relationship** (where the company lends or invests money) **or a debtor relationship** (where the company borrows money or issues securities).

Treatment of trading loan relationships

2.23 If the company is a party to a **loan relationship for trade purposes, any debits – ie interest paid or other debt costs – charged through its accounts are allowed as a trading expense** and are therefore deductible in computing Schedule D Case I profits.

2.24 Similarly **if any credits – ie interest income or other debt returns – arise on a trading loan these are treated as a trading receipt and are taxable under Schedule D Case I.** This is not likely to arise unless the trade is one of money lending.

Treatment of non-trading loan relationships

2.25 **If a loan relationship is not one to which the company is a party for trade purposes any debits or credits must be pooled. A net credit on the pool is chargeable as income under Schedule D Case III. A net deficit on the pool may be:**

   (a) **set against other income of the same accounting period**

   (b) **carried back and set against any surpluses on non-trading loan relationships** (taxed under Schedule D Case III) **for the previous twelve months**

   (c) **carried forward and set against future non-trading profits**

   Any deficit remaining after the above claims is automatically carried forward as an opening DIII debit of the next accounting period.

   We will look at the reliefs available for non trading deficits later in this text.

Accounting methods

2.26 The following bases are acceptable for recognising debits or credits.

   (a) the accruals basis; or
   (b) the mark to market basis.

   The mark to market basis places a fair value on the loan relationship for each accounting period and determines the credit or debit on the change in the value.

   If neither the accruals or mark to market method is used in the accounts, the accruals basis must be used for tax purposes. In this study text, we assume that the accruals basis applies. The mark to market basis is only likely to be used by companies in the financial sector such as banks.

Charges on income

2.27 **Having arrived at a company's total profits, charges on income are deducted to arrive at the profits chargeable to corporation tax (PCTCT). Certain charges, for example patent royalties, are paid net of basic rate income tax. Other charges, for example payments under the gift aid scheme (see below), are paid gross.**

2.28 The full amount of the charges paid in an accounting period, before the deduction of any income tax at source, is deducted from the total profits. The income tax deducted at source must be accounted for to the Inland Revenue. The method used to account for the income tax deducted is covered in the next chapter. Essentially, **any tax deducted from charges must be paid to the Inland Revenue if it cannot be matched with tax suffered on income received net.**

Activity 14.3: The calculation of PCTCT (1)

A company had the following results in the year ended 31 March 2001.

	£
Trading profits	85,000
Bank deposit interest income	6,000
Building society interest income	1,500
Debenture interest income (net amount)	2,560
Capital gains	2,950
Patent royalties - net amount paid in December	11,856

All interest received was on non-trading investments.

What were the company's profits chargeable to corporation tax?

Donations to charities

2.29 Almost all donations of money to charity can qualify as charges on income under the **gift aid scheme** whether they are one off donations or are regular donations made, for example, under a deed of covenant. **Gift aid donations are paid gross by companies.**

2.30 **Donations to charities which are incurred wholly and exclusively for the purposes of the trade are Schedule D Case I deductions** instead of charges on income.

Activity 14.4: The calculation of PCTCT

The following is a summary of the profit and loss account of A Ltd for the year to 31 March 2001.

	£	£
Gross profit on trading		180,000
3½% War Loan interest (non-trading investment)		700
Dividends from UK companies (net)		3,600
Loan interest from UK company (gross) (non-trading investment)		4,000
Building society interest received (non-trading investment)		292
Less: trade expenses (all allowable)	62,000	
patent royalties paid (gross)	1,000	
gift aid donation paid	100	
		(63,100)
		125,492

The capital allowances for the period total £5,500. There was also a capital gain of £13,867.

Compute the profits chargeable to corporation tax.

---

3 CHARGE TO CORPORATION TAX

3.1 **The rates of corporation tax are fixed for financial years. A financial year runs from 1 April to the following 31 March and is identified by the calendar year in which it begins. For example, the year ended 31 March 2001 is the financial year 2000 (FY 2000). This should not be confused with a tax year, which runs from 6 April to the following 5 April.**

3.2 The full rate of corporation tax is 31% for FY 1997 and FY 1998 and 30% for FY 1999 and FY 2000.

Activity 14.5: Corporation tax payable

A company had profits chargeable to corporation tax of £2,000,000 in the year ended 31 March 2001. What was the corporation tax payable?

The small companies rate (SCR)

3.3 **The SCR of corporation tax (20% for FY 1999 and FY 2000) applies to the profits chargeable to corporation tax of companies whose 'profits' are not more than £300,000.**

3.4 **'Profits' means profits chargeable to corporation tax plus the grossed-up amount of dividends received from UK companies.** The grossed-up amount of UK dividends is the net dividend plus the tax credit which an individual investor would receive. We gross up by multiplying by 100/90 post 5.4.1999 and 100/80 before 6.4.1999. You may see the grossed up amount of dividend received referred to as franked investment income.

Activity 14.6: The small companies rate

B Ltd had the following results for the year ended 31 March 2001.

	£
Schedule D Case I	42,000
Dividend received 1 May 2000	9,000

Compute the corporation tax payable.

The starting rate

3.5 **A new 10% starting rate of corporation tax was introduced with effect from 1 April 2000 (FY 2000). It applies to companies with 'profits' of up to £10,000.**

Activity 14.7: The starting rate of corporation tax

Dexter Limited has tho following income for the year ended 31 March 2001.

(a) Schedule D, Case I income of £9,500; and
(b) Franked investment income of £300.

Calculate the corporation tax liability for the year.

Marginal relief

3.6 **Small companies marginal relief (sometimes called taper relief) applies where the 'profits' of an accounting period are over £300,000 but under £1,500,000. We first calculate the corporation tax at the full rate and then deduct:**

$(M - P) \times I/P \times$ **marginal relief fraction**

where M = **upper limit (currently £1,500,000)**
               P = **'profits' (see above)**
              I = **PCTCT**

The marginal relief fraction is 1/40 for FY 1997 to FY 2000 inclusive.

173

DEVOLVED ASSESSMENT ALERT

You will be given the above marginal relief formula in your assessment.

Activity 14.8: Small companies marginal relief

Lenox Ltd has the following results for the year ended 31 March 2001.

	£
PCTCT	296,000
Dividend received 1 December 2000	12,600

Calculate the corporation tax liability.

3.7 **For companies with 'profits' between £10,001 and £50,000 the small companies rate less a starting rate marginal relief applies from 1 April 2000.** The formula for calculating this marginal relief is the same as that given above except that 'M' is the upper limit for starting rate purposes. (£50,000 – FY 2000). The small companies rate only applies in full when 'profits' exceed £50,000.

Activity 14.9: Starting rate marginal relief

Armstrong Ltd has the following income for its year ended 31 March 2001:

		£
(a)	Schedule D, Case I	29,500
(b)	Franked investment income	3,000

Calculate the corporation tax liability.

Changes in the rate - Accounting periods straddling 31 March

3.8 **If there is a change in the corporation tax rate, and a company's accounting period does not fall entirely within one financial year, the profits of the accounting period are apportioned to the two financial years on a time basis.** Note that the profits as a whole are apportioned. We do not look at components of the profit individually, unlike apportionment of profits of a long period of account to two accounting periods.

Activity 14.10: A change in the rate

Frances Ltd makes up accounts to 31 December each year. For the year ended 31 December 1999 its profit and loss account was as follows.

	£
PCTCT	644,000
Dividends plus tax credits	10,000
'Profits'	654,000

Calculate the corporation tax liability for the year.

3.9 The 'profits' falling into each financial year determines the rate of corporation tax that applies to the PCTCT of that year. This could be the full rate, the small companies' rate or, for periods falling into FY 2000, the starting rate.

Activity 14.11: Period straddling 1 April 2000

Hewson Ltd had the following results for its year ended 30 September 2000.

Schedule D Case I	£9,500
Franked investment income	£300

Calculate the corporation tax liability for the year.

Associated companies and short accounting periods

KEY TERM

The expression 'associated companies' in tax has no connection with financial accounting. For tax purposes a company is associated with another company if either controls the other or if both are under the control of the same person or persons (individuals, partnerships or companies). Whether such a company is UK resident or not is irrelevant.

3.10 **If a company has one or more 'associated companies', then the profit limits for starting rate and small companies rate purposes are divided by the number of associated companies + 1 (for the company itself).**

3.11 Companies which have only been associated for part of an accounting period are deemed to have been associated for the whole period for the purpose of determining the profit limits.

3.12 An associated company is ignored for these purposes if it has not carried on any trade or business at any time in the accounting period (or the part of the period during which it was associated). This means you should ignore any dormant companies.

Activity 14.12: Associated companies

J Ltd has two associated companies. In the year ended 31 December 2000, it had profits chargeable to corporation tax of £400,000. Dividends received of £45,000 were received on 30 September 2000. What is the corporation tax payable for the year?

3.13 **The profit limits are reduced proportionately if an accounting period lasts for less than 12 months.**

Activity 14.13: Short accounting periods

For the nine months to 31 January 2001 a company with no other associated companies had PCTCT of £278,000 and no dividends received. Compute the corporation tax payable.

4 THE CORPORATE VENTURING SCHEME

4.1 **The corporate venturing scheme allows an investing company to obtain corporation tax relief at 20% on amounts invested in the new ordinary shares of certain unquoted 'small high risk trading companies'.**

4.2 The investing company can defer any chargeable gains made on corporate venturing investments that it reinvests in another shareholding under the scheme. Any capital loss (net of corporation tax relief) arising on a disposal of the shares can be set against the company's income.

4.3 Tax relief is withdrawn if the shares are not held for three years.

Activity 14.14: End of chapter activity

(a) Traders Ltd's profit and loss account for the year to 31 March 2001 was as follows.

	£		£
General expenses	73,611	Gross trading profit	250,000
Repairs and renewals	15,000	Bad debts recovered	
Legal and accountancy charges	1,200	(previously written off)	373
Subscriptions and donations	2,000	Commissions	800
Bad debts written off	500	Profit on sale of investment	1,515
Directors' remuneration	20,000	Interest on gilts (net, received 1	
Salaries and wages	18,000	December)	80
Patent royalties (gross)	5,000	Loan interest (gross)	1,000
Depreciation	15,000		
Rent and rates	1,500		
Net profit	101,957		
	253,768		253,768

Notes

(i) General expenses include the following.

	£
Travelling expenses of staff, including directors	1,000
Entertaining suppliers	600

(ii) Repairs and renewals include the following.

	£
Redecorating existing premises	300
Renovations to new premises to remedy wear and tear of previous owner (the premises were usable before these renovations)	500

(iii) Legal and accountancy charges are made up as follows.

	£
Debt collection service	200
Staff service agreements	50
Tax consultant's fees for special advice	30
45 year lease on new premises	100
Audit and accountancy	820
	1,200

(iv) Subscriptions and donations include the following.

	£
Donations under the gift aid scheme	200
Donation to a political party	500
Sports facilities for staff	500
Contribution to a local enterprise agency	200

(v) The commissions received were not incidental to the trade.

(vi) The chargeable gain arising on the sale of investments was £770.

(vii) All interest received was on investments made for non-trading purposes. The amounts received were the same as the amounts accrued in the year.

The tax written down value of all the equipment in use at 31 March 2000 was £14,000. The tax written down value of the car pool was £1,000.

Required

Compute Traders Ltd's profits chargeable to corporation tax for the accounting period to 31 March 2001, and the corporation tax thereon.

(b) Dealers plc had profits chargeable to corporation tax of £420,000 for its year ended 31 December 2000.

Required

Compute Dealers plc's mainstream corporation tax for the year.

(c) Springer had profits chargeable to corporation tax of £6,200 in the year to 31 December 2000.

Required

Calculate Springer Ltd's mainstream corporation tax liability for the year.

Key learning points

- Companies pay corporation tax on their profits for each accounting period, but rates of tax are set for financial years. The profits chargeable to corporation tax are income plus gains minus charges.

- Companies may be entitled to the starting rate, the small companies rate or to marginal relief, depending on their 'profits' (chargeable profits plus grossed up dividends received).

Quick quiz

1   When does an accounting period end?

2   How are profits of a long period of account divided between accounting periods?

3   How is taxed income dealt with in a corporation tax computation?

4   What charitable donations are deductible?

5   Which companies are entitled to the starting rate of corporation tax?

6   How is tax calculated when an accounting period straddles a change in the small companies rate limits?

7   What is an associated company?

Quick quiz answers

1   An accounting period finishes on the earliest of:

- 12 months after its start;
- the end of the company's period of account;
- the commencement of the company's winding up;
- the company's ceasing to be resident in the UK;
- the company's ceasing to be liable to corporation tax.

2   Profits are divided between the relevant periods as follows:

- Trading income before capital allowances is apportioned on a time basis.
- Capital allowances and balancing charges are calculated for each accounting period.
- Other income is allocated to the period to which it relates (for example rents to the period when due). Schedule D Case VI income, however, is apportioned on a time basis.
- Chargeable gains are taken into account for the accounting period in which they are realised.
- Charges on income are deducted from the profits of the accounting period in which they are paid.

3   Income which suffers a deduction of tax at source is included within the profits chargeable to corporation tax at its gross equivalent. If tax suffered on income received net exceeds tax deducted

from charges and interest paid net, the difference is subtracted from the corporation tax to find the final amount due.

4   Companies may make donations of money to charities and obtain deductions for them under the gift aid scheme as charges on income.

Donations to charities which are incurred wholly and exclusively for the purposes of the trade are Schedule D Case I deductions instead of charges on income.

5   Companies whose 'profits' are not more than £10,000.

6   The accounting period is split into two parts and the tax is calculated for each part separately. All of the items going into the calculation are apportioned on a time basis, ignoring entirely the dates when amounts were earned, received or paid.

7   A company is associated with another company if either controls the other or if both are under the control of the same person or persons (individuals, partnerships or companies). Whether such a company is UK resident or not is irrelevant.

Answers to activities _____

Activity 14.1

	1.1.99 - 31.12.99	1.1.00 - 31.5.00
	£	£
Schedule D Case I (12:5)	241,200	100,500
Schedule A	6,000	4,200
Chargeable gains	10,800	6,200
	258,000	110,900

Activity 14.2 _____

	£
Premium received by D	30,000
Less £30,000 × 2% × (10-1)	(5,400)
Premium treated as rent	24,600

Activity 14.3 _____

	£
Schedule D Case I	85,000
Schedule D Case III £(6,000 + 1,500 + 2,560 × 100/80)	10,700
Chargeable gains	2,950
	98,650
Less charges £11,856 × 100/78	(15,200)
Profits chargeable to corporation tax	83,450

Activity 14.4

	£	£
Net profit per accounts		125,492
Less: 3½% War Loan interest	700	
dividends received	3,600	
building society interest	292	
loan interest received	4,000	
		8,592
		116,900
Add: royalties paid	1,000	
gift aid donation	100	
		1,100
		118,000
Less capital allowances		5,500
Schedule D Case I		112,500
Schedule D Case III £(700 + 292 + 4,000)		4,992
Chargeable gain		13,867
		131,359
Less charges paid: royalties	1,000	
gift aid donation	100	
		1,100
Profits chargeable to corporation tax (PCTCT)		130,259

Note: UK dividends received never form part of a company's profits chargeable to corporation tax.

Activity 14.5

£2,000,000 × 30% = £600,000

Activity 14.6

	£
Schedule D Case I	42,000
Dividend plus tax credit £9,000 × 100/90	10,000
'Profits' (below £300,000 limit)	52,000
Corporation tax payable	
£42,000 × 20%	£8,400

Activity 14.7

	£
Schedule D, Case I	9,500
Franked investment income	300
'Profits'	9,800
Corporation tax on PCTCT £9,500 × 10%	£950

Activity 14.8

	£
PCTCT	296,000
Dividend plus tax credit £12,600 × 100/90	14,000
'Profits'	310,000

'Profits' are above £300,000 but below £1,500,000, so small companies' marginal relief applies.

	£
Corporation tax at full rate £296,000 × 30%	88,800
Less small companies' marginal relief	
£(1,500,000 – 310,000) × 296,000/310,000 × 1/40	(28,406)
	60,394

Activity 14.9

	£
Schedule D Case I	29,500
Franked investment income	3,000
Profits	32,500

	£
Corporation tax at small companies rate:	
£29,500 × 20%	5,900
Less: starting rate marginal relief -	
1/40 × ((£50,000 – £32,500) × £29,500/£32,500)	(397)
Corporation tax payable	5,503

Activity 14.10

	FY 1998 3 months to 31 March 1999	FY 1999 9 months to 31 December 1999
	£	£
PCTCT (divided 3:9)	161,000	483,000
'Profits' (divided 3:9)	163,500	490,500
Lower limit for SCR		
FY 1998 £300,000 × 3/12	75,000	
FY 1999 £300,000 × 9/12		225,000
Upper limit for SCR		
FY 1998 £1,500,000 × 3/12	375,000	
FY 1999 £1,500,000 × 9/12		1,125,000
	£	£
Tax on PCTCT		
FY 1998: £161,000 × 31%		49,910
Less small companies' marginal relief		
£(375,000 – 163,500) × 161,000/163,500 × 1/40		(5,207)
		44,703
FY 1999: £483,000 × 30%	144,900	
Less small companies' marginal relief		
£(1,125,000 – 490,500) × 483,000/490,500 × 1/40	(15,620)	
		129,280
Corporation tax payable		173,983

Activity 14.11

	FY 1999 6 months to 31.3.00 £	FY 2000 6 months to 30.9.00 £
'Profits' (£9,800)	4,900	4,900
Profit chargeable to corporation tax	4,750	4,750
Lower limit for starting rate (– : 6m)	-	5,000
Lower limit for SCR (6m : 6m)	150,000	150,000
Corporation tax payable		
£4,750 × 20%		950
£4,750 × 10%		475
Total corporation tax payable for 12 months APE 30.9.00		1,425

Activity 14.12

Year ended 31.12.2000 falls 3 months into FY 1999 and 9 months into FY 2000

	Total £
Profits chargeable to corporation tax	400,000
Profits for small companies rate purposes (400,000 + 45,000 × 100/90)	450,000
Lower limit for small companies rate (both years)	100,000
Upper limit for small companies rate (both years)	500,000

Small companies marginal relief applies in both years.

	£
FY 1999	
£400,000 × 3/12 × 30%	30,000
Less	
$£(500,000 - 450,000) \times \dfrac{400,000}{450,000} \times \dfrac{1}{40} \times \dfrac{3}{12}$	(278)
FY 2000	
£400,000 × 30% × 9/12	90,000
Less	
$£(500,000 - 450,000) \times \dfrac{400,000}{450,000} \times \dfrac{1}{40} \times \dfrac{9}{12}$	(834)
	118,888

Activity 14.13

(a) Reduction in the lower limit as the accounting period is only nine months long

£300,000 × $9/12$ = £225,000

(b) Reduction in the upper limit

£1,500,000 × $9/12$ = £1,125,000

(c) 'Profits' = £278,000

(d) Corporation tax

	£
£278,000 × 30%	83,400
Less small companies' marginal relief £(1,125,000 – 278,000) × 1/40	(21,175)
Corporation tax	62,225

Activity 14.14

(a) CORPORATION TAX COMPUTATION

	£	£
Net profit per accounts		101,957
Add: entertaining	600	
tax consultancy	30	
lease on new premises	100	
gift aid donation	200	
political donation	500	
patent royalties payable	5,000	
depreciation	15,000	
		21,430
		123,387
Less: commissions (chargeable under Schedule D Case VI)	800	
profit on sale of investment	1,515	
loan interest	1,000	
interest on gilts	80	
capital allowances (W)	3,750	
		7,145
Schedule D Case I		116,242
Schedule D Case III £1,000 + £80 × 100/80		1,100
Schedule D Case VI		800
Chargeable gain		770
		118,912
Less charges paid (patent royalties and gift aid)		5,200
Profits chargeable to corporation tax		113,712

The profits for small companies rate purposes are below the lower limit, so the small companies rate applies.

The corporation tax liability is £113,712 × 20% = £22,742

Working: capital allowances

Equipment £15,000 × 25%	£3,750

The tax written down value of the car pool is transferred to the main pool at the start of the year.

(b) Dealers plc's profits for small companies rate purposes are £420,000 so tax is payable at the marginal rate in both FY 99 and FY 00.

	FY 1999 and FY 2000
	£
Profits chargeable to corporation tax	420,000
Profits for small companies rate purposes	420,000
Upper limit	1,500,000
Lower limit	300,000
Corporation tax	
FY 1999 and 2000	
£420,000 × 30%	126,000
Less marginal relief	
£(1,500,000 – 420,000) × 1/40	(27,000)
Mainstream corporation tax	99,000

(c) Springer Ltd's 'profits' are £6,200. This means they qualify for the lower rate in FY 2000 and the small companies rate in FY 1999:

	£
FY 1999	
£6,200 × 3/12 × 20%	310
FY 2000	
£6,200 × 9/12 × 10%	465
	775

Chapter 15 Payment of tax by companies

Chapter topic list

1 Returns under the corporation tax self assessment system

2 Payment of tax and interest

3 Income tax suffered or withheld from charges and interest

4 Company return forms

Learning objectives

On completion of this chapter you will be able to:

	Performance criteria	Range Statement
• give advice on the maintenance of accounts and the recording of information relevant to tax returns	18.5.6	18.5.1
• ensure corporation tax returns are completed correctly and submitted on time	18.5.3 18.5.5	18.5.1 18.5.7
• ensure payments of tax are made on time	18.5.7	18.5.1
• account for income tax on quarterly returns	18.4.4	18.4.1

BPP
PUBLISHING

1 RETURNS UNDER THE CORPORATION TAX SELF ASSESSMENT SYSTEM

1.1 A company's tax return (CT600) must include a self assessment of any tax payable.

DEVOLVED ASSESSMENT ALERT

A copy of the CTSA return form (CT 600) is included in the appendix to this text.

Returns

1.2 **An obligation to file a return arises only when the company receives a notice requiring a return.** A return is required for each accounting period.

1.3 A company that does not receive a notice requiring a return must, if it is chargeable to tax, **notify the Revenue within twelve months of the end of the accounting period.** Failure to do so results in a maximum penalty equal to the tax unpaid twelve months after the end of the accounting period.

1.4 A return for each of the company's accounting periods is due on or before the filing date. This is the later of:

(a) **12 months after the end of the accounting period**

(b) **if the accounting period ends in a period of account which is not more than 18 months long, 12 months from the end of the period of account**

(c) **if the accounting ends in a period of account which is more than 18 months long, 30 months from the start of the period of account; and**

(d) **three months from the date on which the notice requiring the return was made.**

Activity 15.1: Filing date

A Ltd prepares accounts for the eighteen months to 30 June 2000. Assuming a notice requiring a return was issued to A Ltd in good time, state the periods for which A Ltd must file a tax return and the filing dates.

1.5 There is a £100 penalty for a failure to submit a return on time, rising to £200 if the delay exceeds three months. These penalties become £500 and £1,000 respectively when a return was late (or never submitted) for each of the preceding two accounting periods.

1.6 An additional tax geared penalty is applied if a return is more than six months late. The penalty is 10% of the tax unpaid six months after the return was due if the total delay is up to 12 months, but 20% of that tax if the return is over 12 months late.

1.7 There is a mitigatable tax geared penalty for a fraudulent or negligent return and for failing to correct an innocent error without unreasonable delay. The maximum penalty is equal to the tax that would have been lost had the return been accepted as correct. If a company is liable to more than one tax geared penalty, the total penalty is limited to the maximum single penalty that could be charged.

1.8 A company may amend a return within twelve months of the filing date. The Revenue may correct obvious errors in a return or amendment within nine months of the day it was filed.

The company may amend its return so as to reject the correction. If the time limit for amendments has expired, the company may reject the correction by giving notice within three months.

1.9 Wherever possible claims must be made on a tax return or on an amendment to it and must be quantified at the time the return is made.

Records

1.10 Companies must keep records until the latest of:

(a) six years from the end of the accounting period;
(b) the date any enquiries are completed;
(c) the date after which enquiries may not be commenced.

All business records and accounts, including contracts and receipts, must be kept.

1.11 If a return is demanded more than six years after the end of the accounting period, any records which the company still has must be kept until the later of the end of any enquiry and the expiry of the right to start an enquiry.

1.12 Failure to keep records can lead to a penalty of up to £3,000 for each accounting period affected. However, this penalty does not apply when the only records which have not been kept are ones which could only have been needed for the purposes of claims, elections or notices not included in the return.

1.13 The Revenue do not generally insist on original records being kept but original records relating to payments made net of tax must be preserved.

Enquiries

1.14 The Revenue may enquire into a return or an amendment, provided that they give written notice that they are going to enquire by a year after the later of:

(a) the filing date;

(b) the 31 January, 30 April, 31 July or 31 October next following the actual date of delivery of the return or amendment.

Only one enquiry may be made in respect of any one return or amendment.

1.15 If a notice of an enquiry has been given, the Revenue may demand that the company produce documents. Documents relating to an appeal need not be produced and the company may appeal against a notice requiring documents to be produced.

1.16 If the Revenue demand documents, but the company does not produce them, there is a penalty of £50. There is also a daily penalty, which applies for each day from the day after the imposition of the £50 penalty until the documents are produced.

1.17 The Revenue may amend a self assessment at any time during an enquiry if they believe there might otherwise be a loss of tax. The company may appeal against such an amendment

1.18 An enquiry ends when the Revenue give notice that it has been completed and notify what they believe to be the correct amount of tax payable. Before that time, the company may ask the Commissioners to order the Revenue to notify the completion of its enquiry by a specified date. Such a direction will be given unless the Revenue can demonstrate that they have reasonable grounds for continuing the enquiry.

1.19 The company has 30 days from the end of an enquiry to amend its self assessment in accordance with the Revenue's conclusions. If the Revenue are not satisfied with the company's amendments, they have a further 30 days to amend the self assessment. The company then has another 30 days in which it may appeal against the Revenue's amendments.

Determinations and discovery assessments

1.20 If a return is not delivered by the filing date, the Revenue may issue a determination of the tax payable. There is no appeal against this but it is automatically replaced by any self assessment made by the company by the later of five years from the filing date and 12 months from the determination.

1.21 If the Revenue believe that not enough tax has been assessed they can make a discovery assessment. When a tax return has been delivered this power is limited:

(a) No discovery assessment can be made on account of an error as to the basis on which the tax liability ought to be computed, if the basis generally prevailing at the time when the return was made was applied.

(b) A discovery assessment can only be made if either:

(i) the loss of tax is due to fraudulent or negligent conduct; or

(ii) the Revenue could not reasonably be expected to have been aware of the loss, given the information so far supplied to them, when their right to start an enquiry expired or when they notified the company that an enquiry had finished.

2 PAYMENT OF TAX AND INTEREST

Tax

2.1 Corporation tax is due for payment **by small and medium sized companies nine months after the end of the accounting period.**

2.2 A system of quarterly payments on account for corporation tax liabilities applies **for large companies.**

2.3 The quarterly payments system is being phased in over a four year period. For the first accounting period ending after 30.6.99 a large company paid 60% of its corporation tax by four equal instalments each of 15% with the remaining 40% as a balancing payment nine months after the accounting end. Then:

- **72% in instalments (4 × 18%), 28% as a balance in year 2**
- **88% in instalments (4 × 22%), 12% as a balance in year 3**
- **100% in instalments (4 × 25%) in year 4 and thereafter**

2.4 The instalments are to be paid on the 14th day of the month, starting in the seventh month. Provided that the accounting period is twelve months long subsequent instalments are due in the tenth month during the accounting period and in the first and fourth months after the end of the accounting period. If the accounting period is less than twelve months long subsequent instalments are due at three monthly intervals but with the final payment being due in the fourth month of the next accounting period.

2.5 EXAMPLE

X Ltd is a large company with a 31 December accounting year end.

Instalments of corporation tax will be due to be paid by X Ltd on:

- 14 July and 14 October in the accounting period
- 14 January and 14 April after the accounting period ends

Thus for the year ended 31 December 2000 instalment payments are due on 14 July 2000, 14 October 2000, 14 January 2001 and 14 April 2001.

2.6 Instalments are based on the estimated corporation tax liability for the current period (not the previous period). The company is therefore required to estimate its corporation tax liability before the end of the accounting period, and must revise its estimate each quarter.

2.7 Broadly, a 'large company' is a company that pays corporation tax at the full rate (profits exceed £1.5 million where there are no associated companies). A company is not required to pay instalments in the first year that it is 'large', unless its profits exceed £10 million (reduced proportionately if there are associated companies).

2.8 There is a de minimis limit in that any company whose liability does not exceed £10,000 need not pay by instalments.

Interest

2.9 Interest is charged on corporation tax paid late and interest is paid to companies on corporation tax overpaid or paid early. This interest paid/received is dealt with under Schedule D Case III as interest paid /received on a non trading loan relationship.

2.10 Interest runs from the due date on over/underpaid instalments. The position is looked at cumulatively after the due date for each instalment. The Revenue calculate the interest position after the company submits its corporation tax return.

2.11 EXAMPLE

X plc prepared accounts to 31.12.00. The company has always prepared accounts to 31 December each year. It paid CT instalments of:

Date	Amount £
14.7.00	3.5m
14.10.00	6.5m
14.01.01	3.5m
14.4.01	3.5m
	17m

X plc's CT return showed a CT liability of £25m. The £8m balance was paid on 1.10.01. £18m (72% × £25m) should have been paid in instalments. The under(over) payments were:

Date	Paid £	Correct £	Under(over) paid £
14.7.00	3.5m	4.5m	1m
14.10.00	6.5m	4.5m	
	10m	9m	(1m)
14.1.01	3.5m	4.5m	
	13.5m	13.5m	-
14.4.01	3.5m	4.5m	
	17m	18m	1m

Interest would be charged (received) as follows.

14.7.00 - 13.10.00	Interest charged on £1m
14.10.00 - 13.1.01	Interest received on £1m
14.1.01 - 13.4.01	No interest
14.4.01 - 30.9.01	Interest charged on £1m

3 INCOME TAX SUFFERED OR WITHHELD FROM CHARGES AND INTEREST

3.1 **Companies may receive some income which has suffered 20% or 22% income tax at source.** This is known as taxed income, or unfranked investment income (UFII). The cash income plus the income tax suffered, that is the gross figure, forms part of a company's profits chargeable to corporation tax. The income tax suffered is deductible from the corporation tax liability.

3.2 **When the company pays interest or a charge on income it deducts the gross amount in its corporation tax computation. For items paid net** (such as debenture interest, and patent royalties), **it acts as an agent for the Revenue and retains income tax at 20% (interest) or 22% (charges) on the gross amount for payment to the Revenue.** The *net* amount is then payable to the payees (for example the debenture holders).

3.3 **Note that income tax is accounted for on amounts paid and received, even though interest is dealt with on an accruals basis in working out profits.**

3.4 A company must deduct 20% tax from interest paid unless it is interest on a loan for a year or less or interest payable to a bank.

Quarterly accounting for income tax

3.5 **Income tax is accounted for by companies on a quarterly basis on a return form CT 61. Returns are made for each of the quarters to 31 March, 30 June, 30 September and 31 December.** If the end of a company's accounting period does not coincide with one of these dates, a fifth return must be made to the end of the accounting period (and a new return period started at the beginning of the company's next accounting period).

Activity 15.2: Quarterly returns

S Ltd makes up accounts to 31 May each year. Show the income tax quarterly return periods for this company for the year to 31 May 2000.

3.6 Each quarterly return has details of income tax suffered and income tax withheld from interest and charges.

3.7 The company must submit the CT 61 and account to the Revenue for any income tax payable 14 days after the end of the return period. Interest runs from this date.

3.8 The overall amount of income tax due is reduced by that suffered on income received.

3.9 If a company has tax suffered on income exceeding its tax deducted from payments, it can reclaim the income tax suffered by recovering income tax payments already made through the quarterly accounting system or by reducing its corporation tax liability. If appropriate a repayment of income tax will be made after the corporation tax computation has been submitted.

3.10 Workings for income tax returns should be maintained in terms of the tax deducted and tax suffered rather than gross income and payment figures. Let us have a look at an example.

3.11 EXAMPLE

Y Ltd paid a patent royalty of £8,481 on 13 June 2000, and received debenture interest of £3,200 on 15 June 2000. The company prepares accounts to 31 March 2001. Show the CT 61 return for the quarter ended 30 June 2000 and state by what date income tax should have been paid over to the Revenue.

3.12 ANSWER

Return period	Income tax Suffered	Income tax withheld	Income Tax due	Due date for income tax
	£	£	£	
1.4.00 - 30.6.00	800	2,392	1,592	14.7.00

The tax suffered on the debenture interest received was $£3,200 \times \dfrac{100}{80} \times 20\% = £800$

The tax withheld from the patent royalty paid was $£8,481 \times \dfrac{100}{78} \times 22\% = £2,392$

Activity 15.3: Quarterly accounting for income tax

Income plc has the following income and payments for the year to 31 March 2001.

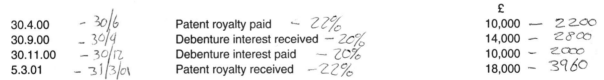

			£	
30.4.00	$-\,30/6$	Patent royalty paid $-\,22\%$	10,000	2200
30.9.00	$-\,30/9$	Debenture interest received $-\,20\%$	14,000	2800
30.11.00	$-\,30/12$	Debenture interest paid $-\,20\%$	10,000	2000
5.3.01	$-\,31/3/01$	Patent royalty received $-\,22\%$	18,000	3960

All of the above figures are gross.

Set out the relevant CT 61 income tax returns.

---

4 COMPANY RETURN FORMS

4.1 A copy of the corporation tax self assessment return form (CT 600) is included in the appendix at the end of this text. You may be asked to complete this return form as part of your Devolved Assessment and you should start to familiarise yourself with it now. Note that the supplementary pages to the return are not included here as you will not be required to deal with them in your Devolved Assessment. Please see page (x) of this text for a note regarding the version of the form that we have used.

4.2 A copy of the CT61 form is also included in the appendix to this text. Familiarise yourself with it now. The form may be given in your assessment as a source document from which income tax information must be identified or as a document which you have to complete.

4.3 You will be able to practice using both of the above forms when you try the Devolved Assessments in BPP's Unit 18 Devolved Assessment Kit.

Activity 15.4: End of chapter activity

(a) Bean Ltd is a trading company that regularly pays corporation tax at the full rate. It has always prepared accounts to 31 December each year. Its profits chargeable to corporation tax for the year to 31.12.00 were £2,150,000.

Required

State the dates and amounts of corporation tax due in respect of the above period.

(b) Barnett Ltd, a UK trading company, was formed in 1992 with the following capital structure which has remained unchanged since that date.

	£
£1 ordinary shares issued at par	256,000
50 pence 10% preference shares	80,000
12% debentures 2001/05	100,000

During the year to 31 March 2001 the following transactions occurred. The amounts stated are the actual cash amounts paid or received.

Payments

15 April	Six months' debenture interest to 31 March 2000
16 October	Six months' debenture interest to 30 September 2000
31 March	£425 patent royalty

Receipts

20 May	£1,000 bank deposit interest
15 June	£3,404 patent royalties
16 February	£11,062 patent royalties

Required

Schedule the details to be included on form CT 61 (quarterly returns) for all relevant periods, stating the due dates of payment where applicable and how any balances outstanding at 31 March 2001 would be dealt with.

Key learning points

- Returns must, in general, be filed within twelve months of the end of an accounting period.

- The Revenue can enquire into returns.

- In general, corporation tax is due nine months after the end of an accounting period but large companies must pay their corporation tax in four quarterly instalments.

- Income tax is accounted for quarterly, but income tax suffered is always recovered in full for each accounting period.

Quick quiz

1   What are the initial flat rate penalties for failure to deliver a corporation tax return on time?

2   For how long must a company keep records?

3   When must the Revenue give notice that it is going to start an enquiry?

4   State the due dates for the payment of quarterly instalments of corporation tax for a 12 month accounting period to 31.12.00.

5   Which companies must normally pay quarterly instalments of their corporation tax liability?

6   For which periods are CT61s due?

Quick quiz answers _____

1   £100 then rising to £200 if the return is more than three months late. These penalties rise to £500 and £1,000 respectively if a return was late or never submitted in each of the two previous accounting periods.

2   Companies must keep records until the latest of:

   (a)   six years from the end of the accounting period;
   (b)   the date any enquiries are completed;
   (c)   the date after which enquiries may not be commenced.

   All business records and accounts, including contracts and receipts, must be kept.

   If a return is demanded more than six years after the end of the accounting period, any records which the company still has must be kept until the later of the end of any enquiry and the expiry of the right to start an enquiry.

3   The Revenue must give written notice that they are going to enquire by a year after the later of:

   (a)   the filing date;

   (b)   the 31 January, 30 April, 31 July or 31 October next following the actual date of delivery of the return or amendment.

4   14 July 2000, 14 October 2000, 14 January 2001 and 14 April 2001.

5   Companies which are liable to corporation tax at the full rate.

6   CT 61s are due for each of the quarters to 31 March, 30 June, 30 September and 31 December. A return is also due for the period ending on the company's accounting date if it is not one of these dates.

Answers to activities _____

Activity 15.1

The company must file a return for each of the two accounting periods. The first accounting period is the twelve months to 31 December 1999 and the second is the six months to 30 June 2000. The filing date is twelve months after the end of the period of account, 30 June 2001 for both returns.

Activity 15.2 _____

   (a)   1 June 1999 to 30 June 1999
   (b)   1 July 1999 to 30 September 1999
   (c)   1 October 1999 to 31 December 1999
   (d)   1 January 2000 to 31 March 2000
   (e)   1 April 2000 to 31 May 2000

Activity 15.3

Return period	Tax on payments £	Tax on income £	Income tax Due £	Income tax Repayable £	Due date
1.4.00 - 30.6.00	2,200	0	2,200	0	14.7.00
1.7.00 - 30.9.00	0	2,800	0	(2,200) (a)	14.10.00
1.10.00 - 31.12.00	2,000	0	1,400 (b)	0	14.1.01
1.1.01 - 31.3.01	0	3,960	0	(1,400) (a)	14.4.01
	4,200	6,760			
		4,200			
		2,560 (c)			

Notes

(a) The repayment is restricted to income tax already paid in the same accounting period. The return is due by the date shown, but there is no set date by which the Revenue must make the repayment.

(b) Up to the end of the previous quarter, the net tax suffered is £(2,800 – 2,200) = £600. The tax to be accounted for is therefore £(2,000 – 600) = £1,400.

(c) £2,560, the net income tax suffered over the year, will be set against the company's corporation tax liability. If that liability is less than £2,560, the company will receive a repayment of income tax suffered.

Activity 15.4

(a) Corporation tax due:

£2,150,000 × 30%   £645,000

The year to 31 December 2000 is the second accounting period ending after 30.6.99 and Bean Ltd is a large company. This means that 72% of the full liability, £464,400 (72% × £645,000) must be paid in four quarterly instalments as follows.

Due date	Amount
14.7.00	116,100
14.10.00	11116,100
14.1.01	116,100
14.4.01	116,100
	464,400

The balancing payment of £180,600 is due on 1 October 2001.

(b) *Income tax*

Return period	Tax on payments £	Tax on income £	Income tax Due £	Income tax Repayable £	Due date
1.4.00 - 30.6.00	1,200	960	240	0	14.7.00
1.7.00 - 30.9.00 No return	0	0	0	0	
1.10.00 - 31.12.00	1,200	0	1,200	0	14.1.01
1.1.01 - 31.3.01	120	3,120	0	1,440	14.4.01*

* This is the due date for the return. There is no due date for the Inland Revenue to make a repayment.

The net income tax suffered over the year (£1,560) will be deducted from the company's corporation tax liability for the year. No amount is carried forward.

Chapter 16 Corporation tax losses

Chapter topic list

1   Reliefs for losses

2   Loss relief against future income: s 393(1) ICTA 1988

3   Loss relief against total profits: s 393A(1) ICTA 1988

4   Reliefs for deficits on non trading loan relationships

Learning objectives

On completion of this chapter you will be able to:

	Performance criteria	Range Statement
• discuss the various reliefs available for a trading loss made by a company	18.5.1	18.5.2
• compute the effect of carrying a loss forward or backwards on the taxable profits of a company	18.5.1	18.5.2
• show how a non trading deficit on a loan relationship is relieved	18.5.1	18.5.2

BPP PUBLISHING

1 RELIEFS FOR LOSSES

Trading losses

1.1 **The following reliefs are available for trading losses incurred by a company.**

(a) **Set-off against current profits**
(b) **Carry back against earlier profits**
(c) **Carry forward against future trading profits**

Reliefs (a) and (b) must be claimed, and are given in the order shown. Relief (c) is given for any loss for which the other reliefs are not claimed.

Capital losses

1.2 **Capital losses can only be set against capital gains in the same or future accounting periods,** never against income. Capital losses must be set against the first available gains.

Schedule D Case VI losses

1.3 Where in an accounting period a company makes a loss in a transaction taxable under Schedule D Case VI, **the company can set the loss against any income from other transactions taxable under Case VI in the same or later accounting periods.** The loss must be set against the earliest income available.

2 LOSS RELIEF AGAINST FUTURE INCOME: S 393(1) ICTA 1988

2.1 **A company must set off a trading loss not otherwise relieved against income from the same trade in future accounting periods. Relief is given against the first available profits.**

2.2 Further relief (under s 393(9) ICTA 1988) is available for trade charges which are unrelieved in an accounting period. These **unrelieved trade charges are carried forward and set off against future trading profits in the same way** as a s 393(1) loss. In practice, such unrelieved trade charges are added to any trading losses being carried forward under s 393(1). Computations can then include a single line for 's 393(1)(9) relief'.

2.3 Relief under s 393(9) is only available in respect of payments made wholly and exclusively for the purposes of the trade (such as patent royalties). Payments not made wholly and exclusively for trading purposes (such as payments under a charitable deed of covenant) are set against current year profits before trade charges in the first instance, but if a loss is brought back under s 393A(1) (see below) and trade charges have already been set against profits, those trade charges are not set free to carry forward.

Activity 16.1: Carrying forward losses

A Ltd has the following results for the three years to 31 March 2001.

	Year ended		
	31.3.99	*31.3.00*	*31.3.01*
	£	£	£
Trading profit/(loss)	(8,000)	3,000	6,000
Non-trade charges	300	400	700
Trade charges	400	150	200

Calculate the profits chargeable to corporation tax for all three years showing any losses available to carry forward at 1 April 2001.

3 LOSS RELIEF AGAINST TOTAL PROFITS: S 393A(1) ICTA 1988

3.1 **A company may claim to set a trading loss incurred in an accounting period against total profits (before deducting any charges) of the same accounting period.** The result may be that trade charges become unrelieved, and available to carry forward.

3.2 **Such a loss may then be carried back and set against total profits (after deducting trade charges but before deducting non-trade charges) of an accounting period falling wholly or partly within the 12 months of the start of the period in which the loss was incurred.**

In each such period, enough profits must be left to match against trade charges, so that trade charges do not become unrelieved and available to carry forward.

If a period falls partly outside the 12 months, loss relief is limited to the proportion of the period's profits (before all charges) equal to the proportion of the period which falls within the 12 months.

3.3 **The 12 month carry back period is extended to 36 months where the trading loss arose in the 12 months immediately before the company ceased to trade.**

3.4 Any possible s 393A(1) claim for the period of the loss must be made before any excess loss can be carried back to a previous period.

3.5 Any carry-back is to more recent periods before earlier periods. Relief for earlier losses is given before relief for later losses.

3.6 A claim for relief against current or prior period profits must be made within two years of the end of the accounting period in which the loss arose. Any claim must be for the *whole* loss (to the extent that profits are available to relieve it). The loss can however be reduced by not claiming full capital allowances, so that higher capital allowances are given (on higher tax written down values) in future years. Any loss remaining unrelieved may be carried forward under s 393(1) to set against future profits of the same trade.

Activity 16.2: S393A loss relief

Helix Ltd has the following results.

	Year ended			
	30.9.98	*30.9.99*	*30.9.00*	*30.9.01*
	£	£	£	£
Trading profit/(loss)	2,000	11,500	10,000	(35,000)
Bank interest	400	500	500	500
Chargeable gains	800	0	0	4,000
Charges on income:				
trade charges	0	1,000	1,000	1,000
non-trade charges	250	250	250	250

Show the PCTCT for all the years affected assuming that s 393A(1) loss relief is claimed. Assume the provisions of FA 2000 continue to apply.

4 RELIEFS FOR DEFICITS ON NON-TRADING LOAN RELATIONSHIPS

4.1 A deficit on a non-trading loan relationship may be set, in whole or part, against any profit of the same accounting period. Relief is given after relief for any trading loss brought forward but before relief is given for a trading loss of the same or future period.

Activity 16.3: S393A loss relief

Witherspoon Ltd has the following results for the two years ended 31 December 2001:

	2000	*2001*
	£	£
Trading profit/(loss)	40,000	(12,000)
Trading losses brought forward	(20,000)	-
Bank interest receivable	2,000	
Interest payable on a loan for non-trading purposes	(11,000)	

Show how relief may be given for the deficit on the non-trading loan relationship in the year ended 31.12.00. Assume that the FA 2000 provisions continue to apply.

4.2 A deficit may be set against non-trading income arising from loan relationships in the previous twelve months provided the income has not been reduced by:

(a) loss relief in respect of a period prior to the deficit period
(b) trade charges

4.3 A deficit may be set against the non-trading profits of the company in the following accounting period. Non-trade profits represent PCTCT less Schedule D Case I.

4.4 Any deficits unrelieved after claiming the above reliefs are automatically carried forward and treated as a deficit for the next accounting period.

4.5 A claim under 4.1 or 4.2 above must be made within two years of the deficit period. A claim under 4.3 must be made within two years of the accounting period in which the deficit is used.

4.6 A company can choose how much deficit to relieve in the current period, how much to carry back and how much to carry forward: unlike s 393A relief, these are not all or nothing claims, and the company can choose to carry back a deficit even if it does not claim current period relief.

Activity 16.4: End of chapter activity

Ferraro Ltd has the following results.

	y/e 31.12.96 £	y/e 31.12.97 £	9m to 30.9.98 £	y/e 30.9.99 £	y/e 30.9.00 £
Trading profit (loss)	10,000	34,480	6,200	4,320	(100,000)
Bank deposit interest accrued	100	200	80	240	260
Rents receivable	3,000	1,200	1,420	1,440	1,600
Capital gain				12,680	
Allowable capital loss		5,000			9,423
Patent royalties (gross)	1,000	1,000	0	1,000	1,500

Required

Compute all profits chargeable to corporation tax, claiming loss reliefs as early as possible. State any amounts carried forward as at 30 September 2000.

Key learning points

- Trading losses may be relieved against current total profits, against total profits of earlier periods or against future trading income.

- Relief against current total profits can lead to trade charges becoming unrelieved and available to carry forward. This does not happen with relief against profits of an earlier period.

- Loss relief can lead to non-trade charges being wasted.

- There are similar reliefs for deficits on non-trading loan relationships, but the setoffs are against different profits.

Quick quiz

1   Against what profits may trading losses carried forward be set?

2   What charges may be carried forward?

3   To what extent may trade losses be carried back?

Quick quiz answers

1   Profits from the same trade.

2   Trade charges which are unrelieved in an accounting period.

3   A Schedule D Case I loss can be carried back and set against total profits (after deducting trade charges but before deducting non-trade charges) of accounting periods falling wholly or partly within the 12 months before the accounting period in which the loss arose. A carryback claim cannot be made unless a claim to set the loss off in the current period is made first.

Answers to activities

Activity 16.1

	Year ended		
	31.3.99	*31.3.00*	*31.3.01*
	£	£	£
Schedule D Case I	0	3,000	6,000
Less: s 393(1) loss relief		(3,000)	(5,550)
non-trade charges			(450)
PCTCT	0	0	0
Unrelieved non-trade charges	300	400	250

Loss memorandum

	£
Loss for y/e 31.3.99	8,000
Unrelieved trade charges y/e 31.3.99	400
Loss carried forward at 1.4.99	8,400
Less s 393(1)(9) relief y/e 31.3.00	3,000
	5,400
Unrelieved trade charges y/e 31.3.00	150
Loss carried forward at 1.4.00	5,550
Less s 393(1)(9) relief y/e 31.3.01	5,550
	0
Unrelieved trade charges y/e 31.3.01	200
Loss carried forward at 1.4.01	200

Activity 16.2

The loss of the year to 30.9.01 is relieved under s 393A ICTA 1988 against current year profits and against profits of the previous twelve months.

	Year ended			
	30.9.98	*30.9.99*	*30.9.00*	*30.9.01*
	£	£	£	£
Schedule D Case I	2,000	11,500	10,000	0
Schedule D Case III	400	500	500	500
Chargeable gains	800	0	0	4,000
	3,200	12,000	10,500	4,500
Less s 393A current period relief	0	0	0	(4,500)
	3,200	12,000	10,500	0
Less: trade charges	0	(1,000)	(1,000)	0
	3,200	11,000	9,500	0
Less s 393A carryback relief	0	0	(9,500)	0
	3,200	11,000	0	0
Less: Non-trade charges	(250)	(250)	0	0
PCTCT	2,950	10,750	0	0
Unrelieved non-trade charges			250	250

	£
S 393A (1) loss memorandum	
Loss incurred in y/e 30.9.01	35,000
Less s 393A (1): y/e 30.9.01	(4,500)
y/e 30.9.00	(9,500)
Remaining loss	21,000
Unrelieved trade charges y/e 30.9.01	1,000
Loss available to carry forward under s 393(1)(9)	22,000

Activity 16.3

	2000
	£
Schedule D Case I	40,000
s 393(1) losses brought forward	(20,000)
	20,000
Less: non-trading deficit £(11,000 – 2,000)	(9,000)
	11,000
Losses carried back s 393A	(11,000)
Chargeable profits	Nil

Activity 6.4

	Accounting periods				
	12m to	12m to	9m to	12m to	12m to
	31.12.96	31.12.97	30.9.98	30.9.99	30.9.00
	£	£	£	£	£
Schedule D Case I	10,000	34,480	6,200	4,320	0
Schedule D Case III	100	200	80	240	260
Schedule A	3,000	1,200	1,420	1,440	1,600
Chargeable gain (12,680 – 5,000)	0	0	0	7,680	0
	13,100	35,880	7,700	13,680	1,860
Less s 393A - current	0	0	0	0	1,860
	13,100	35,880	7,700	13,680	0
Less charges	1,000	1,000	0	1,000	0
	12,100	34,880	7,700	12,680	0
Less s 393A - c/b				(12,680)	(0)
PCTCT	12,100	34,880	7,700	0	0

The loss carried forward against future profits of the same trade is £100,000 – £ (12,680 + 1,860) + £1,500 trade charges = £86,960.

The allowable capital loss of £9,423 during the year ended 30 September 2000 is carried forward against future chargeable gains.

BPP PUBLISHING

Appendix

INDEX TO TAX FORMS

SELF EMPLOYMENT PAGES

Income for the year ended 5 April 2001

Inland Revenue

SELF-EMPLOYMENT

Fill in these boxes first

Name

Tax reference

If you want help, look up the box numbers in the Notes

Business details

Name of business

3.1

Description of business

3.2

Address of business

3.3

Postcode

Accounting period - read the Notes, page SEN2 before filling in these boxes

Start

3.4 / /

End

3.5 / /

- Tick box 3.5A if you entered details for all relevant accounting periods on last year's Tax Return and boxes 3.11 to 3.70 and 3.93 to 3.109 will be blank (read step 3 on page SEN2)

  3.5A

- Tick box 3.6 if details in boxes 3.1 or 3.3 have changed since your last Tax Return

  3.6

- Tick box 3.7 if your accounts do not cover the period from the last accounting date (explain why in the 'Additional information' box below)

  3.7

- Tick box 3.8A if your accounting date has changed (only if this is a permanent change and you want it to count for tax)

  3.8A

- Tick box 3.8B if this is the second or further change (explain why you have not used the same date as last year in the 'Additional information' box)

  3.8B

- Date of commencement if after 5 April 1997

  3.9 / /

- Date of cessation if before 6 April 2001

  3.10 / /

Additional information

Income and expenses - annual turnover below £15,000

*If your annual turnover is £15,000 or more, **ignore** boxes 3.11 to 3.13.*

Now fill in Page SE2

*If your annual turnover is below £15,000, **fill in boxes 3.11 to 3.13 instead of Page SE2**. Read the Notes, page SEN2*

- Turnover, other business receipts and goods etc. taken for personal use (and balancing charges) **3.11**

- Expenses allowable for tax (including capital allowances) **3.12**

Net profit (put figure in brackets if a loss)

box 3.11 *minus* box 3.12

3.13

Now fill in Page SE3

SA103

BPP PUBLISHING

Appendix

Income and expenses - annual turnover £15,000 or more

You must fill in this Page if your annual turnover is £15,000 or more - read the Notes, page SEN2

If you were registered for VAT, do the figures in boxes 3.16 to 3.51, include VAT? **3.14** ▢   or exclude VAT? **3.15** ▢

Sales/business income (turnover)

3.16 ▢

	Disallowable expenses included in boxes 3.33 to 3.50	Total expenses
● Cost of sales	**3.17**	**3.33**
● Construction industry subcontractor costs	**3.18**	**3.34**
● Other direct costs	**3.19**	**3.35**

box 3.16 *minus* (box 3.33 + box 3.34 + box 3.35)
Gross profit/(loss) **3.36**
Other income/profits **3.37**

	Disallowable	Total expenses
● Employee costs	**3.20**	**3.38**
● Premises costs	**3.21**	**3.39**
● Repairs	**3.22**	**3.40**
● General administrative expenses	**3.23**	**3.41**
● Motor expenses	**3.24**	**3.42**
● Travel and subsistence	**3.25**	**3.43**
● Advertising, promotion and entertainment	**3.26**	**3.44**
● Legal and professional costs	**3.27**	**3.45**
● Bad debts	**3.28**	**3.46**
● Interest	**3.29**	**3.47**
● Other finance charges	**3.30**	**3.48**
● Depreciation and loss/(profit) on sale	**3.31**	**3.49**
● Other expenses	**3.32**	**3.50**

Put the total of boxes 3.17 to 3.32 in box 3.53 below

Total expenses

total of boxes 3.38 to 3.50
3.51

boxes 3.36 + 3.37 minus box 3.51
Net profit/(loss) **3.52**

Tax adjustments to net profit or loss

	total of boxes 3.17 to 3.32
● Disallowable expenses	**3.53** £
● Goods etc. taken for personal use and other adjustments (apart from disallowable expenses) that increase profits	**3.54** £
● Balancing charges	**3.55** £

Total additions to net profit (deduct from net loss)

box 3.53 + 3.54+3.55
3.56 £

● Capital allowances	**3.57** £
● Deductions from net profit (add to net loss)	**3.58** £

boxes 3.57 + 3.58
3.59 £

Net business profit for tax purposes (put figure in brackets if a loss)

boxes 3.52 + 3.56 minus box 3.59
3.60 £

Now fill in Page SE3

> **You must fill in this Page (leave blank any boxes that do not apply to you)**

Capital allowances - summary

		Capital allowances	Balancing charge
● Motor cars (Separate calculations must be made for each motor car costing more than £12,000 and for cars used partly for private motoring.)		3.61 £	3.62 £
● Other business plant and machinery		3.63 £	3.64 £
● Agricultural or Industrial Buildings Allowance (A separate calculation must be made for each block of expenditure.)		3.65 £	3.66 £
● Other capital allowances claimed (Separate calculations must be made.)		3.67 £	3.68 £
		total of column above	total of column above
● **Total capital allowances/balancing charges**		3.69 £	3.70 £

Adjustments to arrive at taxable profit or loss

Basis period begins   3.71 / /   and ends   3.72 / /

- ● Tick box 3.72A if the figure in box 3.88 is provisional — 3.72A £
- ● Tick box 3.72B if the special arrangements for certain trades detailed in the guidance notes apply (see Notes, pages SEN8 and SEN10) — 3.72B £
- ● Profit or loss of this account for tax purposes (box 3.13 or 3.60) — 3.73 £
- ● Adjustment to arrive at profit or loss for this basis period — 3.74 £
- ● Overlap profit brought forward 3.75 £   Deduct overlap relief used this year 3.76 £
- ● Overlap profit carried forward 3.77 £

Adjustment for farmers' averaging (see Notes, page SEN8 if you made a loss for 2000-2001) — 3.78 £

Adjustment on change of basis — 3.78A £

Net profit for 2000-2001 (if loss, enter '0') — 3.79 £

Allowable loss for 2000-2001 (if you made a profit, enter 0) — 3.80 £

- ● Loss offset against other income for 2000-01 — 3.81 £
- ● Loss to carry back — 3.82 £
- ● Loss to carry forward (that is allowable loss not claimed in any other way) — 3.83 £
- ● Losses brought forward from earlier years — 3.84 £
- ● Losses brought forward from earlier years used this year — 3.85 £

Taxable profit after losses brought forward — box 3.79 *minus* box 3.85 3.86 £

- ● Any other business income (for example Business Start-up Allowance received in 2000-01) — 3.87 £

Total taxable profits from this business — box 3.86 *minus* box 3.87 3.88 £

Please turn over

Class 4 National Insurance Contributions

● Tick this box if exception or deferment applies — **3.89** ☐

● Adjustments to profit chargeable to Class 4 National Insurance Contributions — **3.90** £

Class 4 National Insurance Contributions due — **3.91** £

Subcontractors in the construction industry

● Deductions made by contractors on account of tax (you must send your SC60s/C1525s to us). — **3.92** £

Summary of balance sheet

Leave these boxes blank if you do not have a balance sheet

■ *Assets*

● Plant, machinery and motor vehicles — **3.93** £

● Other fixed assets (premises, goodwill, investments etc.) — **3.94** £

● Stock and work in progress — **3.95** £

● Debtors/prepayments/other current assets — **3.96** £

● Bank/building society balances — **3.97** £

● Cash in hand — **3.98** £ — total of boxes 3.93 to 3.98 **3.99** £

■ *Liabilities*

● Trade creditors/accruals — **3.100** £

● Loans and overdrawn bank accounts — **3.101** £ — total of boxes 3.100 to 3.102

● Other liabilities — **3.102** £ — **3.103** £

■ *Net business assets* (put the figure in brackets if you had net business liabilities) — box 3.99 minus box 3.103 **3.104** £

■ *Represented by*

Capital Account

● Balance at start of period* — **3.105** £

● Net profit/(loss)* — **3.106** £

● Capital introduced — **3.107** £

● Drawings — **3.108** £

● Balance at end of period* — total of boxes 3.105 to 3.107 minus 3.108 **3.109** £

* If the Capital Account is overdrawn, or the business made a net loss, show the figure in brackets.

Tax deducted from trading income

● Any tax deducted (excluding deductions made by contractors on account of tax) from trading income — **3.120** £

Note: box numbers 3.110 to 3.119 are not used

Additional information

**Now fill in any other supplementary Pages that apply to you.
Otherwise, go back to Page 2 of your Tax Return and finish filling it in.**

PARTNERSHIP (SHORT) PAGES

Income for the year ended 5 April 2001

Inland Revenue

PARTNERSHIP (SHORT)

Fill in these boxes first

Name

Tax Reference

If you want help, look up the box numbers in the notes

Partnership details

Partnership reference number

4.1

Partnership trade or profession

4.2

● Date you started being a partner (if during 2000-2001) **4.3** £ / /

● Date you stopped being a partner (if during 2000-2001) **4.4** £ / /

Your share of the partnership's trading or professional income

Basis period begins **4.5** £ / / and ends **4.6** £ / /

● Your share of the profit or loss of this year's account for tax purposes **4.7** £

● Adjustment to arrive at profit or loss for this basis period **4.8** £

● Overlap profit brought forward **4.9** £   Deduct overlap relief used this year **4.10** £

● Overlap profit carried forward **4.11** £

● Adjust for farmers' averaging (see notes, page PN 3 if the partnership made a loss in 2000-2001 or foreign tax deducted, if tax credit relief not claimed **4.12** £

Adjustment on change of basis **4.12A** £

Net profit for 2000-01 (if loss, enter '0' in box 4.13 and enter the loss in box 4.14) **4.13** £

Allowable loss for 2000-01 **4.14** £

● Loss offset against other income for 2000-2001 **4.15** £

● Loss to carry back **4.16** £

● Loss to carry forward (that is, allowable loss not claimed in any other way) **4.17** £

● Losses brought forward from last year **4.18** £

● Losses brought forward from last year used this year **4.19** £

Taxable profit after losses brought forward box 4.13 minus box 4.19 **4.20** £

● Add amounts not included in the partnership accounts that are needed to calculate your taxable profit (for example Enterprise Allowance (Business Start-up Allowance) received in 2000-2001) **4.21** £

Total taxable profits from this business box 4.20 + box 4.21 **4.22** £

Class 4 National Insurance Contributions

● Tick this box if exception or deferment applies **4.23** £

● Adjustments to profit chargeable to Class 4 National Insurance Contributions **4.24** £

Class 4 National Insurance Contributions due **4.25** £

BPP PUBLISHING

Your share of taxed income

- Share of taxed income (liable at 20%)   4.70 £

Your share of Partnership Trading and Professional Profits

from box 4.22

- Share of partnership profits (other than that liable at 20%)   4.73 £

Your share of tax paid

- Share of income tax paid   4.74 £

- Share of SC60/CIS25 deductions   4.75 £

- Share of tax deducted from trading income (not SC 60/CIS25 deductions)   4.75A £

box 4.74 + box 4.75 + box 4.75A

4.77 £

Additional information

Now fill in any other supplementary Pages that apply to you.
Otherwise, go back to page 2 in your Tax Return and finish filling it in

PARTNERSHIP TAX RETURN

Inland Revenue

Partnership Tax Return

for the year ended 5 April 2001

Tax reference

Date

Tax Office address

Officer in Charge

Issue address

Telephone

For Reference

*T*his Notice requires you by law to send me a Tax Return for the year from 6 April 2000 to 5 April 2001. Give details of all the income and disposals of chargeable assets on which the partners may be charged to tax using:

- this form and any supplementary Pages you need; or
- other Inland Revenue approved forms; or
- the Electronic Lodgement Service (ELS).

Make sure your Tax Return, and any documents asked for, reaches me by **31 January 2002** (you may have slightly longer if the partnership includes a company as a partner). You should ensure that the information individual partners need in order to complete their personal Tax Returns is given to them as quickly as possible. Some partners may wish to send in their personal Tax Returns by 30 September 2001.

Each partner who was a member of the partnership during the return period is liable to automatic penalties if the Partnership Tax Return does not reach me by 31 January 2002. They will have to pay interest and may have to pay a surcharge on any tax they pay late. All Tax Returns will be checked and there are penalties for supplying false or incomplete information.

Who should send me the Partnership Tax Return? If this Partnership Tax Return has been issued in the name of the partnership, then the partner nominated by the other members of the partnership during the period covered by the Tax Return is required by law to complete it and send it back to me. If the partners are unable to nominate someone, they should ask me to nominate one of them.

If this Partnership Tax Return has been issued in the name of a particular partner, that partner is required by law to send it back to me.

European Economic Interest Groupings (EEIGs) are also required by law to send me a Partnership Tax Return. See page 5 of the Partnership Tax Return Guide for details.

You are not required by law to send me a Partnership Tax Return if all the members of the partnership are chargeable to Corporation Tax, and the partnership accounts are made up to a date that ends on or before 30 June 2000, but it will help the assessment of the members if you do so.

The Partnership Tax Return

I have sent you pages 1 to 8 of the Partnership Tax Return; these cover common types of partnership income, such as trading income. There are other Pages, which I have not sent you, for other types of income and disposals.

You are responsible for making sure you have the right Pages. Answer the questions in this form to find out if you have the right ones.

I have sent you a Partnership Tax Return Guide to help you fill it in.

If you need help:
- refer to the Partnership Tax Return Guide, or
- ring the number above - most questions can be answered by telephone, or
- when the office is closed, phone our Helpline on 0845 9000 444 for general advice. It is open each evening and at weekends, or
- if you do not want to explain your question on the phone, call in at an Inland Revenue Enquiry Centre - look under 'Inland Revenue' in the phone book.

The green arrows and instructions will guide you through the Partnership Tax Return.

SA800

Please turn over

BPP PUBLISHING

Inland Revenue — PARTNERSHIP BUSINESS AND INVESTMENT INCOME *for the year ended 5 April 2001*

Answer Questions 1 to 6 on this page and Question 7 on page 5 to check that you have the Pages you need to make a complete return of partnership income and related information for the year ended 5 April 2001. If you answer 'No', go to the next question. If you answer 'Yes', you must make sure that you have the right Pages and then fill in the relevant boxes.

Ring the Orderline on 0845 9000 404 (fax 0845 9000 604) between 8am and 10pm for any supplementary Pages you need.

Check to make sure you have the right supplementary Pages (including the Partnership Savings Pages - see Question 7) and then tick the box below

Q1 Did the partnership receive any rent or other income from land and property in the UK? NO ☐ YES ☐   LAND & PROPERTY YES ☐

Q2 Did the partnership have any foreign income? NO ☐ YES ☐   FOREIGN YES ☐

Q3 Did the partnership business include a trade or profession at any time between 6 April 2000 and 5 April 2001? NO ☐ YES ☐   If yes, complete boxes 3.2 to 3.120 on pages 2 to 5 as appropriate.

Q4 Did the partnership dispose of any chargeable assets? NO ☐ YES ☐   CHARGEABLE ASSETS YES ☐

Q5 During the return period has the partnership included any member who is:

- a company? NO ☐ YES ☐

- not resident in the UK? NO ☐ YES ☐

- a partner in a business controlled and managed abroad and who is not domiciled in the UK or is a Commonwealth citizen (or a citizen of the Republic of Ireland) not ordinarily resident in the UK? NO ☐ YES ☐   If yes, read page 5 of the Partnership Tax Return Guide.

Q6 Are you completing this Tax Return on behalf of a European Economic Interest Grouping (EEIG)? NO ☐ YES ☐   If yes, read page 5 of the Partnership Tax Return Guide.

TRADING AND PROFESSIONAL INCOME *for the year ended 5 April 2001*

Remember, you have to fill in a set of boxes for each trade carried on by the partnership and you may have to fill in a separate set if partnership accounts were made up to more than one date in the year ended 5 April 2001. Check the rules beginning on page 5 of the Partnership Tax Return Guide. *Note box numbers 3.1, 3.3 and 3.6 are not used.*

■ *Partnership details*

Name

Description of partnership trade or profession

3.2 [ ]

Accounting period - *read the notes on page 6 of the Partnership Tax Return Guide*

Start **3.4** [/ /]   End **3.5** [/ /]

- Date of commencement (if after 5 April 1998) **3.9** [/ /]

- Date of cessation (if before 6 April 2001) **3.10** [/ /]

- Tick box 3.5A if you are not required to complete boxes 3.11 to 3.80 and 3.93 to 3.109 **3.5A** [ ]

- Tick box 3.7 if the partnership's accounts do not cover the period from the last accounting date (explain why in the 'Additional information' box on page 8) **3.7** [ ]

- Tick box 3.8A if your accounting date has changed (only if this is a permanent change and you want it to count for tax) **3.8A** [ ]

- Tick box 3.8B if this is the second or further change (explain why you have not used the same date as last year in the 'Additional information' box). **3.8B** [ ]

■ *Income and expenses for this accounting period*

If your annual turnover is £15,000 or more, **ignore** boxes 3.11 to 3.13.   *Now fill in page 3* ➤

If your annual turnover is below £15,000, **fill in boxes 3.11 to 3.13 instead of page 3**.

- Turnover, other business receipts, and goods etc. taken for personal use (and balancing charges) **3.11** £

- Expenses allowable for tax (including capital allowances) **3.12** £

    box 3.11 *minus* box 3.12

Net profit for this accounting period (put figure in brackets if a loss) **3.13** £

BMSD 12/99net   PARTNERSHIP TAX RETURN: PAGE 2

TRADING AND PROFESSIONAL INCOME *for the year ended 5 April 2001, continued*

■ *Income and expenses for this accounting period*

You must fill in this page if your annual turnover is £15,000 or more. If your annual turnover is more than £15 million, fill in boxes 3.16 and 3.60 and send the partnership accounts and computations. Read the notes on page 8 of the Partnership Tax Return Guide.

If you were registered for VAT, do the figures in boxes 3.16 to 3.51 include VAT? **3.14** [ ] or exclude VAT? **3.15** [ ]

Sales/business income (turnover)

3.16 £ [ ]

	Disallowable expenses included in boxes 3.33 to 3.50	Total expenses	
● Cost of sales	**3.17** £	**3.33** £	
● Construction industry subcontractor costs	**3.18** £	**3.34** £	
● Other direct costs	**3.19** £	**3.35** £	

box 3.16 *minus* (box 3.33 + box 3.34 + box 3.35)

Gross profit/(loss) **3.36** £ [ ]

Other income/profits **3.37** £ [ ]

● Employee costs	**3.20** £	**3.38** £
● Premises costs	**3.21** £	**3.39** £
● Repairs	**3.22** £	**3.40** £
● General administrative expenses	**3.23** £	**3.41** £
● Motor expenses	**3.24** £	**3.42** £
● Travel and subsistence	**3.25** £	**3.43** £
● Advertising, promotion and entertainment	**3.26** £	**3.44** £
● Legal and professional costs	**3.27** £	**3.45** £
● Bad debts	**3.28** £	**3.46** £
● Interest	**3.29** £	**3.47** £
● Other finance charges	**3.30** £	**3.48** £
● Depreciation and loss/(profit) on sale	**3.31** £	**3.49** £
● Other expenses including partnership charges	**3.32** £	**3.50** £

Put the total of boxes 3.17 to 3.32 in box 3.53 below

total boxes 3.38 to 3.50

Total expenses **3.51** £ [ ]

boxes 3.36 + 3.37 *minus* box 3.51

Net profit/(loss) **3.52** £ [ ]

■ *Tax adjustments to net profit or loss for this accounting period*

boxes 3.17 to 3.32

● Disallowable expenses	**3.53** £
● Goods, etc. taken for personal use and other adjustments (apart from disallowable expenses) that increase profits	**3.54** £
● Balancing charges	**3.55** £

box 3.53 + box 3.54 + box 3.55

Total additions to net profit (deduct from net loss) **3.56** £ [ ]

● Capital allowances	**3.57** £
● Deductions from net profit (add to net loss)	**3.58** £

box 3.57 + box 3.58

3.59 £ [ ]

boxes 3.52 + 3.56 *minus* box 3.59

Net business profit for tax purposes for this accounting period (put figure in brackets if a loss) **3.60** £ [ ]

TRADING AND PROFESSIONAL INCOME *for the year ended 5 April 2001, continued*

You must fill in this page (leave blank any boxes that do not apply to you)

■ Capital allowances - summary

	Capital allowances	Balancing charge
● Motor cars (Separate calculations must be made for each motor car costing more than £12,000 and for cars used partly for private motoring.)	**3.61** £	**3.62** £
● Other business plant and machinery	**3.63** £	**3.64** £
● Agricultural or Industrial Buildings Allowance (A separate calculation must be made for each block of expenditure.)	**3.65** £	**3.66** £
● Other capital allowances claimed (Separate calculations must be made.)	**3.67** £	**3.68** £
	total of column above	total of column above
Total capital allowances/balancing charges	**3.69** £	**3.70** £

■ Taxable profit or loss for this accounting period

Note: box numbers 3.71 and 3.72 and 3.74 to 3.78 are not used

Tick box 3.72A if the figure in box 3.73 is provisional **3.72A**

Profit or loss from box 3.13 or 3.60 **3.73** £

Adjustment on change of basis **3.79A** £   *Copy this figure to box 11A in the Partnership Statement*

Net profit for this accounting period (if loss, enter '0' here) from box 3.73 **3.79** £   *Copy this figure to box 11 in the Partnership Statement*

Allowable loss for this accounting period (if profit enter '0' here) from box 3.73 **3.80** £   *Copy this figure to box 12 in the Partnership Statement*

Additional information

TRADING AND PROFESSIONAL INCOME *for the year ended 5 April 2001, continued*

Boxes 3.81 to 3.91 are not used

■ *Subcontractors in the construction industry*

● Deductions made by contractors on account of tax for **the period 6 April 2000 to 5 April 2001**
3.92 £

Copy this figure to box 24 in the Partnership Statement

See page 4 of the Partnership Tax Return Guide if you are a 'CT Partnership'

Remember to send in SC60s/CIS25s received by the partnership

■ *Summary of balance sheet for this accounting period*

Leave these boxes blank if you do not have a balance sheet or your annual turnover is more than £15 million.

Assets		
● Plant, machinery and motor vehicles	**3.93** £	
● Other fixed assets (premises, goodwill, investments etc.)	**3.94** £	
● Stock and work in progress	**3.95** £	
● Debtors/prepayments/other current assets	**3.96** £	
● Bank/building society balances	**3.97** £	
● Cash in hand	**3.98** £	total of boxes 3.93 to 3.98 **3.99** £

Liabilities		
● Trade creditors/accruals	**3.100** £	
● Loans and overdrawn bank accounts	**3.101** £	
● Other liabilities	**3.102** £	total of boxes 3.100 to 3.102 **3.103** £

Net business assets (put the figure in brackets if you had net business liabilities)

box 3.99 minus box 3.103 **3.104** £

Represented by

Partners' current and capital accounts

● Balance at start of period*	**3.105** £	
● Net profit/(loss)*	**3.106** £	
● Capital introduced	**3.107** £	
● Drawings	**3.108** £	boxes 3.105 to 3.107 minus box 3.108
● Balance at end of period*		**3.109** £

* If the Capital Account is overdrawn, or the business made a net loss, show the figure in brackets.

■ *Partnership trade charges*

● Net partnership charges paid in the period 6 April 2000 to 5 April 2001 (not the accounting period)
3.110 £

Copy the figure in box 3.110 to box 30 in the Partnership Statement

Boxes 3.111 to 3.119 are not used

■ *Tax deducted from trading income*

● Any tax deducted (excluding deductions made by contractors on account of tax) from trading income
3.120 £

Copy this figure to box 24A in the Partnership Statement

See page 4 of the Partnership Tax Return Guide if you are a 'CT Partnership'

Q7 **Did the partnership receive any other income which you have not already included elsewhere in the Partnership Tax Return?**
Make sure you fill in the Pages for Questions 1 to 4 before answering Question 7

NO [ ] **YES** [ ] *If yes, read the note below*

If you ticked the 'Yes' box and the only other income was interest with tax deducted, from banks, building societies or deposit takers, fill in boxes 7.7A to 7.9A below. Otherwise phone the Orderline and ask for the Partnership Savings Pages and leave boxes 7.7A to 7.9A below blank.

● Interest from UK banks, building societies, and deposit takers paid with tax deducted for the period 6 April 2000 to 5 April 2001 (not the accounting period)

Amount after tax deducted	Tax deducted	Gross amount before tax
7.7A £	**7.8A** £	**7.9A** £
	Copy this figure to box 25 in the Partnership Statement	*Copy this figure to box 22 in the Partnership Statement*

Appendix

PARTNERSHIP STATEMENT (SHORT) *for the year ended 5 April 2001*

Please read these instructions before completing the statement

Use these pages to allocate partnership income if the only income for the relevant return period was trading and professional income or taxed interest from banks, building societies or deposit takers. Otherwise you must ask the Orderline for the full Partnership Statement pages to record details of the allocation of all the partnership income.

Step 1 Fill in boxes 1 to 29 and boxes A and B as appropriate. Get the figures you need from the relevant boxes in the Partnership Tax Return. Remember to complete a separate Statement for each accounting period covered by this Partnership Tax Return and for each trade or profession carried on by the partnership.

Step 2 Then allocate the amounts in boxes 11 to 29 attributable to each partner using the allocation columns on this page and page 7 (see pages 14 to 16 of the Partnership Tax Return Guide for help). If the partnership has more than three partners, please photocopy the allocation pages.

Step 3 Each partner will need a copy of their allocation of income to fill in their personal Tax Return.

PARTNERSHIP INFORMATION

If the partnership business includes a trade or profession, enter here the accounting period for which appropriate items in this statement are returned.

Start **1** / /

Finish **2** / /

Nature of trade **3**

MIXED PARTNERSHIPS

Tick here if this statement is drawn up using Corporation Tax Rules **4**

Tick here if this statement is drawn up using tax rules for non residents **5**

Individual partner details

6 Name of partner

Address

Postcode

Date appointed as a partner (if during 2000-2001) **7** / /

Partner's tax reference **8**

Date ceased to be a partner (if during 2000-2001) **9** / /

Partner's National Insurance number **10**

Partnership's profits, losses, income, tax credits etc.

Partner's share of profits, losses, income, tax credits, etc.

Tick this box if the items entered in the box had foreign tax deducted

Copy figures in boxes 11 to 29 to boxes in the individual's Partnership Pages as shown below

• for an accounting period ended in 2000-2001 ▼

from box **3.79** Profit from a trade or profession **A**	**11** £	Profit **11** £		Copy this figure to box 4.7
from box **3.79A** Adjustment on change of basis	**11A** £	**11A** £		Copy this figure to box 4.12A
from box **3.80** Loss from a trade or profession **B**	**12** £	Loss **12** £		Copy this figure to box 4.7

• for the period 6 April 2000 to 5 April 2001*

from box **7.9A** UK taxed interest	**22** £	**22** £	Copy this figure to box 4.70
from box **3.92** SC60/CIS25 deductions made by contractors on account of tax	**24** £	**24** £	Copy this figure to box 4.75
from box **3.120** Other tax deducted from trading income	**24A** £	**24A** £	Copy this figure to box 4.75A
from box **7.8A** Income Tax deducted	**25** £	**25** £	Copy this figure to box 4.74
from box **3.110** Partnership charges	**29** £	**29** £	Copy this figure to box 15.9 in your personal Tax Return

* see page 4 of the Partnership Tax Return Guide if you are a 'CT Partnership'

BMSD 12/99net   PARTNERSHIP TAX RETURN: PAGE 6

PUBLISHING   **214**

PARTNERSHIP STATEMENT (SHORT) *for the year ended 5 April 2001, continued*

Individual partner details

6	Name of partner
	Address
	Postcode

Date appointed as a partner (if during 2000-2001)	Partner's tax reference
7 / /	**8**

Date ceased to be a partner (if during 2000-2001)	Partner's National Insurance number
9 / /	**10**

Partner's share of profits, losses, income, tax credits, etc.

Copy figures in boxes 11 to 29 to boxes in the individual's Partnership Pages as shown below

Profit	**11** £	Copy this figure to box 4.7
	11A £	Copy this figure to box 4.12A
Loss	**12** £	Copy this figure to box 4.7
	22 £	Copy this figure to box 4.70
	24 £	Copy this figure to box 4.75
	24A £	Copy this figure to box 4.75A
	25 £	Copy this figure to box 4.74
	29 £	Copy this figure to box 15.9 in your personal Tax Return

Individual partner details

6	Name of partner
	Address
	Postcode

Date appointed as a partner (if during 2000-2001)	Partner's tax reference
7 / /	**8**

Date ceased to be a partner (if during 2000-2001)	Partner's National Insurance number
9 / /	**10**

Partner's share of profits, losses, income, tax credits, etc.

Copy figures in boxes 11 to 29 to boxes in the individual's Partnership Pages as shown below

Profit	**11** £	Copy this figure to box 4.7
	11A £	Copy this figure to box 4.12A
Loss	**12** £	Copy this figure to box 4.7
	22 £	Copy this figure to box 4.70
	24 £	Copy this figure to box 4.75
	24A £	Copy this figure to box 4.75A
	25 £	Copy this figure to box 4.74
	29 £	Copy this figure to box 15.9 in your personal Tax Return

BPP PUBLISHING

OTHER INFORMATION *for the year ended 5 April 2001*

Q8 Are the details on the front of the Partnership Tax Return wrong? **NO** [ ] **YES** [ ]   If yes, make any corrections on the front of the form

Q9 **Please give a daytime telephone number in boxes 9.1 and 9.2.**
It is often simpler to phone if we need to ask you about your Tax Return.

Your telephone number **9.1** [ ]

or, if you prefer, your agent's phone number
(also give your agent's name and reference in the
'Additional information' box below). **9.2** [ ]

Q10 Please tick box 10.1 if this Partnership Tax Return contains figures that are provisional because you do not yet have final figures. Page 16 of the Partnership Tax Return Guide explains the circumstances in which Tax Returns containing provisional figures may be accepted and tells you what you must enter in the box below.   **10.1** [ ]

Additional information

Q11 **Declaration**

I have filled in and am sending back to you the following pages:

	Tick		Tick
1 TO 5 OF THIS FORM	[ ]	PARTNERSHIP FOREIGN	[ ]
6 & 7 PARTNERSHIP STATEMENT (SHORT)	[ ]	PARTNERSHIP TRADING	[ ]
6 & 7 PARTNERSHIP STATEMENT (FULL)	[ ]	PARTNERSHIP DISPOSAL OF CHARGEABLE ASSETS	[ ]
PARTNERSHIP LAND AND PROPERTY	[ ]	PARTNERSHIP SAVINGS	[ ]

I attach **11.1** [ ] additional copies of page 7 showing details of the allocation of profits to partners who were members of the partnership during the period for which information has been returned. There were **11.2** [ ] partners in this partnership for that period.

Before you send the completed Tax Return back to your Tax Office, you must sign the statement below.

If you give false information or conceal any part of the partnership's income or details of the disposal of chargeable assets, you may be liable to financial penalties and/or you may be prosecuted.

11.3 The information I have given in this Partnership Tax Return, as the nominated partner, is correct and complete to the best of my knowledge and belief.

Signature   Date

Print name
in full here: _____

If you have signed for someone else, please also
• state the capacity in which you are signing (for example, as executor or receiver)

11.4 [ ]

• give the name of the person you are signing for and your name and address in the 'Additional information' box above.

CAPITAL GAINS PAGES

Inland Revenue

For the year ended 5 April 2001

CAPITAL GAINS

Name

Tax reference

Fill in these boxes first

Use this page if all your transactions were in quoted shares or securities unless taper relief is due on any of them, or you are claiming a relief, for example, Enterprise Investment Scheme deferral relief. Otherwise you must use Pages CG2 to CG6 to work out all of your capital gains or allowable losses.

A Enter details of quoted shares or securities disposed of	B Tick box if estimate or valuation used	C Tick box if asset held at 31 March 1982	D Enter the date of disposal	E Disposal proceeds	F Gain or loss after indexation allowance is due (enter loss in brackets)	G Further information, including any elections made
1			/ /	£	£	
2			/ /	£	£	
3			/ /	£	£	
4			/ /	£	£	
5			/ /	£	£	
6			/ /	£	£	
7			/ /	£	£	
8			/ /	£	£	

Total gains **F1** £ — *Total your gains in column F and enter the amount in box F1*

Total losses **F2** £ — *Total your losses in column F and enter the amount in box F2*

Net gain or loss **Box F1 minus box F2** **F3** £ — *If your net gains exceed £7,200, carry on. If they are below £7,200 there is no liability. If you have a net loss, please fill in the losses summary on page CG8*

Minus income losses set against gains **F4** £ — *If your gains are now below £7,200, there is no liability. Otherwise carry on.*

Minus losses brought forward **Box F3 minus box F4** **F5** £ — *Enter losses brought forward up to the smaller of either the total losses brought forward or the figure in box F5 minus £7,200*

F6 £

Total taxable gains **Box F5 minus box F6** **F7** £ — *Copy this figure to box 8.7 on page Cg8*

Note:
This page is only for transactions in shares or securities quoted on the London Stock Exchange

Go to page CG8

Page CG1

BPP PUBLISHING

Appendix

A	AA*	B	C	D	E	F	G
Brief description of asset	Type of disposal. Enter Q, U, L or O	Tick box if estimate or valuation used	Tick box if asset held at 31 March 1982	Insert the later of date of acquisition and 16 March 1998	Insert the date of disposal	Disposal proceeds	Enter claims or any elections made, reliefs claimed or due and state amount (£)

Gains on assets without mixed (business and non-business) use

1				/ /	/ /	£	
2				/ /	/ /	£	
3				/ /	/ /	£	
4				/ /	/ /	£	
5				/ /	/ /	£	
6				/ /	/ /	£	
7				/ /	/ /	£	
8				/ /	/ /	£	

Gains on assets with mixed (business and non-business) use (see the notes on page CGN4)

9				/ /	/ /	£	
10				/ /	/ /	£	

* Column AA: for transactions in
- quoted shares or securities, enter Q
- unquoted shares or securities, enter U
- land and property, enter L
- other assets (for example, goodwill). enter O

Complete Page CG4 to CG6 for all U, L and O transactions

Losses

Description of asset	Type of * Disposal Enter Q, U, L or O	Tick box if estimate or valuation used	Tick box if asset held at 31 March 1982	Enter the later of date of acquisition and 16 March 1998	Enter the date of disposal	Disposal proceeds	Enter details of any elections made, reliefs claimed or due and state amount (£)
13				/ /	/ /	£	
14				/ /	/ /	£	
15				/ /	/ /	£	
16				/ /	/ /	£	

Total losses of year

H	I	J	K			L	M
Chargeable Gains after reliefs but before losses and taper	Enter 'Bus' if business asset	Taper rate	Losses deducted			Gains after losses	Tapered gains (gains from column L x % in column J)
			K1 Allowable losses of the year	K2 Income losses of 2000-2001 set against gains	K3 Unused losses b/f from earlier years		
£		%	£	£	£	£	£
£		%	£	£	£	£	£
£		%	£	£	£	£	£
£		%	£	£	£	£	£
£		%	£	£	£	£	£
£		%	£	£	£	£	£
£		%	£	£	£	£	£
£		%	£	£	£	£	£
£	Bus	%	£	£	£	£	£
£		%	£	£	£	£	£
£	Bus	%	£	£	£	£	£
£		%	£	£	£	£	£

8.1 £
Total column H

8.5 £
Total column K2

8.6 £
Total column K3

8.3 £
Total column M

Losses arising	
	11 **Attributed gains from UK resident trusts** *(enter the name of the Trust on Page CG7)* £
	12 **Attributed gains from non UK resident trusts** *(enter the name of the Trust on Page CG7)* £
£	
£	*Total of attributed gains* **8.4** £
£	box 8.3 + box 8.4
£	**Total Taxable Gains** £
8.2 £	Copy to box 8.7 on Page CG8 and complete Pages CG4 to CG6 for all U, L and O transactions

Appendix

If you have more that two transactions of this type of asset to return, please photocopy this Page before completion. (Please also complete Pages CG2 and CG3.)

1st transaction

Description of shares or securities - including name of company, company registration number (if known), number, class and nominal value of shares. Also, if possible, give a history of the shares disposed of, for instance, if there has been a reorganisation or takeover (give details of the original company and shares held in that company)

Tick box if you have already submitted form CG34 ☐

State any connection between you and the person who acquired the asset (See Notes, page CGN13)

If you have used an estimate or valuation in your capital gains computation, please enter the date to which the valuation relates, the amount (£) and the reason for the estimate or valuation. Please also attach a copy of any valuation obtained.

2nd transaction

Description of shares or securities - including name of company, company registration number (if known), number, class and nominal value of shares. Also, if possible, give a history of the shares disposed of, for instance, if there has been a reorganisation or takeover (give details of the original company and shares held in that company)

Tick box if you have already submitted form CG34 ☐

State any connection between you and the person who acquired the asset (See Notes, page CGN13)

If you have used an estimate or valuation in your capital gains computation, please enter the date to which the valuation relates, the amount (£) and the reason for the estimate or valuation. Please also attach a copy of any valuation obtained.

Page CG4

Land and property (L) - Further information

If you have more that two transactions of this type of asset to return, please photocopy this Page before completion. (Please also complete Pages CG2 and CG3.)

1st transaction

Full address of land/property affected (attach a copy of any plan if this helps identification)

Description of land/property disposed of, including details of your ownership, for example freehold/leasehold and any tenancies affecting your ownership and the date of transaction or any other date for which a valuation has been made.

Tick box if you have already submitted form CG34 ☐

State any connection between you and
the person who acquired the asset
(See Notes, page CGN13)

If you have used an estimate or valuation in your capital gains computation, please enter the date to which the valuation relates, the amount (£) and the reason for the estimate or valuation. Please also attach a copy of any valuation obtained.

2nd transaction

Full address of land/property affected (attach a copy of any plan if this helps identification)

Description of land/property disposed of, including details of your ownership, for example freehold/leasehold and any tenancies affecting your ownership and the date of transaction or any other date for which a valuation has been made.

Tick box if you have already submitted form CG34 ☐

State any connection between you and
the person who acquired the asset
(See Notes, page CGN13)

If you have used an estimate or valuation in your capital gains computation, please enter the date to which the valuation relates, the amount (£) and the reason for the estimate or valuation. Please also attach a copy of any valuation obtained.

Page CG5

BPP
PUBLISHING

Appendix

If you have more that two transactions of this type of asset to return, please photocopy this Page before completion. (Please also complete Pages CG2 and CG3.)

1st transaction

Full description of the asset (other than shares or land/property) affected and any other information which helps identify the asset.

Tick box if you have already submitted form CG34 ☐

State any connection between you and
the person who acquired the asset
(See Notes, page CGN13)

If you have used an estimate or valuation in your capital gains computation, please enter the date to which the valuation relates, the amount (£) and the reason for the estimate or valuation. Please also attach a copy of any valuation obtained.

2nd transaction

Full description of the asset (other than shares or land/property) affected and any other information which helps identify the asset.

Tick box if you have already submitted form CG34 ☐

State any connection between you and
the person who acquired the asset
(See Notes, page CGN13)

If you have used an estimate or valuation in your capital gains computation, please enter the date to which the valuation relates, the amount (£) and the reason for the estimate or valuation. Please also attach a copy of any valuation obtained.

Page CG6
Page CG7 is blank

Chargeable gains and allowable losses

Once you have completed Page CG1, or Pages CG2 to CG6, fill in this Page

Have you 'ticked' any row in Column B, 'Tick box if estimate or valuation used' on Pages CG1 or CG2?   **NO**   **YES**

Have you given details in Column G on Pages CG2 and CG3 of any Capital Gains reliefs claimed or due?   **NO**   **YES**

Enter the number of transactions from Page CG1 or column AA on Page CG2 for:

- Transactions in quoted shares or securities   **Box Q**
- Transactions in unquoted shares or securities   **Box U**
- Transactions in land and property   **Box L**
- Other transactions   **Box O**

Total taxable gains (from Page CG1 or Page CG3)   **8.7** £

Your taxable gains minus the annual exempt amount   **box 8.7 minus £7,200** **8.8** £

Additional liability in respect of non-resident or dual resident trusts (see Notes, page CGN6)   **8.9** £

Capital losses

(Remember if your loss arose on a transaction with a connected person, see Notes page CGN13, you can only set that loss against gains you make on disposals to that same connected person)

■ **This year's losses**

- Total (from box 8.2 on Page CG3 or box F2 on Page CG1)   **8.10** £
- Used against gains (total of column K1 on Page CG3, or the smaller of boxes F1 and F2 on Page CG1)   **8.11** £
- Used against earlier years' gains (generally only available to personal representatives, see Notes, page CGN11)   **8.12** £
- Used against income (only losses of the type described on page CGN9 can be used against income)   **8.13A** £ amount claimed against income of 2000-2001
  8.13B £ amount claimed against income of 1999-2000   **box 8.13A + box 8.13B** **8.13** £
- This year's unused losses   **box 8.10 minus (boxes 8.11 + 8.12 + 8.13)** **8.14** £

■ **Earlier years' losses**

- Unused losses of 1997-98 and later years   **8.15** £
- Used against year (losses from box 8.15 are used in priority to losses from box 8.18) (column K3 on Page CG3 or box F6 on Page CG1))   **8.16** £
- Remaining unused losses of 1997-98 and later years   **box 8.15 minus box 8.16** **8.17** £
- Unused losses of 1996-97 and earlier years   **8.18** £
- Used this year (losses from box 8.15 are used in priority to losses from box 8.18) (column K3 on Page CG3 or box F6 on Page CG1))   **box 8.6 minus box 8.16 (or box f6 minus box 8.16)** **8.19** £

■ **Total of unused losses to carry forward**

- Carried forward losses of 1997-98 and later years   **box 8.14 + box 8.17** **8.20** £
- Carried forward losses of 1996-97 and earlier years   **box 8.18 minus box 8.19** **8.21** £

SA 108

Page CG8

BPP PUBLISHING

CT600 RETURN FORM

Inland Revenue

Company Tax Return
Form CT 600 (1999) Version 1
For accounting periods ending on or after 1 July 1999

This form (or an Inland Revenue approved substitute for it), together with any relevant *Supplementary Pages,* must be used whenever a company is required by form CT 603 *Notice to deliver a company tax return (*the *Notice)* for any period ended on or after 1 July 1999.

Company information

Company Name

Company registration number *(if registered)*

Reference - *as shown on notice*
/ /

Address -*If different from that shown on the notice*

Postcode

Period covered by this return (cannot exceed 12 months)
From dd/mm/yyyy
/ /

To
/ /

Before you begin completing the form, read the notes on page 2 and then go to Section 1 on page 3 as this will help you decide whether you need to obtain and complete any of the Supplementary Pages which form part of the return. Fill in the 'Summary' and 'Declaration' below once you have completed the relevant sections, and before you send back the return to the issuing Tax Office.

Summary of return information

Put an 'X' in box if 'Yes'

Are you making a repayment claim
• **for this period**

• **for an earlier period**

Put an 'X' in box if 'Yes'

Are you filing more than one return for this company now?

Are you seeking approved investment trust company status under S842(1) ICTA 1998?
Attach a schedule showing how the company has met all the conditions. See note 26.

I attach
• **accounts for the period to which this return relates**

• **for an earlier period**

• **if no accounts, say why not**

I am sending you the following completed *Supplementary Pages* **as part of this return form**
Put an 'X' in appropriate box(es)

Loans to participators by close companies (CT600A)

Controlled foreign companies (CT600B)

Group and consortium (CT600C)

Insurance (CT600D)

Charity (CT600E)

Declaration

Warning
Giving false information in the return, or concealing any part of the company's profits or tax payable, can lead to the company and you being prosecuted.

Declaration
The information I have given on this form and the accompanying Supplementary Pages is correct and complete to the best of my knowledge and belief.

Signature

Date *(dd/mm/yyyy)*

Status

Name *(in capital letters)*

Except where a liquidator has been appointed, any person who is authorised to do so may sign on behalf of the company. A photocopy of a signature is not acceptable.

CT600(1999)

Important points

- **As soon as you receive the *Notice to deliver a company tax return* (the *Notice*)** make sure you obtain all the *Supplementary Pages* you need. The information on page 3 in Section 1 should help you decide which you will need and how to get them. Please contact the Tax Office shown on the *Notice* if you need more help.

- **Members' clubs, societies and voluntary associations** may only need to complete the *Company information, Summary* and *Declaration* sections on page 1, and the short calculation on pages 4 and 5. Note 1 in the *Company Tax Return Guide (Guide)* gives more detail about what to complete but our leaflet '*Clubs, societies and voluntary associations' (IR46)* gives information and includes an example of a completed form *CT600*. The leaflet is available from any Inland Revenue Enquiry Centre or Tax Office (see 'Inland Revenue' in your local Phone Book).

- **'Company' includes** every kind body, club, society, association or organisation that is chargeable to corporation tax, whether or not it is incorporated.

- **Please do not** make an entry where the company did not have the item specified in the return form. Complete the boxes with whole figures only, except where pence or decimals are indicated.

- **The Guide** and the further notes on this form will help you complete this return.

Which sections you need to complete

After reading the notes on this page, start at Section 1.

All trading companies must complete Section 2. All companies must then complete either the Short Calculation (Section 3) or the Detailed Calculation (Section 4). The notes at the beginning of each Calculation will help you decide which one is appropriate.

Complete Section 5 if you want to claim capital allowances.

Complete Section 6 if, in this period, the company has any of the losses or excess amounts listed there. Group companies must also show the maximum amounts available for surrender by way of group or consortium relief.

Complete Section 7 if there is a repayment claim attached to this return.

If the company charges directors' remuneration in the accounts please complete Section 8.

What to do when you have completed the return

When you have completed the appropriate sections make sure you give us all the information requested on page 1. Once you have done this, sign and date the *Declaration* and send the **whole** form to us. Attach any supporting calculations, claims or surrender documentation. Send them along with the relevant completed *Supplementary Pages*, company accounts and, where prepared, directors' and auditors' reports. Note 3 in the *Guide* advises you of the date by which you must do this (the filing date).

It is a good idea to keep a copy of the completed return for your own records.

You must pay any tax outstanding that you calculate is due. A payslip is attached to the *Notice*. Note 20 in the *Guide* tells you about payment dates.

Do not send back the *Guide* but please keep it for reference purposes.

When we receive the return - *see note on page 12 of the Guide*

When we receive your completed return we will process it, based on your figures, and record the amount you have shown in the return as the tax due for this period. At this stage we will acknowledge receipt of the return.

The *Guide* tells you the time limits by which you can amend the return, and the time limits applying to us for correcting or enquiring into it.

Remember

- **Interest is charged on tax paid late.**
- **The company may be liable to penalties if its return is late or incorrect.**

Section 1 : Which *Supplementary Pages* must be completed?

This page will help you decide if you need any *Supplementary Pages*. The notes in the *Guide* will also help you. Most company agents have supplies but if you do not have an agent, or your agent does not hold stocks, please call the CTSA Orderline on 0845 300 6555, or fax on 0845 300 6777. Make a note of the name and form number of the *Supplementary Page(s)* you want before calling. The CTSA Orderline is open 7 days a week between 8am and 10pm.

If you need further help please contact the Tax Office shown on the *Notice*.

Members' clubs, societies and voluntary associations are unlikely to need any *Supplementary Pages*.

Close companies

If the company is close and made a loan, or loans, to an individual participator, or associate of a participator, in the return period which has not been repaid within the return period, **you must complete** the detailed calculation on pages 6 to 8 and the *Loans to participators by close companies Supplementary Pages (form CT600A)*

Controlled foreign companies (CFCs)

If, in this period, the company had an interest of 25% or more in a foreign company which was controlled from the UK, **you must complete** the *Controlled foreign companies Supplementary Pages (form CT600B)*, and , if there is a charge under S747 ICTA 1988, the detailed calculation on pages 6 to 8.

Further guidance on CFCs is available - see *'Other publications of interest'* on page 12 of the *Guide*.

Group and/or consortium companies

If the company is claiming or surrendering any amounts under the group or consortium relief provisions for this period **you must complete**
- Section 4, the detailed calculation on pages 6 to 8, if you are claiming group or consortium relief
- Section 6 on page 9 if you surrendering relief and
- the *Group and consortium Supplementary Pages (form CT600C)*

Insurance companies and friendly societies

If, in this period, the company or society
- made claims under Sch 19AB ICTA 1988 to provisional payments (including notional repayments in respect of tax on gilt interest) or
- has entered into business in the accounting period which it treats as overseas life assurance business (OLAB)
you must complete the detailed calculation on pages 6 to 8 and the *Insurance Supplementary Pages (form CT600B)*

Charities

If, in this period, the charity is claiming exemption or partial exemption for tax **you must complete** any relevant section of the CT600 for taxable income and the *Charity Supplementary Pages (form CT600E)*

Section 2 : Turnover of the company

You must complete this Section if the company has trading or professional income
Members' clubs, societies and voluntary associations that do not trade outside their membership need not complete this Section
Investment companies and Unit Trusts need not complete this Section.

Turnover

1   **Total turnover from trade or profession**
    Enter the total for this return period. See note 4

    1 £ _____

2   **Banks, building societies, insurance companies and other financial concerns**
    Put an 'X' in this box

    2 [   ]

This is the end of Section 2. Please now complete either Section 3 on pages 4 and 5, or Section 4 on pages 6 to 8.

Section 3 : Short Calculation

You may complete this section if it covers all the entries you need to make and any entry is less than £10 million.

In all other cases, or if you prefer, complete Section 4 instead. You should enclose explanations and calculations of any figures you have estimated or which are not immediately recognisable from the company's accounts. If you include a valuation you should state from where you obtained it. The figures to be entered are those adjusted for tax purposes, after deducting capital allowances and adding balancing charges, where appropriate. **References to** *notes* **are to those in the** *Guide.*

If the company is close and has made loans to an individual participator, or associate of a participator, in this period that were not repaid within the period, you need to complete Section 4 instead.

Please note that certain numbered boxes are missing from the short calculation.

Income

3   **Trading and professional profits**
    See note 5. Complete Section 6 if there is a loss
    3 £

4   **Trading losses brought forward claimed against profits**
    Only include losses made in the same trade. Include charges treated as losses. **Do not enter an amount larger than is needed to cover the profits in box 3**. *See notes 5 and 6.*
    4 £

5   **Net trading and professional profits**
    If box 4 equals box 3, enter '0'. Leave this box blank if there are no trading profits in box 3.
    box 3 minus box 4
    5 £

7   **Profits and gains from non-trading loan relationships**
    Include bank, building society or other interest, and any other profits and gains even if tax has been deducted. You will need to complete the 'Detailed calculation' at Section 4, and Section 6, if you have deficits on non-trading loan relationships from this, earlier or later accounting periods to include. See note 8
    7 £

8   **Annuities, annual payments and discounts not arising from loan relationships and from which income tax has not been deducted**
    Exclude any amount included in box 7
    8 £

10 **Income from which income tax has been deducted**
    Enter the gross amount before tax and exclude any amount included in box 7. See note 9.
    10 £

12 **Income from UK land and buildings**
    Enter the amount net of allowable expenses. Complete Section 6 if there is a loss. See note 10. .
    12 £

13 **Annual profits and gains not falling under any other heading**
    Enter amount net of losses. Complete Section 6 if there is a loss. See note 7. .
    13 £

Chargeable gains

14 **Gross gains**
    See note 11. Complete Section 6 if there is a loss
    14 £

15 **Allowable losses including losses brought forward**
    Do not enter an amount larger than the amount of gross gains shown in box 14. *See note 11.*
    15 £

16 **Net chargeable gains**
    If box 15 equals box 14, enter '0'
    box 14 minus box 15
    16 £

19 **Profits before other deductions and reliefs**
    total of boxes 5, 7, 8, 10, 12, 13 and 16
    19 £

Deductions and reliefs

26 **Trading losses of this or a later accounting period**
&   **under S393A ICTA1988**
27 *Put an 'X' in box 26 if amounts carried back from later accounting periods are included in box 27. See box 12*
    26   **27** £

30 Profits before charges
    box 19 minus box 27
    30 £

31 **Charges paid**
    This figure must not exceed profits shown in box 30. See note 13
    31 £

Corporation tax profits
33 Profits chargeable to corporation tax
    box 30 minus box 31
    33 £

Carry forward the figure in box 33 to the box at the top of page 5.

Appendix

Section 3 : Short Calculation continued

Profits chargeable to corporation tax *Enter the figure from box 33 on page 4*

£ [   ]

Tax calculation   If you claim tax is chargeable at the small companies' rate, or if you are claiming marginal small companies' relief, complete boxes 34-38. If there are no associated companies, franked investment income or foreign income dividends, please enter the financial year(s) in boxes 35 and 37, and '0' in boxes 34, 36 and, if necessary, 38. *See note 15.*

34   **Franked investment income and foreign income dividends arising in the period covered by the return.** *See note 15*

34 £ [   ]

35 - 38   Number of companies associated with this company in the/each financial year(s) covered by this return
Exclude this company. See note 15

Financial year (yyyy)	Number of associated companies
35 [ ]	**36** [ ]
37 [ ]	**38** [ ]

39 - 59 Corporation tax chargeable *See note 16*

Financial years beginning 1 April (yyyy)	Amounts of profit	Rates of tax *See note 31*	Tax
39 [ ]	**40** £ [ ]	**41** [• %]	**42** £ [ ] p
49 [ ]	**50** £ [ ]	**51** [• %]	**52** £ [ ] p

box 42 plus box 52
59 £ [   ] p

59   Corporation tax chargeable.

Reliefs and deductions in terms of tax

60   **Marginal small companies' relief**
Attach your computation. See notes 15 and 16

60 £ [   ] p

62   **Advance corporation tax (restricted if necessary under S239(2) ICTA 1998)** *See notes 17*

62 £ [   ] p

63   **Total reliefs and deductions in terms of tax**
Cannot exceed box 59 amount

total of boxes 60 and 62
63 £ [   ] p

68   **Tax chargeable**

box 59 minus box 63
68 £ [   ] p

69   **Income tax deducted from gross income included in profits**
Do not include deductions used to cover income tax for which the company was liable to account to the Inland Revenue on payments it has made. See note 18.

69 £ [   ] p

70   **Income tax repayable to the company**
Complete if box 69 is greater than box 68. Also complete Section 7

70 £ [   ] p

72   Tax payable
Enter '0.00' if you have completed box 70. See note 20
This figure is the amount of your self-assement

box 68 minus box 69
72 £ [   ] p

Tax reconciliation

73   **Deductions under the Construction Industry Scheme**
Enclose forms SC60 / CIS25. See note 19

73 £ [   ] p

74   **Construction industry deductions repayable**
Complete Section 7

box 73 minus box 72
74 £ [   ] p

75   **Tax already paid (and not repaid)**
Exclude amounts entered in boxes 69 and 73. See note 21

75 £ [   ] p

76   **Tax outstanding**
This amount is payable to the Accounts Office. See note 23

box 72 minus boxes 73 and 75
76 £ [   ] p

77   **Tax overpaid**
Complete Section 7

box 75 plus box 73 minus box 72
77 £ [   ] p

Indicators

79   Put an 'X' in this box if the company should have made quarterly instalment payments under the Corporation Tax (Instalment Payments) Regulations 1998
See note 20

79 [   ]

80   Put an 'X' in this box if the company is within a group payment arrangement for this period.

80 [   ]

This is the end of the Short Calculation

Section 4 : Detailed Calculation

Complete this section if you have not completed Section 3. You should enclose explanations and calculations of any figures you have estimated or which are not immediately recognisable from the company's accounts. If you have included a valuation you should state from where you obtained it. The figures to be entered are those adjusted for tax purposes, after deducting capital allowances and adding balancing charges where appropriate. **References to** *notes* **are to those in the** *Guide.*

Income

3 Trading and professional profits
See note 5. Complete Section 6 if there is a loss

3 £ _____

4 Trading losses brought forward claimed against profits
Only include losses made in the same trade. Include charges treated as losses. **Do not enter an amount larger than is needed to cover the profits in box 3.** *See notes 5 and 6.*

4 £ _____

5 Net trading and professional profits
If box 4 equals box 3, enter '0'. Leave this box blank if there are no trading profits in box 3.

box 3 minus box 4
5 £ _____

6 Profits and gains from non trading loan relationships,
& exchange fluctuations and certain financial instruments
7 *Include bank, building society or other interest, and any other profits and gains even if tax has been deducted. Also include intra-group income under S247(4) ICTA 1998 which represents interest on loan relationships. Put an 'X' in box 6 if income is stated net after carrying back deficits on non-trading loan relationships. Complete Section 6 if there are net deficits. See note 8.*

6 ____ **7** £ _____

8 Annuities, annual payments and discounts not arising from loan relationships and from which income tax has not been deducted
Exclude any amount included in box 7

8 £ _____

9 Overseas income within Sch D Case V
Complete Section 6 if there is a loss.

9 £ _____

10 Income from which income tax has been deducted.
Enter the gross amount before tax and exclude any amount included in box 7. See note 9.

10 £ _____

11 Intra-group income under S247(4) ICTA 1988 election where tax has not been deducted
Exclude any amount included in box 7

11 £ _____

12 Income from UK land and buildings
Enter the amount net of allowable expenses. Complete Section 6 if there is a loss. See note 10. .

12 £ _____

13 Annual profits and gains not falling under any other heading
Enter amount net of losses. Complete Section 6 if there is a loss. See note 7. .

13 £ _____

Chargeable gains

14 Gross gains
See note 11. Complete Section 6 if there is a loss

14 £ _____

15 Allowable losses including losses brought forward
Do not enter an amount larger than the amount of gross gains shown in box 14. *See note 11.*

15 £ _____

16 Net chargeable gains
If box 15 equals box 14, enter '0'

box 14 minus box 15
16 £ _____

Deductions specifically from non trade profits

17 Losses brought forward against certain investment income .

17 £ _____

18 Non-trade deficits on loan relationships (including interest), exchange fluctuations and certain financial instruments brought forward
See note 8. Amount cannot exceed total of boxes 7, 8, 9, 10, 11, 12, 13 and 16. .

18 £ _____

19 Profits before other deductions and reliefs

total of boxes 5, and the net sum of boxes 7 to 13 and 16 minus boxes 17 and 18
19 £ _____

Carry forward the figure in box 19 to the box at the top of page 7

BPP
PUBLISHING

Section 4 : Detailed calculation continued

Profits chargeable to corporation tax *Enter the figure from box 19 on page 6* £ ___

Deductions and reliefs

20 Losses on unquoted shares
20 £ ___

21 Management expenses under S75 ICTA 1988
21 £ ___

22 Interest distributions under S468L ICTA 1988 *See note 29*
22 £ ___

23 Schedule A losses for this or previous accounting period under S392A ICTA 1988 *See note 10*
23 £ ___

24 Capital allowances for the purposes of management of the business. *S28 CAA 1990. Investment companies only. Complete Section 5.*
24 £ ___

25 Non-trade deficits for this accounting period from loan relationships, exchange fluctuations or certain financial instruments. *See note 8*
25 £ ___

26 & 27 Trading losses of this or a later accounting period under S393A ICTA1988
Put an 'X' in box 26 if amounts carried back from later accounting periods are included in box 27. See box 12
26 ___ **27** £ ___

28 Non-trade capital allowances
S145(3) CAA 1990. Complete Section 5
28 £ ___

29 Total of deductions and reliefs
This figure must not exceed profits shown in box 19
total of boxes 20 - 25, 27 and 28
29 £ ___

30 **Profits before charges and group relief**
box 19 minus box 29
30 £ ___

31 Charges paid
This figure must not exceed profits shown in box 30. See note 13
31 £ ___

32 Group relief
This figure must not exceed box 30 minus box 31. Complete and attach the 'Group and consortium Supplementary Pages'. See note 14
32 £ ___

33 **Profits chargeable to corporation tax**
box 30 minus boxes 31 and 32
33 £ ___

Tax calculation If you claim tax is chargeable at the small companies' rate, or if you are claiming marginal small companies' relief, complete boxes 34-38. If there are no associated companies, franked investment income or foreign income dividends, please enter the financial year(s) in boxes 35 and 37, and '0' in boxes 34, 36 and, if necessary, 38. *See note 15.*

34 Franked investment income and foreign income dividends arising in the period covered by the return. *See note 15*
34 £ ___

35 - 38 Number of companies associated with this company in the/each financial year(s) covered by this return
Exclude this company. See note 15

Financial year (yyyy)	Number of associated companies
35 ___	**36** ___
37 ___	**38** ___

39 - 59 Corporation tax chargeable *See note 16*

Financial years beginning 1 April (yyyy)	Amounts of profit	Rates of tax *See note 31*	Tax
39 ___	**40** £ ___	**41** • ___ %	**42** £ ___ p
	43 £ ___	**44** • ___ %	**45** £ ___ p
	46 £ ___	**47** • ___ %	**48** £ ___ p
49 ___	**50** £ ___	**51** • ___ %	**52** £ ___ p
	53 £ ___	**54** • ___ %	**55** £ ___ p
	56 £ ___	**57** • ___ %	**58** £ ___ p

total of boxes 42, 45, 48, 52, 55 and 58
Carry forward the figure in box 59 to the box at the top of page 8 **59** £ ___ p

Section 4 : Detailed calculation continued

Corporation tax chargeable *Enter the figure from box 59 on page 7*   £ [ ] p

60-63 Reliefs and deductions in terms of tax

60 **Marginal small companies' relief**
    Attach your computation. See notes 15 and 16.   **60** £ [ ] p

61 **Double taxation relief**
    Exclude any amount included in box 67   **61** £ [ ] p

61A **Put an 'X' in this box if box 61 includes
    an Underlying Rate relief claim**   **61A** [ ]

62 **Advance corporation tax (restricted if
    necessary under S239(2) ICTA1988)**
    See note 17   **62** £ [ ] p

63 **Total reliefs and deductions in terms of tax**
    Cannot exceed corporation tax chargeable amount in box 59.   total of boxes 60,61 and 62
    63 £ [ ] p

64-78 Calculation of tax outstanding or overpaid

64 **Net corporation tax liability.**   box 59 minus box 63
    64 £ [ ] p

65 **Tax payable under S419 ICTA 1988**
&   *Complete and attach the 'Loans to participators by close companies*
66 *Supplementary Pages.' Put an 'X' in box 65 if you completed box A11
    in the Supplementary Pages. Copy the figure from box A13 to box 66*   **65** [ ]   **66** £ [ ] p

67 **Tax payable under S747 ICTA 1988**
    Enter the total figure of tax from the 'Controlled foreign companies Supplementary Pages'   **67** £ [ ] p

68 **Tax chargeable**   total of boxes 64, 66 and 67
    68 £ [ ] p

69 **Income tax deducted from gross income included in profits**
    *Do not include deductions used to cover income tax for which the company was
    liable to account to the Inland Revenue on payments it has made. See note 18*   **69** £ [ ] p

70 **Income tax repayable to the company**
    Complete if box 69 is greater than box 68. Also complete Section 7   **70** £ [ ] p

71 **Advance corporation tax on foreign income dividends and
    set off to the extent that corporation tax is otherwise unpaid**
    See note 22   **71** £ [ ] p

72 **Tax chargeable**
    Enter '0.00' if you have completed box 70. See note 20
    This figure is the amount of your self-assesment   box 68 minus boxes 69 and 71
    72 £ [ ] p

Tax reconciliation

73 **Deductions under the Construction Industry Scheme**
    Enclose forms SC60/CIS25. See note 19   **73** £ [ ] p

74 **Construction industry deductions repayable**
    Complete Section 7   box 73 minus box 72
    74 £ [ ] p

75 **Tax already paid (and not repaid)**
    Exclude amounts entered in boxes 69, 71 and 73. See note 21.   **75** £ [ ] p

76 **Tax outstanding**
    This amount is payable to the Accounts Office. See note 23   box 72 minus boxes 73 and 75
    76 £ [ ] p

77 **Tax overpaid**
    Complete Section 7   box 75 plus box 73 minus box 72
    77 £ [ ] p

78 **Tax refunds surrendered to the company under S102 FA 1989**
    Enclose a copy of the joint Notice. See note 24.   **78** £ [ ] p

Indicators

78 **Put an 'X' in this box if the company should have made quarterly instalment
    payments under the Corporation Tax (Instalments Payments) Regulations 1998**
    See note 20   **79** [ ]

80 **Put an 'X' in this box if the company is within a group payment arrangement
    for this period**   **80** [ ]

This is the end of the Detailed Calculation

BPP PUBLISHING

Section 5 : Claims for capital allowances and details of balancing charges

You must complete this section if you want to claim capital allowances. You should also show balancing charges taken into account in Section 3 or 4 calculations. Show details of qualifying expenditure on which writing-down allowances may be claimed, even if you do not want to claim any allowances for this period. *See note 25*

Notice of expenditure on machinery and plant *See note 25*

81   Expenditure on which first year allowance is claimed.   **81** £

82   Qualifying expenditure on long-life assets.   **82** £

83   Qualifying expenditure on other assets.   **83** £

Charges and allowances included in calculation of trading profits or losses

	Balancing charges	Capital allowances
84-85 **Cars** *Including leased out and 'expensive' cars*	**84** £	**85** £
86-87 **Machinery and plant - long-life assets**	**86** £	**87** £
88-89 **Machinery and plant - other assets.**	**88** £	**89** £
90-91 **Industrial buildings and structures** *Including qualifying hotels, and commercial buildings and hotels in enterprise zones*	**90** £	**91** £
92-93 **Other charges and allowances** *For example agricultural buildings, mineral extraction, scientific research, patents*	**92** £	**93** £

Charges and allowances not included in calculation of trading profits or losses

	Balancing charges	Capital allowances
94-95	**94** £	**95** £

Section 6 : Losses, deficits and excess amounts

Complete this section if the company has incurred, in this period, any of the losses or deficits shown below, or if it has, for this period, any of the excess amounts shown below. Companies that are proposing to surrender any amount as group or consortium relief should also complete the second column. *See note 27.*

	Arising	Maximum available for surrender as group relief
96-97 **Trading losses Case I** *See note 5*	calculated under S393 ICTA 1988 **96** £	calculated under S393A ICTA 1988 **97** £
98 **Trading losses Case V**	calculated under S393 ICTA 1988 **98** £	
99-100 **Non-trade deficits on loan relationships** *See note 8*	calculated under S82 FA 1996 **99** £	calculated under S83 FA 1996 **100** £
101-102 **Schedule A losses** *UK land and buildings. See note 10*	calculated under S392A ICTA 1988 **101** £	calculated under S403 FA 1988 **102** £
103 **Overseas property business losses Case V**	calculated under S392A ICTA 1988 **103** £	
104 **Losses Case VI**	calculated under S396 ICTA 1988 **104** £	
105 **Capital losses**	calculated under S16 TCGA 1992 **105** £	

	Excess	
106 **Excess non-trade capital allowances** *Excess over income in period*		calculated under S403 ICTA 1988 **106** £
107 **Excess charges** *See note 13*		calculated under S403 ICTA 1988 **107** £
108-109 **Excess management expenses**	calculated under S75(3) ICTA 1988 **108** £	calculated under S403 ICTA 1988 **109** £
110 **Excess interest distributions**	calculated under S468L(7) ICTA 1988 **110** £	

Section 7 : Overpayments and repayment claims

Complete this section if you are claiming a repayment. If you have competed boxes 70, 74 and 77 in Section 3 or 4, attach your calculations. Do not forget to put an 'X' in the appropriate box of the *Summary of return information* section on page 1. *See note 28*

Please note there is no box 113 in this section.

111 **Repayment of corporation tax**
Include construction industry deductions repayable and enclose forms SC60/CIS25

111	£		p

112 **Repayment of income tax**

112	£		p

114 **Repayment of advance corporation tax**
See note 22

114	£		p

Bank details (for person to whom the repayment is to be made)

Repayments of corporation tax (but not income tax, advance corporation tax or construction industry deductions) can be made quickly and safely by direct credit (BACS) to a bank or building society account.

You should provide details of the account which is to be credited. If the details are those of the nominee you want to receive the repayment, remember to complete the authority overleaf.

Name of bank or building society

115	

Branch sort code · Account number

116			117	

Name of account

118	

Building society reference

119	

Signature

120	

Except where a liquidator has been appointed, any person who is authorised to do so may sign the BACS details on behalf of the company. A photocopy of the signature is not acceptable.

Name (*In capital letters*)

120A	

Section 7 : Overpayments and repayment claims continued

Repayment claim

121 The following amount is to be repaid
either

121	£		p

122 ·   to the company
or

122	

(put an 'X' in
either box 122 or
123 **but not both**)

123 ·   to the nominee in the authority given below

123	

124 The following amount is to be surrendered
under S102 Finance Act 1989, and

124	£		p

either

125 ·   the joint notice is attached
or

125	

(put an 'X' in
appropriate box))

126 ·   will follow
Repayments of advance corporation tax cannot be surrendered

126	

127 Please stop repayment of the following amount until I send you the Notice

127	£		p

Payments to a person other than a company

Complete the authority below if you want the repayment to be made to a person **other than the company.** The
Inland Revenue reserves the right not to make a repayment to a nominee and will not normally make a repayment
to an overseas nominee.

I, as *(enter status - company secretary, treasurer, liquidator or authorised agent, etc.)*

128	

of *(enter name of company)*

129	

authorise *(enter name)*

130	

(enter address)

131	

Postcode

Nominee reference

132	

to receive on the company's behalf the amount due.

Signature

133	

Except where a liquidator has been appointed, any person
who is authorised to do so may sign the BACS details on
behalf of the company. A photocopy of a signature is not acceptable.

Name (*In capital letters*)

133A	

This is the end of Section 7

Section 8 : Directors' remuneration - optional section

Please complete this section if directors' remuneration is charged in the accounts supporting this form Ct600
Attach a continuation sheet if you need more space

Company name

| 134 | |

PAYE District		**PAYE Reference**	
135		136	

Accounts for the period

Remuneration claimed as a deductions in the accounts
Show total figure for all directors

From *(dd/mm/yyyy)*	To	
137 / /	138 / /	139 £

Date when account laid before the company in general meeting or, if resolved not to lay accounts, the date on which the accounts were approved by the directors

| 140 | / | / |

Analysis
Net remuneration voted after adjustments

Enter the net figure of remuneration after deducting employers' National Insurance contributions, employers' and employees' superannuation contributions and any benefits which have been included in the accounts' figure

141	Name of director	National Insurance number	Salary	Bonus, fees or commission
			£	£
			£	£
			£	£
			£	£
			£	£
			£	£
			£	£
			£	£

Put an 'X' here if a continuation sheet is used 142

143	Adjustments to reconcile the analysis above with total accounts' deductions claimed - please give details	
		£
		£
		£
		£
		£

Date of commencement or cessation of directorship during the period of account

144	Name of director	National Insurance number	Date commenced	Date ceased

CT61 RETURN FORM

Return *of company payments*
and **interest**

Please use this reference if
you write to or telephone the
Accounts Office

1

Accounts Office ref.

2 3 4

Company regn. no.   Accounting date

Income tax on annual payments and interest paid (and manufactured payments from abroad)

- Please use this form when you next need to make a return of annual payments and interest
- The enclosed CT61 Notes (1999) will help you. Page 2 of the notes explain when a return is needed.
- When a return is needed, you must give all the information asked for on this page and sign the declaration below. But you need only fill in the other parts of the return which are relevant to your company.
- Send the return to me within 14 days after the end of the return period. A reply envelope is enclosed.

  If tax is payable use the payslip on the enclosed CT61 Notice.

Company details

Name of company

If you wish future CT61 Returns to be sent to a new address, enter this here

Address _____

_____

_____

_____

_____ Postcode_____

Please tick if this
is a change of
Registered Office

Leave this box blank if the address is the same as printed above.

Period covered by this return

Return periods are fixed by law. See CT61 Notes page 5 for guidance.

Example: Interest paid on 25 April 1999 and the
accounting period is year to 31 March 2000. Enter:

	Day	Month	Year		Day	Month	Year
Return period ▶		.		to			
being part of the **Accounting Period** ▶				to			

Return period ▶	01	04	1999	to	30	06	1999
being part of the **Accounting Period** ▶	01	04	1999	to	31	03	2000

For official use only

901

Declaration   *False statements can results in prosecution*

To the best of my knowledge the information given in this return
is correct and complete

Signature

It would assist if you can state your daytime telephone number
and extension here

Name *in CAPITALS*

State in what capacity you make this return

Date

CT61 Return (New)

1

- Part 1 calculates the tax due on payments the company has **made**.
- Part 2 is for tax on any 'manufactured' interest received from abroad.
- Part 3 records tax suffered at source on payments the company has **received.**

Tax in Part 2 can be set-off to reduce the tax due in Part 1.

If you need more room please attach a schedule

1 Income tax on annual payments and interest paid   See Notes page 3

	Date	Description	Gross amount £	Lower rate income tax £
Annual payments etc **made** under deduction of income tax at **lower rate** *See Notes page 3* *Include 'manufactured' interest*	/ / / / / / / / / / / / / /		01	02

	Date	Description	Gross amount £	Basic rate income tax £
Annual payments etc **made** under deduction of income tax at **basic rate** *See Notes page 3*	/ / / / / / / / / /		03	04

	Date	Gross amount £	Reduced rate income tax £
Annual payments etc to **non-residents** made under deduction of **reduced rate** tax under a Double Taxation Agreement *See Notes page 6* Ref. no. of the authority ▶ [ ]	/ / / / / /	05	06

Total annual payments etc above   01 + 03 + 05   07

Total income tax on annual payments etc above . . . . 02 + 04 + 06   08 [ ]

Interest paid by deposit-takers
Interest and dividends paid by building societies

			Gross amount £	Lower rate income tax £
Enter the **Gross amount paid** from which you deducted tax and the **lower rate Income Tax** you deducted *See Notes page 3*	{	Before 6 April	09 [ ]	10 [ ]
		From 6 April	11 [ ]	12 [ ]
Do not enter any interest you paid gross			*When the return period does not include 6 April use boxed 09 and 10*	

Total income tax   08 + 10 + 12   13 [ ]

Less income tax deducted from income received now claimed as a **set-off**   From Part 3, box 25   14 [ ]

Income tax now payable on annual payments and interest   13 - 14   15 [ ]

Include this figure at box 18 below

2 Income tax on 'manufactured' interest from abroad   See Notes page 6

	Gross amount £		Income tax £
Manufactured interest received from abroad by UK resident companies and by UK branches of overseas companies	16 [ ]	Income Tax payable at a lower rate	17 [ ]

Include this figure at box 18 below

                                           Income tax £

Total income tax now payable . . . . 15 + 17   18 [ ]

Carry to payslip on CT 61 Notice

BPP PUBLISHING

If you need more room please attach a schedule

3   Income tax deducted from annual payments and interest received   See Notes page 4

Running record for this accounting period

Income tax £

Amount of income tax **brought forward** from last return **for this accounting period.**   19 [   ]

Adjustment, if any, agreed with Inspector .... *Enter 'MINUS' if appropriate*   20 [   ]

19 + or - 20   21 [   ]

Income **received** under deduction of tax, since last return for this **accounting period**

You can include income received in earlier return periods **in this accounting period** if you did not need to submit a form for those periods. *See Notes page 2* If you need more room please attach a schedule

Date	Description	Gross amount	Income tax
/ /			
/ /			
/ /			
/ /			
/ /	Totals 22	23	

Running total now available for set-off or repayment below   21 + 23   24 [   ]

Amount set-off against income tax From 24 or 13, whichever is smaller   25 [   ]   ◀ *Carry this figure to Part 1, box 14*
in Part 1

Repayment now claimed of tax paid on annual payments etc in an earlier return **within this accounting period only**   26 [   ]

Total income tax used for set-off or repayment ....   25 + 26   27 [   ]

Amount **not used** for set-off or repayment   24 - 27   28 [   ]

Amount to be **carried forward** to next return **within this accounting period only**   *cannot exceed 28*   29 [   ]

Amount **not carried forward**, for example at the end of the accounting period   28 - 29   30 [   ]

Before sending back this return, please

- check you have signed the declaration on page 1
- check that your Accounts Office reference appears at the top of page 1, and
- if tax is payable, tick below to show how you will be paying

When we receive this form we will send you a further form for your next return.

Payment method
It will assist if you can tick to show how you will be paying

[✓] By BACS / CHAPS

➤ [ ] By Bank Giro

[ ] By Girobank transfer

[ ] By post to the Inland Revenue Accounts Office

These payment methods are explained on the back of the CT61 notice.

Please note
If the Inspector considers that any payments, etc have been omitted from this return, or is in any way dissatisfied with it, the Inland Revenue can issue an appropriate assessment.

Key terms
and index

BPP PUBLISHING

ORDER FORM

Any books from our AAT range can be ordered by telephoning 020-8740-2211. Alternatively, send this page to our address below, fax it to us on 020-8740-1184, or email us at **publishing@bpp.com.** Or look us up on our website: www.bpp.com

We aim to deliver to all UK addresses inside 5 working days; a signature will be required. Order to all EU addresses should be delivered within 6 working days. All other orders to overseas addresses should be delivered within 8 working days.

To: BPP Publishing Ltd, Aldine House, Aldine Place, London W12 8AW

Tel: 020-8740 2211   **Fax: 020-8740 1184**   **Email: publishing@bpp.com**

Mr / Ms (full name): _____

Daytime delivery address: _____

_____

Postcode: _____   Daytime Tel: _____

Please send me the following quantities of books.

	5/00 Interactive Text	8/00 DA Kit	8/00 CA Kit
FOUNDATION			
Unit 1 Recording Income and Receipts	☐	☐	
Unit 2 Making and Recording Payments	☐	☐	
Unit 3 Ledger Balances and Initial Trial Balance	☐		☐
Unit 4 Supplying information for Management Control	☐	☐	
Unit 20 Working with Information Technology (8/00 Text)	☐		
Unit 22/23 Achieving Personal Effectiveness	☐		
INTERMEDIATE			
Unit 5 Financial Records and Accounts	☐		☐
Unit 6 Cost Information	☐		
Unit 7 Reports and Returns	☐	☐	
Unit 21 Using Information Technology	☐		
Unit 22: see below			
TECHNICIAN			
Unit 8/9 Core Managing Costs and Allocating Resources	☐		☑
Unit 10 Core Managing Accounting Systems	⬭	☐	☐
Unit 11 Option Financial Statements (Accounting Practice)	☐		
Unit 12 Option Financial Statements (Central Government)	☐		
Unit 15 Option Cash Management and Credit Control	☐	☐	
Unit 16 Option Evaluating Activities	☑	☐	
Unit 17 Option Implementing Auditing Procedures	☑	☑	
Unit 18 Option Business Tax FA00(8/00 Text)	☑	☑	
Unit 19 Option Personal Tax FA00(8/00 Text)	☐	☐	
TECHNICIAN 1999			
Unit 17 Option Business Tax Computations FA99 (8/99 Text & Kit)	☐	☐	
Unit 18 Option Personal Tax Computations FA99 (8/99 Text & Kit)	☐	☐	
TOTAL BOOKS	☐ +	☐ +	☐ = ☐

Postage and packaging: @ £9.95 each = £ ☐
UK: £2.00 for each book to maximum of £10
Europe (inc ROI and Channel Islands): £4.00 for first book, £2.00 for each extra   P & P   £ ☐
Rest of the World: £20.00 for first book, £10 for each extra

▶ Unit 22 Maintaining a Healthy Workplace Interactive Text (postage free)   ☐ @ £3.95   £ ☐

GRAND TOTAL £ ☐

I enclose a cheque for £ _____ (cheques to BPP Publishing Ltd) or charge to **Mastercard/Visa/Switch**

Card number ☐☐☐☐☐☐☐☐☐☐☐☐☐☐☐☐☐☐☐

Start date _____   **Expiry date** _____   **Issue no. (Switch only)** ___

Signature _____

REVIEW FORM & FREE PRIZE DRAW

All original review forms from the entire BPP range, completed with genuine comments, will be entered into one of two draws on 31 January 2001 and 31 July 2001. The names on the first four forms picked out on each occasion will be sent a cheque for £50.

Name: _____   Address: _____

_____

_____

How have you used this Interactive Text?
(Tick one box only)

☐ Home study (book only)

☐ On a course: college _____

☐ With 'correspondence' package

☐ Other _____

Why did you decide to purchase this Interactive Text? *(Tick one box only)*

☐ Have used BPP Texts in the past

☐ Recommendation by friend/colleague

☐ Recommendation by a lecturer at college

☐ Saw advertising

☐ Other _____

During the past six months do you recall seeing/receiving any of the following?
(Tick as many boxes as are relevant)

☐ Our advertisement in *Accounting Technician* magazine

☐ Our advertisement in *Pass*

☐ Our brochure with a letter through the post

Which (if any) aspects of our advertising do you find useful?
(Tick as many boxes as are relevant)

☐ Prices and publication dates of new editions

☐ Information on Interactive Text content

☐ Facility to order books off-the-page

☐ None of the above

Have you used the companion Assessment Kit for this subject?   ☐ Yes   ☐ No

Your ratings, comments and suggestions would be appreciated on the following areas

	Very useful	Useful	Not useful
Introductory section (How to use this Interactive Text etc)	☐	☐	☐
Chapter topic lists	☐	☐	☐
Chapter learning objectives	☐	☐	☐
Key terms	☐	☐	☐
Assessment alerts	☐	☐	☐
Examples	☐	☐	☐
Activities and answers	☐	☐	☐
Key learning points	☐	☐	☐
Quick quizzes and answers	☐	☐	☐
List of key terms and index	☐	☐	☐
Icons	☐	☐	☐

	Excellent	Good	Adequate	Poor
Overall opinion of this Text	☐	☐	☐	☐

Do you intend to continue using BPP Interactive Texts/Assessment Kits? ☐ Yes ☐ No

Please note any further comments and suggestions/errors on the reverse of this page.

Please return to: Nick Weller, BPP Publishing Ltd, FREEPOST, London, W12 8BR

REVIEW FORM & FREE PRIZE DRAW (continued)

Please note any further comments and suggestions/errors below

FREE PRIZE DRAW RULES

1 Closing date for 31 January 2001 draw is 31 December 2000. Closing date for 31 July 2001 draw is 30 June 2001.

2 Restricted to entries with UK and Eire addresses only. BPP employees, their families and business associates are excluded.

3 No purchase necessary. Entry forms are available upon request from BPP Publishing. No more than one entry per title, per person. Draw restricted to persons aged 16 and over.

4 Winners will be notified by post and receive their cheques not later than 6 weeks after the relevant draw date.

5 The decision of the promoter in all matters is final and binding. No correspondence will be entered into.